Florida

A History

Gloria Jahoda

**With a Historical Guide
prepared by the editors of
the American Association for
State and Local History**

W. W. Norton & Company
New York · London

American Association for State and Local History
Nashville

Copyright © 1984, 1976
American Association for State and Local History
Nashville, Tennessee

Published and distributed by W. W. Norton & Company, Inc.
500 Fifth Avenue
New York, New York, 10110

Library of Congress Cataloguing-in-Publication Data

Jahoda, Gloria.
    Florida: A history.

    (The States and the Nation series)
    Bibliography: p. 201
    Includes index.
    1. Florida—History. I. Series.
F311.J33   975.9   76–6468
ISBN 0-393-30178-8

Printed in the United States of America
1 2 3 4 5 6 7 8 9 0

Again, for my husband, Gerald Jahoda

Contents

Original Maps by Harold Faye

Historical Guide

TO FLORIDA

Introduction

The following pages offer the reader a guide to places in this state through which its history still lives.

This section lists and describes museums with collections of valuable artifacts, historic houses where prominent people once lived, and historic sites where events of importance took place. In addition, we have singled out for detailed description a few places that illustrate especially well major developments in this state's history or major themes running through it, as identified in the text that follows. The reader can visit these places to experience what life was like in earlier times and learn more about the state's rich and exciting heritage.

James B. Gardner and Timothy C. Jacobson, professional historians on the staff of the American Association for State and Local History, prepared this supplementary material, and the association's editors take sole responsibility for the selection of sites and their descriptions. Nonetheless, thanks are owed to many individuals and historical organizations, including those listed, for graciously providing information and advice. Our thanks also go to the National Endowment for the Humanities, which granted support for the writing and editing of this supplement, as it did for the main text itself.   —*The Editors*

Historic St. Augustine

St. Augustine

★ Forty-two years before English colonists established Jamestown and fifty-five years before the Pilgrims landed at Plymouth Rock, the Spanish planted their first colony in present-day Florida. The founding of St. Augustine in 1565 secured Spain's claim to Florida and provided an important strategic base for the European

Moat at Castillo de San Marcos

imperial power for nearly two and a half centuries. Although the United States took possession in 1821, the Spanish influence remained strong, contributing to Florida's distinctive historical character. Now fully restored, the old city of St. Augustine and the Castillo de San Marcos vividly bring to life this Spanish heritage.

The Spanish crown established St. Augustine in an effort to stop French encroachment on territory first claimed by Ponce de León in 1513. The specific target was Fort Caroline, a French outpost established in 1564 on the St. Johns River. Spain viewed the fort as a threat to its control over shipping lanes between Nueva España and the home country and authorized Admiral Pedro Menéndez de Avilés to lead an expedition to eliminate the intruders. Menéndez arrived on the west Florida coast in August 1565 and shortly thereafter established a colonial settlement on the small peninsula formed by Matanzas Bay and the San Sebastian River. Since he had spotted the site on August 28, St. Augustine's Day, he named the new colony after the early Christian saint. With an outpost established, Menéndez then turned to the task of eliminating the French intruders. Within two weeks, he took Fort Caroline and reestablished Spain's claim to the Florida peninsula.

In the decades that followed, St. Augustine became the focus of efforts to expand and consolidate the influence of Catholic Spain in the New World. As a military outpost, St. Augustine protected Spanish commerce and blocked the expansion of English colonies established to the north along the Atlantic coast in the seventeenth century. At the same time, the colony provided a base for missionary activities by the Roman Catholic Church. The Church's efforts among the region's Indians expanded Spain's control to the north and the west, beyond the confines of the original colony. Yet despite its function in the imperial system, St. Augustine was long neglected by the Spanish crown. Instead of erecting a permanent installation, the Spaniards financed a succession of wooden forts scarcely defensible against any concerted attack. The outpost's vulnerability was largely ignored, however, until 1668, when pirates raided the town. The next year Queen Mariana, regent for her son King Carlos II, ordered construction of a permanent fortification.

To carry out these orders, a new governor was dispatched to Florida. Don Manuel de Cendaya arrived in St. Augustine in July 1671 and within a month had laborers at work quarrying coquina, a natural shell rock, at Anastasia Island and preparing for construction to begin. On October 2 ground was broken, and the first stone was laid at the end of the month. An assortment of Indian laborers, Spanish peons, convicts, and slaves proceeded with work on the new fort and by midsummer of 1673 the east wall had reached twelve feet in height. Work continued slowly, however, plagued by numerous delays and chronic shortages of funds. Construction was not completed until August 1695—over twenty years after Cendoya initiated the project. Castillo de San Marcos, as the fort was named, reflected Spanish principles of fortification transplanted and adapted to the New World. The square citadel featured diamond-shaped extensions or bastions at each corner, a ravelin protecting the gate, and a surrounding moat, and its thick stone walls enclosed a magazine, storerooms, a chapel, and quarters for the soldiers on duty.

The first test of the new fort's strength came in 1702, when the War of the Spanish Succession spread to America. England had declared war on Spain and France in 1701, and English colonists in the Carolinas decided to follow suit and move against St. Augustine. The Carolinians raided north Florida, occupied the town, and attacked the Castillo, retreating only when Spanish reinforcements arrived. The stone citadel stood impregnable, but the invaders burned St. Augustine to the ground. In an effort to secure the town against a repeat invasion, the Spanish erected earthworks, palisades, and redoubts on its exposed sides. The first of these—the Cubo Line—extended from the fort west to the San Sebastian River, thus controlling the only land route onto the peninsula on which both the town and the fort stood. This defense measure made St. Augustine a virtual walled city.

The new fortifications were completed before another major attack by the English in 1740. Commercial rivalry between England and Spain had erupted in 1739 in the War of Jenkins' Ear, and St. Augustine became a target of British strategy to gain control of the Caribbean. British warships laid siege to the Castillo for thirty-eight days, but problems within the English command made it possible for the Spanish to break the blockade and stymie the takeover effort. Experience again proved an excellent teacher, and the Spaniards proceeded in the 1750s and 1760s to rework and strengthen the old garrison. Masonry vaults, higher walls, and stronger outworks prepared the Castillo for yet another major assault, but the Spanish ended up yielding the fort without a fight. In the Treaty of Paris that concluded the French and Indian Wars, defeated Spain ceded Florida to Britain in order to regain Havana. When the English arrived to take possession of the old Spanish outpost, both the military and the civilian population departed.

The British renamed the Castillo Fort St. Mark and used it as a base of operations for twenty-one years. In a second Treaty of Paris, which ended the Revolutionary War in 1783, Florida once again reverted to Spanish ownership. The former empire had declined considerably by then, however, and involvement in the Napoleonic Wars further weakened the Spanish crown. In 1821 Spain yielded to diplomatic pressure and ceded Florida to the United States. The latter renamed the Castillo Fort Marion and used it as a coastal fortification and military prison until 1900. Declared a national monument in 1924, the old Spanish garrison in 1935 came under the administration of the National Park Service, which today provides tours, talks, and exhibits on the history of the fort and Spanish Florida.

The Castillo's history is integrally tied to that of St. Augustine, and both must be visited in order to gain a better perspective on the blend of military and civilian life in Spanish Florida. As the fort has changed over the centuries, so has the city. For example, residents shifted from traditional board-and-thatch construction to masonry because of the availability of surplus material from the fort project. When Spain's imperial quarrels led to conflict, the city often suffered the worst. This necessitated periodic reconstruction of war-damaged structures and eventually the erection of perimeter fortifications that virtually walled in the eighteenth-century city. But despite such changes, the basic physical form of the community remained relatively constant after 1598, when the governor established the present city plan and laid out the public square in the heart of the still-young settlement.

Nearly four centuries later, St. Augustine is still in many ways a typical Spanish colonial town. Visitors can pass through the old city gates, walk along the narrow, winding streets, and view old coquina and wood structures that date back to the seventeenth and eighteenth centuries. Among the many significant structures are the Gonzalez-Alvarez House, constructed about 1623 and reputedly the oldest house in America; the Llambias House, a late eighteenth-century edifice; the Old Spanish Treasury; and the Cathedral of St. Augustine, erected in 1797 by the oldest Roman Catholic parish in the nation, established in 1594. Within the historic section of the city, the St. Augustine Historical Society operates several historic-house museums, and the Historic St. Augustine Preservation Board owns and administers over twenty original and reconstructed structures. The latter's programs include living history, crafts, exhibits, and publications.

Of course, the Spanish influence was not confined solely to St. Augustine; other cities and regions of Florida celebrate their Spanish origins as well. But the Castillo de San Marcos and St. Augustine clearly functioned as the center of Spanish imperial activity on the Florida peninsula and today provide the most exciting opportunities to relive this colorful chapter in the state's history.

Bulow Plantation Site

Bunnell

★ The tradition of moon-
light and magnolias is as important to Florida history as
it is to that of the rest of the
South. A plantation society
complete with slavery and a
code of chivalry thrived in
Florida in the decades after
Spanish cession of the territory to the United States. One
of the most magnificent and
extensive antebellum estates

Ruins at Bulow Plantation

was Bulow Plantation or Bulowville, situated some forty miles below
St. Augustine near the east coast. The Bulow family's sugar and cotton operations lasted only about fifteen years, until the Seminole Indians destroyed the plantation in early 1836 during the Second Seminole War. The Bulow Plantation State Historic Site thus commemorates
both Florida's plantation heritage and resistance to the infamous Indian
removal policy of the United States government.

James Russell began in 1812 the initial development of what would
later be known as Bulow Plantation. The 2,500 acres of land that he
named "Good Retreat" had been given to him as payment for a
schooner he sold to the Spanish government soon after he and his
household arrived at St. Augustine from the Bahamas. He did not
make much progress in clearing the dense growth of hardwood trees
prior to his death in 1815, and in 1820 his heirs sold the property to
Charles Wilhelm Bulow, a Charleston, South Carolina, planter and
politician. Bulow was a descendant of Baron Joachim Von Bulow,
who had been sent by the Elector of Wurtemburg to establish the Lu-
theran church in the Carolina colonies. By the early nineteenth century
the Bulow family owned Savannah Plantation, Ashley Hall in Charleston, and numerous other properties. Bulow was one of many wealthy
Southerners who augmented their extensive landholdings with new
plantations in Florida about the time the Spanish ceded the territory to

the United States. With land prices low and sugar and cotton prices up, these planters expected high profits from the newest addition to the plantation South.

Altogether Bulow purchased between four and six thousand acres along Smith's Creek. Using slave labor, he proceeded with Russell's plan to clear the densely wooded area and soon planted the first sugarcane, cotton, and indigo crops. With wood and coquina (a soft limestone formed of shells) available on the property, he constructed a residence, slave quarters, and other essential outbuildings. But like Russell, Bulow died before he could see his plans to fruition. At his death in 1823, the property passed to his son and heir John Joachim Bulow. Since the younger Bulow was still a minor, however, trustees operated the estate until about 1828, when John Bulow completed his European education and returned to the United States to succeed his father as Master of Bulowville.

Under John Bulow's management, the plantation developed into one of the largest and most profitable in the area. Although he planted about 1,000 acres of cotton, 1,500 acres of sugarcane became the key to the plantation's operations. The plantation sugar mill may have been the largest in the Florida territory. Here the cane stalks were crushed to extract the juice, which was then reduced to a thick syrup, crystalized, and stored. The mill complex includes a crushing house, steam boiler, kettle room, wooden vats, curing room, and storage sheds. Transportation of the sugar and by-product molasses also required boat slips on Smith's or Bulow Creek, where flats or barges could load up for the eleven mile trip down to the Halifax River and on to Mosquito Inlet to make connections for shipment to distant markets. Other support structures typical of a working plantation included a barn, corn house, gin house, poultry house, cooperage, blacksmith shop, and fodder houses.

A plantation of this scale depended on slave labor. The three hundred slaves owned by Bulow lived in forty houses arranged in a semicircle about two hundred yards from their master's home. These twelve-by-sixteen-foot wooden structures apparently had wooden floors, a rare feature in slave quarters, and were furnished adequately by Bulow. He was reportedly a good master. Although he only gave the slaves ground corn each week, they had enough time on their own to hunt, fish, and cultivate small garden plots.

Bulow himself apparently lived in grand style in the plantation's Big House. Piazzas encircled the two-story coquina structure, and the house had an especially fine library. Bulow, who had spent several years in Paris, became known as a lavish host. The numerous empty ale and wine bottles from his parties were used to reinforce the sides of the boat slips at which he kept canoes and skiffs for fishing and hunting expeditions along interior waterways. Bulow Plantation's hospitality and accessibility to transportation made it a perfect home base for John James Audubon when he visited the area in 1831.

John Bulow maintained good relations with the Seminole Indians in the region and did not support the government's removal policy. During the Second Seminole War, he opposed the army's presence, but Major Benjamin Putnam and his Mosquito Raiders took the plantation by force and set up headquarters there in late December of 1835. With Bulow kept under guard, the army built a small fort of palm logs and fortified the Big House and slave quarters with stacks of baled cotton. Meanwhile Seminole raids were reported closer and closer to the Bulow estate. After Putnam and a sizable number of his men were wounded in a skirmish at Dunlawton plantation in January, such reports caused considerable alarm. Unable to resist attack, Putnam ordered all to abandon the plantation and retreat to St. Augustine on January 23. Although the exact date is not known, within the next week the Seminoles raided and burned the plantation. Bulow died in Paris a few months later at the age of twenty-seven.

With the plantation in ruins, the woods again took over the once profitable fields. When the state secured the property, only the ruins of the mansion, the sugar mill, the spring house, and the slave quarters remained. The Division of Recreation and Parks of the Florida Department of Natural Resources now administers the 109-acre state park. The ruins provide a visual link to Florida's plantation past and a reminder of the infamous Second Seminole War. Related sites include two other examples of antebellum plantations, the Gamble Plantation State Historic Site at Ellenton and the Kingsley Plantation State Historic Site at Ft. George, and the Dade Battlefield State Historic Site at Bushnell, the location of the opening conflict of the Second Seminole War.

Henry Morrison Flagler Museum

Palm Beach

★ No one more deserves to be called "the Father of Florida" than Henry M. Flagler, the central figure in the development of the state's east coast in the late nineteenth and early twentieth centuries. His East Coast Railway opened up new areas to developers, provided the transportation network essen-

Flagler's Whitehall

tial to exploiting the state's agricultural potential, and, together with his hotels, launched the modern tourist industry on Florida's "gold coast." The preeminent symbol of Flagler's wealth and influence is Whitehall, his elaborate Palm Beach home. Now preserved as the Henry Morrison Flagler Museum, it reflects both Flagler's role in developing Palm Beach as a legendary gathering place for America's wealthy and famous and his greater impact on the history of Florida.

When Flagler first became interested in developing Florida in the 1880's, he had already established himself as one of the nation's leading entrepreneurs. His most notable business venture was a partnership with John D. Rockefeller in 1870 to form the Standard Oil Company, one of the world's richest and most powerful corporations. He demonstrated the same business acumen in 1883 when, while honeymooning with his second wife in St. Augustine, he became intrigued by the city's potential as a resort. Struck by the lack of modern facilities, he commissioned architects John M. Carrère and Thomas Hastings to design a luxury hotel in keeping with the city's European background and traditions. The lavish Spanish revival Ponce de Leon Hotel opened in 1888. Flagler soon expanded his operations to the Cordova and Alcazar hotels as well. To insure accessibility and the success of his hotels, he also acquired and improved the East Coast Railway from Jacksonville to St. Augustine. His instincts proved correct, and the historic city soon flourished as a fashionable winter resort.

In the decades that followed, Flagler extended his railroad southward through purchase and construction and added to his chain of luxury resort hotels. First he extended his railroad to Daytona Beach, where he bought and enlarged the Ormond Beach Hotel. Then in 1894 the line reached Palm Beach, a small coastal-island settlement some two hundred miles south of Daytona. The island was named for its palm groves, which date from the wreck of a coconut-laden Spanish ship in 1878. Flagler found the island and its temperate climate well suited to development and in 1893 began work on what would soon become one of America's most famous resorts.

Construction began on the Royal Poinciana Hotel before the railroad even reached Palm Beach. Completed in 1894 on a thirty-two acre site along the shore of Lake Worth, the 1,150-room frame building was one of the world's largest wooden structures and the largest resort hotel in existence. For the construction workers and hotel employees, Flagler directed the layout of the adjoining town of West Palm Beach, complete with water system, paved streets, and landscaping. The East Coast Railway line reached West Palm Beach in 1894, and a railroad bridge across Lake Worth was completed later that year. Shortly thereafter private railroad cars began arriving, bearing the wealthy and famous Americans who would make Palm Beach the country's most fashionable winter gathering place.

As the resort's popularity increased, Flagler added new wings to the Royal Poinciana and in 1896 opened the Palm Beach Inn, which he later enlarged, renovated, and renamed the Breakers. Another landmark of the early years was Bradley's Beach Club, an exclusive gambling casino established in 1899 by Colonel Edward Reilly Bradley. A later addition was the Everglades Club, the first of the famous Boom Spanish structures designed by Addison Mizner for the resort community. Mizner also designed extravagant mansions for the Stotesburys and Wanamakers of Philadelphia and other socially prominent families, who preferred to stay in their own homes rather than hotels during the two months of Palm Beach's winter season. One particularly notable example is Mar-A-Lago, the opulent home of the late Marjorie Merriweather Post and now a national historic site.

In 1901 Flagler erected Palm Beach's most lavish mansion as a wedding present for his third wife, Mary Lily Kenan. Designed and built in just eighteen months at a cost of two and a half million dollars,

Whitehall, as the Flagler home was known, stood south of the Royal Poinciana on a six-acre site at the edge of Lake Worth. Architects Carrere and Hastings incorporated both Spanish and Classical elements in their design. The red tiled roof, stuccoed exterior, and interior courtyard reflected the Spanish influence, but Whitehall's Doric columns and porches were more typical of Southern Greek Revival homes. In addition to designing the Ponce de Leon Hotel for Flagler, Carrere and Hastings became well known as the architects of the New York Public Library, the old Metropolitan Opera House, the Frick Mansion, and the U.S. Senate Office Building. Upon completion of the mansion, the Flaglers spent another one and a half million dollars on furnishings. From 1902 until Flagler's death in 1913, the couple spent their winters there, entertaining lavishly in the style that became synonymous with Palm Beach society.

Palm Beach was not the end of the line for Flagler's East Coast Railway. By 1896, his line extended to Miami, where he again played a central role in establishing a popular resort community. His Royal Palm hotel was the first such establishment in the city now renowned for its resort hotels. The last leg of his railroad construction project took much longer, for his goal of reaching Key West required bridging miles of swampland, barren coral, and ocean. This 156-mile engineering marvel took seven years and twenty million dollars to complete. On January 22, 1912, Flagler rode into Key West on the first train that crossed the overseas bridges to the islands. In a brief speech, the aging entrepreneur declared, ''Now I can die happy; my dream is fulfilled.'' He died less than a year and a half later, on May 20, 1913, and was buried in a mausoleum adjacent to St. Augustine's Memorial Presbyterian Church, which he had built in 1890 in memory of his daughter.

Mrs. Flagler opened Whitehall only one more season before her death in 1917. Subsequently the house was used as a private club and then in 1925 opened as a luxury resort hotel. The mansion itself was used for public rooms and luxury suites, and a ten-story tower provided three hundred sleeping rooms. In 1959 the house was purchased for the Henry Morrison Flagler Museum, and it was opened to the public the following year. Careful restoration and furnishing have returned the house to the elegance of the Flagler era. Visitors can now tour the magnificent marble entrance hall, the walnut-panelled library, the music room where the Flaglers held weekly musicales, the billiard room, the ornate gold and white ballroom, the breakfast room, the dining room, the salon, and a courtyard on the first floor. Second-floor rooms include the master suite with its original Louis XV style furniture, Mrs. Flagler's morning room, and several of the fourteen guest rooms. The lower floors of the 1925 hotel addition have been retained for exhibits, meetings, and community events.

Flagler's private railroad car, "Rambler," also stands on the grounds. Flagler had the car built in 1886 and used it throughout the remainder of his life, including his inaugural trip to Key West in 1912. Later used as a tenant farmer's shack, the car was found and restored in 1967. The exterior bears the yellow and maroon colors of the East Coast Railway, and the interior lounge, stateroom, berths, and kitchen have been accurately restored to the Flagler period.

Whitehall is an impressive symbol of Henry M. Flagler's wealth and influence. His pioneering development of Florida's east coast provided the basis for the boom of the 1920's and firmly established the resort industry that has become so integral a part of the state's economic growth and development. His Palm Beach home and the exhibits and programs of the Henry Morrison Flagler Museum provide a unique opportunity to experience the lavish lifestyle of one of America's most famous resort communities and to learn more about the history of modern Florida.

Other Places of Interest

*The following suggest other places of
historical interest to visit. We recommend that
you check hours of operation in advance.*

DADE BATTLEFIELD SITE AND MUSEUM, *state 476 just west of U.S.
301, Bushnell.* Exhibits and artifacts of the 1835 battle in which Seminoles
killed more than 100 U.S. soldiers.

De SOTO NATIONAL MEMORIAL, *five miles west and two miles north on
75th Street W., Bradenton.* Site visited by De Soto in 1539, with visitor
center where costumed interpreters demonstrate crossbow and arquebus.

FLORIDA STATE MUSEUM, *University of Florida, Gainesville.* Exhibits on
archeology and anthropology from prehistoric times to the present; extensive natural history exhibits.

FORT CAROLINE NATIONAL MEMORIAL, *ten miles east of Jacksonville
and five miles north of state 10.* Museum near the site of the French settlement of 1564, the first European settlement on the North American continent.

FORT GEORGE ISLAND, *twenty-five miles east of Jacksonville.* Several historic sites, including the Huguenot Memorial honoring the French landing
in 1562; Fort Saint George, 1736; and Kingsley Plantation, 1817.

FORT JEFFERSON NATIONAL MEMORIAL, *Dry Tortugas Islands, sixty-
eight miles west of Key West in the Gulf of Mexico.* Incompleted United
States fort begun in 1846, now a ruin.

FORT MATANZAS NATIONAL MONUMENT, *fourteen miles south of St.
Augustine.* Site where the Spanish massacred (matazas-Sp. *slaughters*) the
French in 1565 and constructed a fort in 1740–1742, of which only a rem-
nant stands.

GAMBLE PLANTATION, *U.S. 301, Ellenton.* Greek Revival house built
1845–1850, where Confederate Secretary of State Judah Benjamin hid before escaping to England. Contains antebellum furnishings.

GULF ISLANDS NATIONAL SEASHORE, *south of Pensacola on state 399
on Santa Rosa Island and at the U.S. Naval Air Station, Pensacola.* Includes Fort Pickens, built 1829–1835, where Geronimo was imprisoned
1886–1888; Battery San Antonio, built by the Spanish about 1797; Fort

xxi

Barrancas (1834–1844); the Pensacola Lighthouse (1858); and the Advanced Redoubt of Barrancas (1840s).

HERITAGE PARK, *Largo*. A reconstructed town, including residences, a store, a depot, and a church, all dating from the late nineteenth and early twentieth centuries.

HISTORICAL MUSEUM OF SOUTHERN FLORIDA, *Miami*. General history museum with exhibits on history of the region, including the Caribbean.

INTERNATIONAL SWIMMING HALL OF FAME, *One Hall of Fame Drive, Fort Lauderdale*. Photos, murals, Olympic medals.

JACKSONVILLE MUSEUM OF ARTS AND SCIENCES, *1025 Gulf Life Drive, Jacksonville*. Antique and ethnic dolls; exhibits on pre-Columbian and Florida Indians and early white Florida history.

KEY WEST HISTORIC DISTRICT, *Key West*. Includes the Audubon House, where the painter stayed in 1832; Hemingway House, home of writer Ernest Hemingway from 1931 to 1960, and Civil War forts.

LAUNCH COMPLEX 39, KENNEDY SPACE CENTER, *Titusville area*. Where the first manned voyage to the moon was launched in 1969.

LIGHTNER MUSEUM, *City Hall-Museum Complex, King Street, St. Augustine*. House in the 1889 Alcazar Hotel, built for Henry Flagler; with decorative arts, Tiffany glass, Victorian art glass, and other nineteenth-century material arts.

MARJORIE KINNAN RAWLINGS HOUSE, *state 325 south of Cross Creek, Cross Creek*. Late-nineteenth-century farmhouse, home of the author of *The Yearling*.

MARY McLEOD BETHUNE HOME, *Bethune-Cookman College campus, Daytona Beach*. Clapboard house built in the 1920s, the home of black leader and founder of the college; contains a museum.

MORIKAMI MUSEUM OF JAPANESE CULTURE, *4000 Morikami Park Road, Delray Beach*. Exhibits on the Yamato Colony of Japanese farmers, including bonsai collection and folk art.

MUSEUM OF FLORIDA HISTORY, *R. A. Gray Building, Tallahassee*. General history museum with exhibits on life in Florida, including Spanish trade and maritime artifacts.

OKEECHOBEE BATTLEFIELD, *four miles southeast of Okeechobee on U.S. 441*. Where Zachary Taylor defeated Seminole and Mikasuki soldiers in 1837 in the Second Seminole War.

PELICAN ISLAND NATIONAL WILDLIFE REFUGE, *east of Sebastian in the Indian River*. First federal sanctuary to protect wildlife, established in 1903 by Theodore Roosevelt for the brown pelican.

PENSACOLA HISTORIC DISTRICT, *bounded by Chase Street, Ninth Avenue, Pensacola Bay, and Palafox Street.* Includes houses and buildings from 1800s and 1900s, Museum of West Florida History, Plaza Ferdinand VII, Seville Square, and the Clara Barkley Dorr house.

PENSACOLA HISTORICAL MUSEUM, *405 S. Adams Street, Pensacola.* Local history, including family silver, men's and women's accessories and household items from 1800s, fine art glass, and glass negatives.

ROCHELLE SCHOOL, *off state 234, Rochelle.* An 1885 clapboard school in use until 1935, with Italianate elements; one of few remaining buildings from town's early period.

SAN MARCOS de APALACHE, *on state 363 about two miles south of U.S. 98 just south of St. Marks.* Where the Spanish built three forts between 1565 and 1763; with a portion of the stonework remaining and a museum.

TALLAHASSEE JUNIOR MUSEUM, *3945 Museum Drive, Tallahassee.* Includes an excellent "cracker" homestead with support buildings.

TARPON SPRINGS SPONGE EXCHANGE, *Dodecanese Street, Tarpon Springs.* Greek community and center of United States sponge industry.

TEMPLE MOUND MUSEUM, *139 Miraclestrip Parkway, S.E., Fort Walton Beach.* Interpretive center next to Temple mound of Fort Walton culture; with rock and ceramic artifacts from the area.

TOMOKA MUSEUM, *Tomoka State Park, Ormond Beach.* Exhibits and art on the site of Timucuan village extant in 1605.

VIZCAYA, *3251 S. Miami Avenue, Miami.* Concrete and stucco mansion with formal gardens; the home of industrialist James Deering.

YBOR CITY HISTORIC DISTRICT, *Tampa.* Cuban community, once a famous cigar-making center.

FLORIDA

0   50   100   150   200
Miles

ALABAMA   GEORGIA

ATLANTIC
OCEAN

Escambio R.

Chipola R.

Pensacola Milton   Marianna   St. Mary's R.
        Elgin AFB   Chattahoochee Jackson Lake Monticello White Springs Jacksonville Fernandina
Santa Rosa   Blountstown   Telogia Tallahassee   Ocean Pond Baldwin Fort Caroline
Island   Wakulla Natural Bridge   Live Oak Olustee
        Port St. Joe   St. Marks   Starke   St. Augustine
                    Apalachee Alachua Savannah Palatka
            Apalachicola Bay   Gainesville
                                           St. Johns R.

                              Cedar Key Ocala Daytona
                              Yankeetown Inglis Deland New Smyrna
                    Lake Tsala Apopka   Merritt Island
                         Brooksville Clermont Titusville
G U L F   O F   Masaryktown   Cape Canaveral
                    New Port Richey Green Orlando Banana R.
                    Tarpon Springs Swamp Kissimmee Cocoa Beach
M E X I C O   Safety Harbor Lakeland
                    St. Petersburg Tampa   Indian R.
                              Pinellas Kissimmee
                         Tampa Bay Point Prairie Fellesmere
                              Sarasota
                              Venice
                    Warm   Peace R.   Hobe
                    Mineral Springs   Lake Sound
                                           Okeechobee
                         Caloosahatchee R.   Palm
                              Fort Myers Lake Harbor Beach
                                        Big Boca Raton
                              Naples Cypress Fort
                                    Swamp Lauderdale
                         Marco Island   EVERGLADES Miami

See inset

THE KEYS

Lake   West
Okeechobee   Palm Beach Palm Beach
Lake   Belle Glade
Harbor   Loxahatchee R.
        Hillsborough Delray Beach
        Canal Boca Raton
        New River
        Canal
        Miami Canal Fort Lauderdale
                ATLANTIC
                OCEAN
        Hialeah
E V E R G L Miami Miami Beach
        Coral Gables
                Biscayne Bay

                         Havana

                    CUBA

0   10   50
Miles
Florida Bay

Harold Faye

Invitation to the Reader

IN 1807, former President John Adams argued that a complete history of the American Revolution could not be written until the history of change in each state was known, because the principles of the Revolution were as various as the states that went through it. Two hundred years after the Declaration of Independence, the American nation has spread over a continent and beyond. The states have grown in number from thirteen to fifty. And democratic principles have been interpreted differently in every one of them.

We therefore invite you to consider that the history of your state may have more to do with the bicentennial review of the American Revolution than does the story of Bunker Hill or Valley Forge. The Revolution has continued as Americans extended liberty and democracy over a vast territory. John Adams was right: the states are part of that story, and the story is incomplete without an account of their diversity.

The Declaration of Independence stressed life, liberty, and the pursuit of happiness; accordingly, it shattered the notion of holding new territories in the subordinate status of colonies. The Northwest Ordinance of 1787 set forth a procedure for new states to enter the Union on an equal footing with the old. The Federal Constitution shortly confirmed this novel means of building a nation out of equal states. The step-by-step process through which territories have achieved self-government and national representation is among the most important of the Founding Fathers' legacies.

The method of state-making reconciled the ancient conflict between liberty and empire, resulting in what Thomas Jefferson called an empire for liberty. The system has worked and remains unaltered, despite enormous changes that have taken place in the nation. The country's extent and variety now surpass anything the patriots of '76 could likely have imagined. The United States has changed from an agrarian republic into a highly industrial and urban democracy, from a fledgling nation into a major world power. As Oliver Wendell Holmes remarked in 1920, the creators of the nation could not have seen completely how it and its constitution and its states would develop. Any meaningful review in the bicentennial era must consider what the country has become, as well as what it was.

The new nation of equal states took as its motto *E Pluribus Unum*—"out of many, one." But just as many peoples have become Americans without complete loss of ethnic and cultural identities, so have the states retained differences of character. Some have been superficial, expressed in stereotyped images— big, boastful Texas, "sophisticated" New York, "hillbilly" Arkansas. Other differences have been more real, sometimes instructively, sometimes amusingly; democracy has embraced Huey Long's Louisiana, bilingual New Mexico, unicameral Nebraska, and a Texas that once taxed fortunetellers and spawned politicians called "Woodpecker Republicans" and "Skunk Democrats." Some differences have been profound, as when South Carolina secessionists led other states out of the Union in opposition to abolitionists in Massachusetts and Ohio. The result was a bitter Civil War.

The Revolution's first shots may have sounded in Lexington and Concord; but fights over what democracy should mean and who should have independence have erupted from Pennsylvania's Gettysburg to the "Bleeding Kansas" of John Brown, from the Alamo in Texas to the Indian battles at Montana's Little Bighorn. Utah Mormons have known the strain of isolation; Hawaiians at Pearl Harbor, the terror of attack; Georgians during Sherman's march, the sadness of defeat and devastation. Each state's experience differs instructively; each adds understanding to the whole.

The purpose of this series of books is to make that kind of understanding accessible, in a way that will last in value far beyond the bicentennial fireworks. The series offers a volume on every state, plus the District of Columbia—fifty-one, in all.

Each book contains, besides the text, a view of the state through eyes other than the author's—a "photographer's essay," in which a skilled photographer presents his own personal perceptions of the state's contemporary flavor.

We have asked authors not for comprehensive chronicles, nor for research monographs or new data for scholars. Bibliographies and footnotes are minimal. We have asked each author for a summing up—interpretive, sensitive, thoughtful, individual, even personal—of what seems significant about his or her state's history. What distinguishes it? What has mattered about it, to its own people and to the rest of the nation? What has it come to now?

To interpret the states in all their variety, we have sought a variety of backgrounds in authors themselves and have encouraged variety in the approaches they take. They have in common only these things: historical knowledge, writing skill, and strong personal feelings about a particular state. Each has wide latitude for the use of the short space. And if each succeeds, it will be by offering you, in your capacity as a *citizen* of a state *and* of a nation, stimulating insights to test against your own.

James Morton Smith
General Editor

Florida

A History

1

"It's Snowing in Akron, Ohio!"

WHATEVER else it is and has been, the state of Florida is the Great American Escape. The palm fronds of Hawaii may sway as bravely in their trade winds as those of Florida, but they are expensively far from the mainland. The palms of California wave over urbanization that can be as hectic as anything Manhattan ever offered; moreover, as any dutiful Floridian will affirm, they wave in smog. Florida, still rural in many stretches, for all the tawdry glitter of Miami Beach, is the place to go when you want to get away, at a price you can afford, from life in the rest of the United States.

One of Florida's many utterly enchanting paradoxes is that it is at once un-American and super-American: where else does the weary pilgrim find feudal farming, huge live oaks hung dreamily with thick strands of Spanish moss, and—not far away—the launching pads of moon rockets? There are Seminole Indians in the Everglades who speak no English; there are also ten-foot plastic Santa Clauses on west-coast causeways at Christmas, rubber animatronic rabbits at Easter in gimcrack amusement parks, and jammed fishing-party boats in midsummer that creak, as they return to Gulf and Atlantic shores, with the weight of their catch as well as of their well-fed passengers. There is a Florida for the Savile Row and Gucci elite, behind the casuarina fastnesses of Hobe Sound and Palm Beach. There is also a Florida for what is left of the counter-culture—most of it in the parks of Orlando, a central Florida city that was relatively normal before the coming of Mickey Mouse at Disney World. Orlando police are harried and compassionate, and they heartily wish all the weirdos would go back to Fort Lauderdale for their spring vacations, where they used to go, and not bother the God-fearing Baptists of inland orange groves.

For every social station and for every purse, there is a Florida to suit. The Salvation Army, predictably, cares for the bums. But the dream that Florida offers is, above all, the dream of the American middle class: perfect health and happiness in a balmy latitude where old age is variously referred to as years that are Golden and/or Harvest and where the death-merchants of funeral homes hide becomingly behind lush banana trees in which mockingbirds sing.

The traveler to Florida has been led to expect miracles. In swirling snow, up on the choked highways of New Jersey, he has been taunted by billboards that ask, reasonably, "Wouldn't You RATHER be in Florida?" In 1885, as august an organization as the American Medical Association went on record endorsing Pinellas Point, the site of modern St. Petersburg, as the healthiest spot in the U.S.A.

It is impossible, in Florida, not to be obsessed by the weather; it has created the place and its ambiance, and weather will probably determine, directly or indirectly, any prosperity to come. The sun, promoters agree among themselves, had better go on shining in the Sunshine State. What the accomplished Florida huckster has to sell is a vision of paradise, and in the effort he is assisted by an army of Floridophiles that echoes his myths of tropic bliss like a Greek chorus.

Pre-eminent among such boosters, as far as middle-class America is concerned, is Norman D. Ford, travel editor of *Harvest Years* magazine. *Norman Ford's Florida,* in 1973, reached its sixteenth edition under the auspices of Harian Publications, Inc., of Greenlawn, New York. Norman Ford not only knows what's in Florida, but is able to present his more scientifically oriented readers with reasons for the state's claim to being heaven on earth:

> Modern-day climatologists are almost unanimous that the chief factor in determining the value of a climate lies in the average intensity

of its ultraviolet light. Ultraviolet waves are, of course, those light rays having the shortest wave length. Owing to this fact, they are quickly dispersed by dust and particles held in suspension in the air. When allowed to reach the earth in full measure, their effect is strongly aseptic which may well account for the prevalence of pneumonia and other germs in cities where dust and smog prevent ingress of ultraviolet light. Perfectly free from dust or smog, the wine-clear air of Florida allows a maximum of ultraviolet rays to reach its sandy surface.[1]

There are, admits Mr. Ford, drawbacks, even in Eden. Florida may possess, "for men and women already past middle age," the "one *best* climate" in which "persons of delicate constitution gain strength and weight." But it is also true that

> strong young people are slowed down and forced to live at a slower tempo . . . All persons suffer from slightly diminished mental efficiency . . . This is the price you pay to live in Florida . . . However, it is only a *tendency* and nowadays a great deal of creative and intellectual activity is carried out in Florida's universities and at such research centers as Cape Kennedy.[2]

For victims of diminished mental efficiency, the astronauts have surely managed an enviable record. And Mr. Ford's conclusions are nothing if not heartening:

> Only your doctor can say how the actinic therapy of Florida's sun and the state's warm moist climate can benefit *your* health. Statistics prove beyond doubt that Florida is beneficial to sufferers from heart disease, cancer, TB, arteriosclerosis and diabetes. For your interest we will mention those other ailments which, over and over again, people have told us were held in check or improved through living in Florida. They are: hay fever, colds and chills, ulcers, rheumatism, gout and arthritis, rickets, kidney, liver and stomach complaints, skin ailments, influenza, and pneumonia, asthma, neuritis and catarrh.[3]

The very rich are different from you and me; they seek relief, in Florida, from sinusitis. But the average American stuffy nose is

---

1. Norman D. Ford, *Norman Ford's Florida* (Greenlawn, N.Y.: Harian Publications, Inc., 1973), p. 7.

2. Ford, *Norman Ford's Florida,* p. 9.

3. Ford, *Norman Ford's Florida,* p. 21.

caused by the mysteries of catarrh, as Mr. Ford's readers well know, and it is not only catarrh that vanishes under the ultraviolet rays of the sun of Florida's pale shores. At Warm Mineral Springs, south of west-coast Venice on U.S. Route 41, the earth pours forth water as powerful as any Bernadette ever saw gushing at Lourdes. Rheumatics and arthritics, Norman Ford tells you, arrive in droves, on crutches and in wheelchairs. Then they step gingerly into the waters—which are conveniently "buoyant"—and when they emerge, they are able to walk unaided.[4] Back home, up north, they presumably get worse again —until the next hegira to Warm Mineral Springs.

No matter what you are doing in Florida, and no matter where you are staying, the weather is a pivot. Once, on a soft November evening in Daytona Beach, where palms undulating in the sea breeze were illumined in hot pink, scarlet, and kelly green by strategically placed spotlights, a Palm Beach-suited master of ceremonies strode onto the stage of an outdoor bandshell after the musicians had finished *The Desert Song*. "Ladies and gentlemen!" he announced in victorious tones that resonated above the hums and squeaks of a capricious public address system. "It's snowing in Akron, Ohio! How *about* that?" It's possible that a band concert in Daytona Beach may have been interrupted for bulletins on the Cuban Missile Crisis of 1962, but not likely. For when you know that it's snowing in Akron, you can gloat. Florida newspapers and radio and television stations make sure that no climatic catastrophe anywhere else in the United States goes unreported. A Texas gully-washer can knock the peacemaking efforts of Henry Kissinger off the front page, and what headlines imply is often as significant as what they actually tell: "NO LIVES LOST IN CALIFORNIA BLIZZARD." (Usually, in snow, one infers, Californians die like flies.)

Hurricanes, on the other hand, are "tropical depressions," unless they savage cities. Norman Ford loyally explains that hurricanes frequently hit North Carolina and New England. Four times out of five, Caribbean hurricanes don't hit Florida at

4. Ford, *Norman Ford's Florida*, p. 253.

all. And they can kill in the land of the pilgrims; six hundred people in New England perished in 1938. Until Hurricane Donna washed over the Keys and the lower west coast in 1960, Florida had gone scot-free for a decade. Why blame hurricanes on Florida or associate them together? Not every citizen would agree that, because a Florida town stays standing for ten years, the menace of Caribbean storms is negated. But even on the Keys, where catastrophic orgies of wind and water have leveled resorts and restaurants repeatedly and have blown refrigerators into treetops, the inhabitants of these vulnerable strips of green separating the Atlantic Ocean from the Gulf of Mexico come back for more. On Marco Island, on the lower southwest coast, the Deltona Corporation sells waterfront lots for $50,000 apiece. "Private ownership of ecologically valuable submerged land and wetlands is a major conservation and political problem," declared Ken Woodburn, an environmental aide to Governor Reubin Askew, in 1969.[5] When Florida sand gets in your shoes, goes the proverb, you are driven to return. The legend-makers themselves have stayed to worship at the shrine. Poet Sidney Lanier, in Tampa to write a hack guidebook for a railroad company in the 1870s, was dying of tuberculosis, even as he assured his readers that Florida offered consumptives a cure. Perhaps because he believed this, he lived out some borrowed time before his malady finally felled him, and he had the propriety to perish in Lynn, North Carolina.

Geologically, Florida was an American afterthought. The mainland existed long before the peninsula finally thrust itself a few feet out of the seas that washed it. All of Florida's early fossils are marine: whales and snails, a bewildering variety of now-extinct fish. The oldest fossil ever found in the state was discovered in 1955 during drilling operations near Lake Okeechobee by the Amerada Petroleum Company. It is a partial turtle skeleton dating from the Cretaceous geological epoch of a hundred and twenty million years ago, and it was unearthed from a depth of 9,000 feet underground. Florida has yielded no

5. Quoted in Robert B. Rackleff, *Close to Crisis: Florida's Environmental Problems* (Tallahassee, Fla.: New Issues Press, Inc., 1972), p. 92.

dinosaur remains because, when dinosaurs flourished, it was ocean. It is possible that a Cretaceous dinosaur or two might yet turn up during further drilling, but it is not likely. A dinosaur would have had to be living on an island in those teeming prehistoric waters, and somehow he would have had to manage to get there.

Florida became recognizably Florida as recently—as universal rhythms run—as twenty million years ago. While mainland America was gripped successively four times by ice sheets spreading down from the Arctic, Florida knew only the periods of heavy rainfall that formed the state's rivers and lakes as we see them today and formed also the state's prime water source, the Floridian aquifer. This is a layer of porous limestone filled with fresh water whose level rises and falls with suns and storms, dry seasons and rains. In the past, Florida has been cavalier with her abundance of fresh water. Now, however, man's efforts to turn subtropic wilderness into dazzling expanses of heavily populated kitsch have begun to take their toll. At several points on the peninsula, and even in the Panhandle, the aquifer has suffered some salt-water intrusion. Engineers are not only respected in Florida; they are revered, because they are expected to produce miracles of their own from the miracle of Florida's Mediterranean type of climate: enough fresh water for inhabitants whose numbers increase by 10 percent per year and also for broad fields of reclaimed muck that grow an important share of the rest of America's winter vegetables. Engineers must guard quasi-tropical riches in a state that actually at no point touches the tropics at all. It is another—and stunning—Florida anomaly.

The total area of Florida is approximately 58,000 square miles. About 4,000 of these are water. Florida's tidal coastline is—more or less—3,700 miles long, and 800 of them are tourist-beckoning beach. The fact that all of Florida lies north of the Tropic of Cancer—by a hundred miles at its southernmost point—does not deter sun-seekers who arrive in droves every winter. "Snowbirds," Floridians call them, half in good-natured derision and half in affection capable of astonishment when some madman from Yankeeland braves the Atlantic off

Miami Beach in mid-January. Florida residents swim when they believe God meant them to, from May until October.

In the northern part of the state, the climate—and the atmosphere—are Deep Southern. Here the massive live oaks spread, and, in fitful winds, the undersides of bay tree leaves shimmer silver through their sunlit swamps. Where Florida is not hammock land—rich enough to support a growth of oaks and other trees requiring soil with plenty of humus—it is pinewoods. The dimensions of Florida's pinewoods are staggering to tourists who see them for the first time: mile upon mile of erect trunks of slash and longleaf pine, with an under-story of either saw palmetto, where the soil is sandy, or of gallberry and holly flats, where soil is more acid. A huge portion of central Florida is occupied by the Big Scrub of sand pines immortalized in the writings of Marjorie Kinnan Rawlings. It was in the Big Scrub that Jody Baxter learned to love his yearling and learned also that his love would have to be sacrificed for the crops that were meant to feed his family, not a capricious deer. It is a recurrent theme in Florida's natural history, this question of whether the beauty of wild things outweighs man's requirements for food.

The Keys, a chain of coral islands punctuating sapphire and emerald waters southwest of Miami, are the most nearly tropical part of the state. Here grow mahogany and gumbo-limbo trees; Bahama bananaquits chirp, and mangrove cuckoos perch on telephone wires; in summer, magnificent frigate birds soar in vivid blue skies and poincianas are heavy with scarlet racemes. Banyan trees send down fat aerial roots from their branches in the dooryards of houses with slatted windows and with gardens full of such hot-weather exotica as night-blooming cereus and sapodillas, guava trees and Cattleya orchids, and the miniature Key limes that are the main ingredient in the Key lime pie served from one end of the state to the other. Florida summers are violently hot, though patriotic weathermen have developed ingenious ways of disguising the fact: thermometers, for instance, which register air temperature far above the ground. One's radio may announce that the temperature is eighty-seven; the thermometer down at the little sand-yard grocery not far from the beach may register 112, and that not altogether in sun.

When Florida doesn't feel like accepting a truth, it blissfully ignores it. In winter, in its northern part, the state can be—as Tallahasseans say—colder than a hound dog's nose. Night-time temperatures in the teens have happened there, cutting back garden viburnums and pyracanthas; so has happened snow, if rarely. When snow falls in Tallahassee, it is a festival: men, women, and children get out their cameras and rush over to the Greek-columned governor's mansion to take shots of the governor's orange tree—the state tree, planted farther north than it should be—with its branches weighted down by white stuff. The governor's tree is carefully tended in winter, surrounded by a roofless polyethylene shelter and warmed in crises of temperature by smudgepots. The citrus groves, oceans of them, their dark green leaves glistening in the sun, fill the center of the state, a spreading testimony to America's preoccupation with Vitamin C.

Florida is a rainy state. Measurable annual fall ranges from fifty to about sixty-five inches. Florida housewives—notorious buyers of shower curtains, of which mildew takes its frequent toll—are also veteran bug fighters, though, with resigned gentility, we call flying cockroaches "palmetto beetles." If cockroaches are a disgrace in the North, they are a fact of life in Florida.

So are sometimes more bizarre visitors—the rat snake, for instance, that found its way inside a concrete-block house and made for the toilet bowl, around which it wrapped itself in an ingenious effort to keep cool. Florida has more than its share of water moccasins and rattlesnakes (rattler rodeos are local festivals in various parts of the state), copperheads in the north, and everywhere the particularly lethal little coral snake whose venom can paralyze and kill so quickly.

Less menacingly, there are gnats and tiny sand-flies called no-see-ums, because one can't: one can only itch. Florida's assortment of flies is Gothic in its splendor: deer flies and dog flies and yellow flies that raise welts on human skin not unlike those of poison ivy. In the poetic-looking Spanish moss festooning the oaks and cypresses of north and central Florida dwell redbugs, which can burrow into flesh and sooner or later will.

Termites make a bee-line for unprotected frame houses, and exterminators everywhere rake in fortunes. Gardens play host to fire ants, relative newcomers, whose bites burn raw, and whose mounds spring up too high for lawn mowers to level.

Floridians almost universally discount these hazards of Florida heat and humidity. Nobody really minds. Belts and shoes turn blue in August if the air-conditioning is inefficient. Such perils are not a high price to pay for caressing trade winds, roses in January, creamy orange blossoms in April, and Gulf Stream fishing. Most people who deplore Florida's entomological richness are journalists in search of stories. Northerners who can't make the trip south are comforted by chronicles of the redbugs and the fungi. They are also comforted, presumably, by the often-repeated comment that Florida is a vast and verdant clip joint. "In the chromium-plated slums of Miami Beach," once gravely intoned Nevada newspaper publisher Lucius Beebe, "may be found the true epicenter of world suckerdom, a scene of such carnage among the spenders that even French restaurateurs and hoteliers, themselves among the foremost practitioners of tourist larceny, come here for refresher courses." [6] Perhaps, but Miami Beach has yet to learn the thriving French custom of removing bill-incurring light bulbs from their bathroom sockets. It has also yet to learn the larceny of Las Vegas.

For the past seventy years, Florida has been the scene of ecological donnybrooks. Propaganda leaflets from conservationists and developers could fill freight cars, and do tax the floor space of the State Library in Tallahassee. Even so loyal a Florida-praiser as Norman Ford alludes to the hundreds of miles of finger canals being dug to supply waterfront real estate. Salt water seeps under the porous limestone rock, souring wells and killing vegetation. There are artificial shores where a palm tree's life isn't worth a nickel. The finger canals, in places, are rich repositories of infection. They are not subject to tidal flushing, and thus they trap human fecal matter. A swim in such a canal

6. June Cleo and Hank Mesouf, *Florida: Polluted Paradise* (Philadelphia: Chilton Books, 1964), p. 69.

could reward the swimmer with blood poisoning, dysentery, or
kidney ailments. All this, according to marine biologist Jack
Rudloe of Panacea, in the Panhandle, is "the old Florida rape
job. Hurry up and develop it and sell it to the suckers and
leave." [7] But there are corporations, too, that stay: the Mackle
Brothers, for instance, creators of several resort-in-retirement
ventures. Worriers, though, may well conclude that if pneumonia doesn't get you, paratyphoid may. Even the sun's actinic
therapy has its limits.

But it is vain to try to track down poisoned victims. Waterfront idylls proceed merrily to be created; and, if their marine
life is havocked, few human inhabitants seem the worse for
wear. Because Florida—in its natural and also its man-altered
reaches—possesses an intense and even heartbreaking beauty,
emotions run high. Nobody expects northern New Jersey to be
heaven on earth; Secaucus is allowed to stink of its pigs and
chemical factories with impunity. But because perfection is expected of the Land of Flowers, because Florida must remain a
haven for the discontented of other states, growing ranks of en-
vironmentalists demand of it total fragrance and total purity.
Florida's beauty can also become Florida's burden, and the fact
is nowhere more vividly seen than in its two ranking environmental controversies: the Cross-Florida Barge Canal and the
Central and Southern Florida Flood Control District.

The Barge Canal was a gleam in the eyes of entrepreneurs as
far back as 1821, when the United States acquired the Sunshine
State from Spain. Vast benefits were projected from a channel
that would cut through north-central Florida and bear the barge
traffic of factories and agriculture. Today, the canal works are a
raw scar, nowhere more outrageously apparent than on U.S.
Route 19 as the traveler drives south from Inglis to New Port
Richey. The canal has been begun—more than once—and by
order of President Nixon, in 1971, under the pressure of ecologists, it was again discontinued. Commerce and agriculture
grumble, and romantics hail the rescue of nearby wild rivers.
Meanwhile, the gigantic aborted ditch stretches out to sea, and

7. Quoted in Rackleff, *Close to Crisis,* p. 89.

no carpet of flowers mitigates the austerity of its disused banks. Who is right? There are as many answers as there are Florida causes; in heaven, causes proliferate.

The Central and Southern Florida Flood Control District, the FCD, which has harnessed the water resources of the Kissimmee River network and those of Lake Okeechobee, is as hot an emotional potato as the barge canal. The late Philip Wylie turned his attention from momism to Everglades muck drainage when he wrote that should "the Gulf of Mexico and the Atlantic meet underground" because of this drainage, "a million and more Floridians would have to reach more than 200 miles north for a drink of water." Engineers smiled; was Mr. Wylie a biologist, geologist, or engineer, himself? In February 1959, *Harper's* magazine ran a shocker entitled "The Florida Swamp That Swallows Your Money." The whole thing had been "dreamed up" by the Army Corps of Engineers in 1947, and soft-spoken, venerable Florida Senator Spessard Holland had sold the chimera to Congress. It was not flood control. It was, said *Harper's,* a land-reclamation project that benefited "a few large landowners; their giant farms, resorts, supermarkets, and housing projects are doubling, tripling, and quadrupling in value . . . It will make a killing for a few speculators." Yet Americans of the seventies continue to demand entrance into the Great Escape, and Florida can hardly be blamed for wanting to find a place to put them. It can also hardly be censured for wanting land on which to help feed America as cheaply as it can. Galloping inflation in the supermarket has intruded into American lives and has fostered new reflections on what the National Audubon Society calls *agribusiness.*[8]

In September 1928, a hurricane tore into Lake Okeechobee with tragic waves and gales. In the whole town of Belle Glade, afterwards, only six buildings remained on their foundations. The waters of the lake had gone on an epic rampage that had drowned more than two thousand people. Coffins could not be brought in fast enough. There was no drinking water, nor were there telephone wires or passable roads. Stormy Governor Na-

8. Quoted in Cleo and Mesouf, *Polluted Paradise,* pp. 91, 92.

poleon Bonaparte Broward, a former steamboat captain who took office in 1905, had dreamed of draining the Everglades as early as the turn of the century. There had since been federal investigations, scandals, state politics, charges and countercharges. The phrase "land by the gallon" had become a red flag. By November 1930, the Army Corps of Engineers started construction of an improved levee on the lake's south rim. The swampland sang with dredges and shovels and the rumble of earth-moving equipment. By 1937, the federal government had already spent sixteen million dollars on the project. But from 1931 to 1945, south Florida experienced, not floods, but a drought that bred holocausts. The drained muck-land burned; Miami wells were shut down, as salt water invaded them; and in wild places, deer and raccoons and panthers were consumed, in agony, by ruthless walls of flame. After World War II came large-scale agriculture; this meant a still greater strain on south Florida's water resources. In 1947, another hurricane struck. Damage to agricultural interests was in the hundreds of millions of dollars. The Kissimmee River, to the north, could not handle excessive water any more than the drained muck-land could tolerate unregulated fire. In 1949, the Central and Southern Florida Flood Control District was created to manage water in an area the size of New Jersey, nearly sixteen thousand square miles. Spessard Holland, Florida's courtly former governor and long since its respected senior senator, fought for the FCD project in Congress. Again dredges moved in; so did sportsmen, who found the new canals teeming with bass. Half a million acres of farm land had emerged. But all this was tampering with nature, ecologists rightly asserted. It was, replied the FCD, but "man has had to interfere with nature's cycle of flood and drought to make central and southern Florida habitable. He must continue to change and control the area's topography as long as he lives here. Once he starts, there is no turning back." [9] And he had started to tamper more than a half century before.

The Everglades, avid wilderness enthusiasts maintain, have

9. Richard P. Bush, "Beyond Disaster," undated mimeograph of film script (West Palm Beach, Fla.: Central and Southern Florida Flood Control District), p. 9.

suffered irreparable damage in losing some of their natural water supply at dry seasons, and in being flooded during wet ones. In the summer of 1966, a herd of five thousand deer were stranded in Everglades floods. The FCD and the Army Corps of Engineers got the blame, as bucks, does, and fawns drowned helplessly in the swirling waters. The executive director of the FCD protested that the same thing had happened in 1947, before the FCD had existed; the FCD could not manage south Florida's water resources exclusively for the benefit of animals and fish and birds in the Everglades. Again, beauty in Florida was at war with circumstance. The horror in a drowning deer's eyes had to be weighed against America's need for Florida's potential farm land. That farm land could be beautiful too was seldom mentioned. In 1974, it was determined that Broward and Palm Beach counties on the lower southeast coast were losing a total of eighteen thousand acres yearly to urban development. "This shortage of farm land is going to slip up on us like the gasoline shortage," said Donald E. Vandergrift of the Palm Beach-Broward Soil and Water Conservation District.[10] For, just as lovers of nature and wildlife yearned for the vanishing flocks of wood ibises whose wings beat over the swamps like soft thunder, students of man were beginning to understand that Thomas Robert Malthus had had important things to say about the increase of the world's population. America was no longer able to deal in huge crop surpluses. And the part of the Everglades not contained in the Everglades National Park was potential growing land. Engineers and romantics continue to maintain battle lines. Vegetation changes may not be detrimental to the Glades environment, say the engineers, while the romantics see the fear in the eyes of dying animals and the shrinking of a primeval sawgrass wilderness like no other on earth. It is an issue as old as science: what right has man to seize the territory of his fellow creatures? How shall the land be used? What are the priorities? None of these questions is easy, when you are standing in the magnificence of a Glades hammock of royal palms and watching clouds of white egrets fly overhead to watery feeding

10. *Palm Beach Sun-Sentinel,* January 4, 1974.

grounds that they must have to survive. It is a paradox of the FCD that the perimeter levees of its major conservation areas now protect the heart of the Glades from encroachment, even as they symbolize man's interference with an ecosystem. The ecosystem is tough, say many biologists; yo-yo fluctuations of flood and drought in the Glades are natural. All life, counter the romantics—who have biologists of their own—is fragile; none should be lost, whether insect or vegetable or animal or human. Florida, like the rest of the earth, suffers from human tenancy; its sufferings are heightened, however, by its very mystique. Why must there be problems in paradise?

Florida differs from most of the rest of America also in its heritage. Pilgrim fathers never trod its shores. Until Great Britain acquired the territories of East and West Florida from the Spanish in 1763 for a treaty trade that lasted only two decades, English was, in Florida, an unknown language. The culture of the state was Spanish, where it was not Indian. Florida never had the tidy red-brick governmental palaces of Anglo-Saxon domination. It had Indian *chikees* and Cuban fishing shacks, an offbeat tradition of barbecued red snapper with oranges instead of one of turkey and cranberries and pumpkin pie. When the United States finally acquired Florida as her own, after the lightning raids of Andrew Jackson as the nineteenth century unfolded, she realized that her newest territory was highly un-American. It had no Mullinses or Standishes, no Jeffersons or Madisons. It had Latins, and where they were absent, it was held by the Tustenuggees and Miccos, war and civil chiefs of the Creek Indian nation and their offshoot, the Seminoles. But the Creeks and Seminoles were as much late-comers as the Spanish had been in 1513, at Easter-time, when Ponce de León landed on the peninsula he thought was an island; Florida was inhabited then by Apalachees and Timucuas and Tequestas and Calusas and Ais. They in turn had displaced other groups, which had, in antiquity, displaced the last mastodons. The history of Florida is one of seizures and barbaric romance. America's dreams, the weather, nature, man, and a memory of the conquistadores have all made Florida what it has become. And whatever else it is, it is never static. "No state is under greater pressure," says ecologist Raymond F. Dasmann in his book *No Further Retreat: The Fight To Save Florida,* "from all the forces that place demands upon land, water and life. The United States begins or ends in Florida." [11] It also began with the spoils of Spain. For four hundred years, Florida has been North America's ranking treasure hunt. It is not surprising that this treasure hunt has kept its traditional glamor. Who knows what lies under the beckoning, alien palms unknown to the temperate zone? Besides—it's snowing in Akron, Ohio!

11. Quoted in Archie F. Carr, *The Everglades,* The American Wilderness Series (New York: Time-Life Books, 1973), p. 156.

2

Cutthroats and Crosses

$\mathcal{M}$AN has been in Florida for at least ten thousand years. Probably the migrants from Asia destined to be miscalled Indians were crossing the Bering Strait as early as the biological era of glyptodonts—which were giant armadillos—and mastodons. Some of Florida's treasure consists of fossils that reveal what an astonishing assemblage of animals once inhabited the state: saber-toothed tigers, camels and horses, tapirs, large rodents called capybaras, outsize cave bears, and the doglike direwolves whose shrill barking echoed through the warm nights. If the first men who discovered Florida did not remember ice and snow, the tradition at least of Siberia's austerities must still have been vivid. A peninsula lay waiting: benign, teeming with game, full of deep springs of fresh water, and bordered by salt seas rich in fish. The terrestrial Happy Hunting Ground must have awed the wanderers, even as it made them grateful for their luck.

The Paleo-Indians were not agricultural. They were hunters and fishermen, and Florida was ideally suited to their way of life. Later tribes brought in a mortuary cult; some of their burial mounds have survived, along with their richly decorated pottery. By around A.D. 1500, the burial-mound culture was replaced by one that centered around sun worship. The red men raised imposing temples on elaborately fashioned mounds, higher than the old ones that had contained graves. They began growing corn, beans, and squash. The sun worshippers were

18

artists; they carved intricate birds and animals to represent their totems, they gilded ceremonial objects, they painted vivid ritual masks, and the peninsula echoed with the music of their reed flutes and conch trumpets. In the northwest lived the Apalachees; the large family of Timucuas inhabited the east coast and upper peninsula; and south of Tampa Bay, the warlike Calusas were dominant. Smaller tribes like the Tequestas, who lived at the eastern edge of the Everglades, kept endless vigil for roaming Calusa war parties. War, to the Calusas, was a religion, rather than a means of expanding their territory. There was enough of Florida to support its aboriginal population bountifully, but the Calusas wanted the glory and daring of battle.

It was most likely the Timucuas who saw first the pale invaders at whose hands they were doomed to perish. Florida was named by Juan Ponce de León in 1513; it was the season of Easter when he rounded Cape Canaveral, and he was looking, not for a Fountain of Youth, but for gold. The Fountain-of-Youth legend was created by later Spanish writers who wanted to embellish the simple realities of Ponce's exploration. He was no doddering visionary, but a tough, seasoned soldier, and when he was attacked by Indians on the lower southeast coast in the Land of Mayami, he fought back with savage ardor. He also fought with greyhounds trained to tear their quarry to pieces. It was only twenty-one years since Columbus in the West Indies had seen a race of natives who had, artlessly, welcomed him: he had reported of the Tainos that their manners were decorous and praiseworthy. The decorum did not survive the forays of the first conquistadores, who enslaved any Indians they found, as they searched the New World for booty. Sometimes Spanish caravels and brigantines were wrecked in swirling Florida storms and on treacherous offshore reefs. Some of the Cuban and West Indian slaves managed to swim to shore, and they forewarned the tribes of Florida. When Florida's Indians first saw Juan Ponce de León, they already understood what manner of men the freebooting Spanish were. What they did not understand was that Spain would hound them out of their very existence—with germs, if not with swords.

The history of white Florida thus began with violation. The conquistadores were no mild-mannered religious dissidents, as were the Pilgrims who, in 1620, would claim Massachusetts. Neither were they encumbered by the refinements of seventeenth-century Virginia gentlemen. What they wanted was a fortune, and they were quick to kill. They were also Roman Catholic Christians who justified their contempt for Indians by condemning them as pagans. It was 1528 when a one-eyed, red-bearded giant, Pánfilo de Nárvaez, landed on the shores of Tampa Bay and boomed out to an empty Timucua village a royal proclamation that the Indians could not have understood, even if they had heard it:

> In behalf of the Catholic Caesarean Majesty of Don Carlos, King of the Romans, and Emperor ever Augustus, and Dõna Juana his mother, sovereigns of Leon and Castile, Defenders of the Church . . . I, Pánfilo de Nárvaez his servant, messenger and captain, notify and cause you to know in the best manner I can that God, our Lord, one and eternal, created the heaven and earth, and one man and one woman of whom we all have come. . . . All these nations He gave in charge to one person, called St. Peter, that he might be master and superior over mankind, to be obeyed and head of all the human race . . . Him they call *Papa,* which means admirable, greatest, father and preserver. . . . One of the popes who succeeded him . . . made a gift of these islands and the main of the Ocean Sea to the said Emperor and Queen . . . I entreat and require you to understand this well . . . and that you recognize the Church as Mistress and Superior of the Universe, and the High Pontiff, called *Papa,* in its name, the Queen and King, our masters in their places as Lords, Superiors, and Sovereigns of these islands and main . . . You shall not be required to become Christians except when, informed of the Truth, you desire to be converted . . . as nearly all the inhabitants of the other islands have done . . . when His Highness will confer on you numerous privileges and instruction, with many favors.[1]

After this capsule history of the Holy Catholic Church and the rulers of Spain, Nárvaez, his voice echoing in the deserted village, got down to business:

1. Woodbury Lowery, *The Spanish Settlements Within the Present Limits of the United States* (New York: G. P. Putnam's Sons, 1911), pp. 178–180.

If you do not do this, and of malice you be dilatory, I will enter
with force, making war upon you from all directions and in any
manner that I may be able. I will take the persons of yourselves,
your wives and your children to make slaves, sell and dispose of
you, as Their Majesties shall think fit, and I will take your goods,
doing you all the evil and injury that I may be able . . . and I
declare to you that the deaths and damages that arise therefrom, will
be your fault and not that of His Majesty, nor mine, nor of these
cavaliers who came with me.[2]

The history of white—and thus, ultimately, of black—
America began in Florida, and it began in blood. The Timucuas, when they emerged from the palm thickets bordering
Tampa Bay, ordered Nárvaez with unmistakable signs to leave.
It was a brave gesture; no Timucua had ever seen anything like
these white-faced men in gleaming armor astride their massive
Andalusian horses. But it was not the Timucuas who conquered
Nárvaez; it was the interior wilderness of Florida, and, finally,
the Gulf of Mexico, washing over crude wood-and-horsehide
boats that Nárvaez and his men fashioned for escape, after their
supporting fleet had failed to rendezvous in the country of the
Apalachees. "Apalachen! Apalachen!" the Timucuas had said
to Nárvaez, as they pointed north. *Apalachen,* to the Spanish,
was gold. In quest of it, ultimately, all but two of Nárvaez's
party died. One survivor was Alvar Nuñez Cabeza de Vaca,
who wandered for years among Southern and Southwestern Indians before he climbed the Sierra Madre range toward Spanish
Mexico and freedom. Later, he wrote a book about his experi-
ences; *The Journey of Alvar Nuñez Cabeza de Vaca* is an American classic that captures the rugged splendor of a continent
—and the determination of human will to survive.

Just as modern America's first history emerged from Florida,
so also in Florida there originated the tale that has become
another American classic. We know the participants as Powha-
tan, Pocahontas, and Captain John Smith. But Captain John
Smith was a reader of stirring Spanish adventures, and his rescue by Pocahontas was inserted into the second edition of his

2. Lowery, *Spanish Settlements,* p. 180.

own Virginia narrative, after he had learned about the dramatic deliverance of a Spaniard named Juan Ortiz, in Florida.

Ortiz had come from Cuba in search of the missing Nárvaez. What he found, instead, was a Timucua chief, Hirrihigua, whose nose had been slashed by Nárvaez after the Indian had failed to acknowledge the sovereignty of the High Pontiff called *Papa*. For good measure, Nárvaez had thrown Hirrihigua's mother to snarling dogs, which devoured her. In the Timucua village of Ucita, on Tampa Bay, memories of the Spanish were long. When young Ortiz rowed in from the bay, he met capture. Hirrihigua had him bound and was about to roast him in a torture the Timucuas called *barbacoa*. The searing flames were already blackening Juan's flesh when Hirrihigua's young daughter Ulele pleaded with her father for his life. The chief's wife also interceded, and because Hirrihigua was a good husband and father, he granted the women's wishes. He even permitted Juan to recover under his own royal roof—for a while. But he could not forget what Nárvaez had done to him, nor forget his mother's screams as Spanish greyhounds were eating her alive. Again Hirrihigua vowed to kill Juan, this time by swift arrows, rather than slow fire, as a concession to his family. But Ulele stole out of her father's hut after dark to find the handsome Spaniard and urge him to flee Ucita: she would send a guide into the wilderness, and the guide would lead him to a neighboring chief, Mocoso, who was Hirrihigua's enemy. Juan dared the rattlesnake-infested saw palmettos of Tampa Bay's shores, and the guide came, as Ulele had promised. Mocoso magnanimously took Juan in, and Juan began learning the Timucua language. Americans centuries later would adopt, in form considerably tamer, both the fire ritual and the Timucuans' word for it, in the great American backyard barbecue.

Thus, on the hot and profusely vegetated beach of the bay, when Hernando de Soto later attacked a band of Mocoso's Indians, he was astonished to hear one of them shout: "Do not kill me, Cavalier! I am a Christian! My name is Juan Ortiz and I come from Seville." [3] De Soto thus acquired an interpreter who

3. A Hídalgo of Elvas, *A True Relation of the Vicissitudes That Attended Governor*

promised to accompany his expedition on its pursuit of gold. Juan was a Roman Catholic, and he knew he must leave pagans for Christians. He and de Soto and a band of conquistadores cut their way through Florida's interior up to the Appalachian mountains of southwest Virginia and, ultimately, to the shores of the Mississippi. Both Juan and de Soto died of fever and the elements, though some of the expedition survived. They it was who told of what a Florida chief—they called him a *cacique*—had answered when, through Juan, de Soto had delivered the customary Spanish theological and military oration. "I have long since learned who you Christians are," said Acuera, who ruled forests and dim swamps north of Tampa Bay:

> I already know very well what your customs and behavior are like. To me you are professional vagabonds who wander from place to place, gaining your livelihood by robbing, sacking, and murdering people who have given you no offense. I want no manner of friendship or peace with people such as you. . . . I am a king in my land and it is unnecessary for me to become the subject of a person who has no more vassals than I. I regard those men as vile and contemptible who subject themselves to the yoke of someone else when they can live as free men. . . . I and all my people have vowed to die a hundred deaths to maintain the freedom of our land.[4]

Most of Acuera's people were dead by the time Don Tristan de Luna y Arellano landed at Pensacola in 1559 and, in 1565, Pedro Menéndez de Avilés established America's oldest city, St. Augustine, where he imprisoned wayward Indians who refused to bow before either Spanish might or the High Pontiff called *Papa*.

Along with the conquistadores, another species of Spaniard arrived in Florida—the priest, and through him occurred the founding of the oldest Christianity in America. (Florida abounds in "oldests.") The Floridian altar was, literally, more venerable than the Floridian hearth. Though Ponce de León had had no

Don Hernando de Soto, edited by Edward Bourne (New York: A. S. Barnes, 1904), p. 27.

4. Garciláso de la Vega, "The Inca," *The Florida of the Inca,* translated by John Grier Varner and Jeannette Johnson Varner (Austin: University of Texas Press, 1951), pp. 118–119.

clergy in his party on his first expedition to Florida, when he returned in 1521 to colonize his "island," it was with two hundred men and fifty horses, cats to catch mice in granaries, and dogs for watching and, on occasion, eating refractory pagans. He brought crossbows and guns and spears, implements for tilling the soil, and both secular and monastic clergy. On Apalachee Bay in north Florida, Ponce was met by Apalachees who shot their arrows into him. Mortally wounded, he left Florida with his priests and his menagerie and his equipment to return to Cuba, where he died. One-eyed Pánfilo de Nárvaez, of the stentorian voice that reminded his hearers of someone shouting in a cave, also brought missionaries. It was Nárvaez's fierce temper that had been responsible for the loss of his eye; in Mexico, he had fought with a lieutenant of Hernándo Cortez. The same temper had sliced off Hirrihigua's nose and killed the chief's mother. Father Suarez, who accompanied Nárvaez, could only watch in dismay.

Hernando de Soto came with his own complement of priests and Dominican friars, who carried ashore their vestments and the paraphernalia of the mass. They, too, had to watch in silence as de Soto hewed out his bloody trail up the peninsula. In the country of the defiant Acuera, he cut off fifty Indian noses and then murdered their erstwhile owners. To be a conquistador was to be a very connoisseur of noses. It is one of the riddles of the whole Spanish adventure that, as de Soto was responsible for tortures and slaughter, he was also responsible for the first Christmas service in what would become the United States. On the shores of Tallahassee's Lake Jackson, in north Florida, he and his priests observed mass; it was 1539, and black robes and white billowed in mild December winds while crosses gleamed in the sunlight. De Soto, a religious man, prayed for his enterprise and his little army. Then he went on, but not before he had become a storied scourge in Florida as "the chief tyrant." Of all the conquistadores, he was undoubtedly the most ruthless—and the competition was impressive. Survivors of his expedition told Bartolomé de Las Casas, Bishop of Chiapas in Mexico, what had happened. Bishop de Las Casas was soon writing to Prince Philip of Spain, King Carlos's heir, that de Soto had tormented and killed [the Indians] leading them like animals. When one became tired or fainted, they cut off his head at the neck, in order not to free those in front from the chain that bound them, and the body fell to one side and the head to the other. . . . It is said that the Chief Tyrant had the faces of many Indians cut, so that they were shorn of nostrils and lips, down to the beard; and in particular a group of 200 whom he either summoned or who came voluntarily from a certain town. Thus he dispatched these mutilated, suffering creatures dripping with blood, to carry the news of the deeds and miracles done by those baptized Christians, preachers of the Holy Catholic Faith. It may be judged in what state those people must be, how they must love the Christians, and how they will believe that their God is good and just.[5]

The price of death was too high, Las Casas believed, for a native's wish to keep his land and his failure instantly to acknowledge an unknown Redeemer.

With the pleadings of Las Casas, there came a change in Spain's policy of conversion. What was needed among the heathen were dedicated resident missionaries, it was decided. Fray Luis Cancer de Barbastro, a saintly Dominican who had made many converts among the Mexican Indians of Tampico, arrived in 1549 with three Dominican priests and a lay brother. Unfortunately, he arrived on the shores of Tampa Bay. The Timucuas did not understand his good intentions, and they wasted little time trying. Fray Luis was the first, though unofficial, American saint. The power of his deeply felt God could not erase from Timucua nightmares the spectres of Nárvaez and de Soto. Thirty-six years after Ponce de León had found Cape Canaveral, neither Spain nor its official faith had established permanent roots on Florida soil. In 1559, to what is now Pensacola, Don Tristan de Luna y Arellano brought a band of colonists that included Dominicans with "tried lives, learning, and doctrine" who were young enough to work among the Indians and learn their languages. The weather on Santa Rosa Sound was so gently warm, the scent of wild grapes so heady, that Don Tristan and his men saw no urgent need for houses. A hurricane descended on them with towering waves and wrecked most of

5. Bartolomé de Las Casas, *The Tears of the Indians* (New York: Oriole Editions, 1972), pp. 57–58.

their fleet. The storm, for the survivors, was followed by famine. Soldiers and priests began eating their horses and even the leather of the animals' harnesses. They were not rescued until 1561, when their Father Domingo of the Annunciation prayed for a miracle on a bright and devastated shore full of driftwood and rotting Spanish ship planks. In three days, the miracle came: fresh Spanish ships with food and the promise of deliverance. De Luna gratefully departed. Another attempt to settle Florida had failed ignominiously; by this time, Philip II was king of Spain, and he wondered aloud if Florida were worth all the expense and effort. Spanish treasure fleets on their way home from Mexico and South America still plied the main of the Ocean Sea, but the dreaming land of moss-laden oaks and tall, straight, longleaf pines remained in the hands of its Indians.

Already, however, the Indians had begun to fall victim to such white diseases as smallpox and measles. Then Spain heard that French and English pirates were setting forth for the Florida coast, and King Philip decided that the colonization of Florida was essential to protect Spain's rights in North America. Pedro Menéndez de Avilés, styled the Adelantado of Florida, arrived to found St. Augustine. He also sailed down the St. Johns River, which flowed from south to north and which he knew as the River of May, to find four French warships under the command of Jean Ribault, a Huguenot. On a subsequent expedition, Menéndez marched overland to the embryo French colony of Fort Caroline and, among these protestant settlers, he found things that struck him and his men dumb with horror: "Many packs of playing cards with the figure of the Host and Chalice on the backs, and many saints with crosses on their shoulders and other playing cards burlesquing things of the Church." The sacrilege earned the French a massacre. "Not as Frenchmen but as Lutherans!" exulted a businesslike Menéndez, over their corpses. Then he returned to St. Augustine where, as his brother-in-law and chronicler, Gonzalo Solís de Méras, reported, "Some persons considered him cruel, and others, that he had acted as a very good captain should." The authority and practicality of Menéndez was making St. Augustine stick. He sent for Andalusian Jesuits, and he lavished presents on the Indians. And in the name of the Holy Catholic Faith, under the very eyes of his absent wife's brother, he also had to commit bigamy.[6]

In Calos, capital of the Calusas on the lower southwest coast, Menéndez arrived, with gifts that included gourmet delicacies like quince jam, a complement of musicians with a dancing dwarf to amuse the cacique, dazzling Spanish clothes for the Calusa women, and two hundred arquebusiers to impress Calos's population. The cacique was taken by the quince jam. And these Christians were not killing, even though their weapons of destruction were more efficient than Calusa spears and arrows. Perhaps Christians had changed. The cacique stared at Menéndez's troops, and then announced: "I want to give you for wife my older sister, whom I love very much, in order that you may take her to visit the land of the Christians. If you send her back, I will become a Christian myself, for it appears better to me than to be an Indian." [7] Menéndez was aghast. So was Solís de Méras. If Menéndez took the woman, he won souls for Christ and strengthened the Spanish foothold in Florida. If he refused, he would earn not only the fury of spurned Calusas, but the disgrace of losing sovereignty on the Gulf of Mexico. But the lady was at least in her thirties and ugly, and her nakedness was covered only by a skirt of Spanish moss. The prospect of such an illicit marriage was not appealing.

"Here is my sister," said the cacique. "Go with her into the adjoining room and take her for your wife. If you do not, my Indians will be scandalized and will know that you are laughing at them and her. In this village are more than four thousand Calusas." [8]

Christian men, temporized Menéndez, could not sleep with women who were not Christians.

"We are Christians already," said the cacique, "since we

---

6. Gonzalo Solís de Méras, *Pedro Menéndez de Avilés,* translated and edited by Jeannette Thurber Conner (Deland: Florida Historical Society, 1923), p. 142.

7. Solís, *Pedro Menéndez,* p. 149.

8. Solís, *Pedro Menéndez,* p. 149.

have taken you for our elder brothers." The quince jam and the
dancing dwarf had done their work. Menéndez, his back to the
wall, launched into a discussion of the Trinity, original sin, the
resurrection, and the devil—a nasty cacique who "presides over
Hell." The cacique of Calos listened gravely. Then he spoke:
"Let there be rejoicing. Baptize my sister and give her a Christian name. Then sleep with her, for it shall be a great beginning
to our trusting one another." [9]

Menéndez watched numbly as the Calusa woman's hand-
maidens dressed her in the green silk gown he had brought her.
She looked, reported the understanding Solís de Méras, "much
better than when she was naked." What the first, legitimate,
and absent Señora Menéndez did not know would not hurt her.
Menéndez baptized his red bride himself with the name of Antonia, hoping to appease St. Anthony, to whom he had an espe-
cial devotion. In the morning, Antonia "arose very joyful."
Soon Menéndez deposited her in Cuba for instruction at the
hands of Spanish fathers there. What the fathers told her of
Christian doctrines concerning marriage, divorce, and adultery
is not known. When Menéndez returned from St. Augustine to
Cuba to get supplies for his capital, Antonia greeted him ecstat-
ically. Again he tried to stall her. He was a member of the
Roman Catholic order of Santiago, he said, and Knights of Santiago could not sleep with their wives until eight days after they
had put into port.

Antonia smiled ingenuously. Two of the days, she said, had
already passed. In six she would come to Menéndez's lodgings.
But later that day she decided not to wait. Surely her attractions
were stronger than the Vow of Santiago. She gained admission
to Menéndez's room by telling his porter that the Spanish Adelantado had sent for her. "What is this, sister?" exclaimed a
startled Menéndez as he sat up in his sheets. "Let me lie in a
corner of the bed!" she pleaded. Didn't he want the friendship
of the Calusas? Didn't he want them all to become Roman
Catholic Christians? Sighing, Menéndez opened his trunk to
give her a new chemise, a mirror, and a glass necklace he had

9. Solís, *Pedro Menéndez*, pp. 145 ff.

brought her. Antonia stayed. The Vow of Santiago, presumably, went by the board.[10]

The years that followed Menéndez's viceroyalty saw dedicated missionaries in Florida. They saw conversions, as well as martyrdoms. Menéndez made his peace in confession, and one day he wrote to his nephew: "After the salvation of my soul, there is nothing I desire more than to be in Florida and there end my days saving souls . . . It means all my happiness." Antonia had by then proved to be a disappointment. It turned out that she and her brother had professed love and Christianity in order to persuade Menéndez to kill the inhabitants of Tocobaga, a Timucua village to the north. When he refused, she shouted: "You have two hearts, Adelantado! One for yourself and one for Tocobaga! For me and my brother you have none." But by this time St. Augustine was being built, the Spanish had established a chain of forts and missions in northern Florida, and the cacique of Tocobaga was exclaiming that he had not thought the Christians so good, marveling that they had not slain his people and burned both gods and village.[11]

At Calos, Menéndez left Father Juan Rogel, a Jesuit, who got along well enough with the cacique until he discovered that the cacique was plotting to kill him and the Spanish soldiers who guarded his safety. A Spanish captain summarily executed the cacique. The chief's brother, Don Pedro, was put in his place. Don Pedro attended mass until he found that Father Rogel didn't want him to keep the time-honored Calusa custom of marrying one's sister. Father Rogel, for his part, found that the Calusas became most religious when they were issued the most presents. Eventually, the Calusas reasonably turned on him when he told them to destroy their shrines. He escaped with his life to Tocobaga, but the Indians there burned their village to the ground rather than shelter him; in council, they had decided that it did not pay to harbor Christians, even when they had committed no murders: they still had the potential. On Tampa Bay, Christianity had failed. In northwest and central Florida, it was kept

10. Solís, *Pedro Menéndez*, p. 191.
11. Solís, *Pedro Menéndez*, p. 226.

alive by optimistic friars in shabby, palm-thatched missions. The Franciscans arrived in 1587; Menéndez was then dead, but his nephew, Pedro Menéndez Marques, was Adelantado of Florida in his place.

Throughout most of the seventeenth century, the missions of the gentle fathers in brown prospered as well as they could in a country without gold. Spanish-Catholic Florida was a world away from pilgrim-and-puritan Massachusetts and Church-of-England Virginia. It was certainly a world older; its discovery in 1513 had preceded the landing of the *Mayflower* by a century and seven years, and even Jamestown had not been founded until 1607. Spanish Florida's ties were with Mexico and Central and South America. She looked to Cartagena, not Boston. Her settlers had their eyes on the equator, not the mainland to the north. Francisco Vazquez de Coronado had had his own foray into the Southwest, where he made no permanent settlement among the Pueblo Indians, but paved the way for subsequent Spanish expeditions. The Spanish of the Southwest, too, looked to Mexico and to South America. But Florida had been Spain's first toehold in North America, and at St. Augustine, the first house in America had been built. It is still sturdily standing, on a narrow, shaded street that echoes with the rumble of tourist carriages faithful to bygone originals.

In spite of Florida's antiquity, it remained a frontier. The heat, mosquitoes, and hurricanes guaranteed that. It had no glittering native cities, as Mexico and Peru had had: Tenochtitlan, Machu Picchu. Ultimately, climate controlled Florida's destiny as a possible outpost capable of supporting life in something like comfort. Air conditioning and refrigeration were invented by John Gorrie, a doctor in Apalachicola, in the middle of the nineteenth century. The Land of Mayami began to be built up only in the late nineteenth and early twentieth centuries. Florida, in many parts, is still a frontier. Huge expanses of pine forests in its northern tier are broken only by little towns: Bonifay, Chipley, Bagdad, Two Egg. The city of Tallahassee had no shopping malls until the 1960s, and once, in my early residence there, I had a shock. Talking with the elderly Dr. Mark F. Boyd, a distinguished Florida historian whom I met after having read several of his writings, I said something about his doctorate in history, and he smiled. "My doctorate is in medicine. I came down here, you know, to fight yellow fever." Soon afterward, there arrived at my front door a man who introduced himself as the *Aedes aegypti* Inspector. In the 1960s, Florida still regarded yellow fever as a possibility and was on the alert for the species of mosquito known to cause it. To my horror, the inspector found some in an unused, rain-filled flowerpot and gave me a lecture.

It has shaped Florida differently from the rest of the country, this history of blood and fanaticism and meteorological extremes. The state's theological tradition was originally one of bigotry. Perhaps it is the heat that has also intensified the fundamentalism of the backwoods Protestant sects who have replaced Jesuits and Franciscans, though not entirely displaced them. Florida has always been a country of violent drama. Hapless French Protestants seeking religious freedom on the St. Johns had been handily slain "as Lutherans." Where the Massachusetts pilgrims had been friendly to Squanto, the conquistadores had cut off the nose of Hirrihigua. Where Virginia settled into the genteel piety of Anglicanism, Florida had a turbulent chronicle of martyrdoms. Its first white settlers were Spanish from Spain and, afterward, Spanish Cubans, who established what they called "fishing ranchos" in the territory of the Calusas when time and diseases had killed off all but a tiny remnant of the tribe. Florida was innocent of the logic of British justice until it was traded to the English in 1763 by a weakened Spain. It knew nothing even then of English roast beef and ale. The prevailing drink was West Indian rum.

Florida not only looked different, with its waving palms and wild oranges and swamp alligators and rippling, blue-green waters moving over beaches of white sand: it *was* different; and its legacy of Spanish culture makes it different still. Pensacola restaurants serve Spanish *gazpacho,* though as a salad and not a cold vegetable soup, as the Andalusian original is. Florida is full of Gomezes and Solanas and Martinezes whose family history in the New World is four centuries old. (The other Gomezes and Solanas and Martinezes were to come later, as Cuban cigar workers and as middle- and upper-class refugees from the communism of Fidel Castro.) Florida's waves of Latin settlers have washed over it in successive tides. Florida eats garbanzo-bean soup and saffron-flavored yellow rice. It has no legacy of patroons, as does the Hudson Valley. The people who built the cathedral at St. Augustine were poor. Early fathers referred to the "misery" of the Spanish inhabitants. "Good as their intentions may be, they are and will be helpless as long as His Majesty does not deign to arrange some class of commerce for the development of the province." [12]

Florida, then, has a short history of democracy, and the democracy until 1964 included forbidding drinking fountains and restaurants to blacks. Instead, the patchwork past of the state is rich in excess, Mediterranean intensity, and physical violence. There are Floridians today who say, at the sign of trouble, not "Call the police," but "Get my gun." Somehow, all the heady emotion wore off on the Bible-toting Protestants who came with America in the nineteenth century. They, too, are rigidly sure of paradise. Did lynch mobs have their roots entirely in an ethic generally American-Southern, or did they, when they existed in Florida, not also date back to the do-it-yourself justice of Spain?

Florida has always understood and accepted extremes. Spanish Floridians under the rule of Britain could not fathom why Americans in Boston objected to a tax of pennies on tea. Taxation without representation? Who had ever been represented in the Escorial of Spain? What was, ultimately, meaningful to them was a fire-breathing Andrew Jackson who came down from the north like an avenging angel to wrest Florida from Spain's second period of control, which had begun in 1783. Jackson sacked and burned. He had suspected foes shot without ceremony. He behaved like a conquistador. For this, Latin Florida could accept him; in their torrid, half-trackless wilderness, and in the baroquely fortified site of America's first colony, they comprehended strength where they had never comprehended parliamentary niceties. Later Floridians did not understand the nonviolent legalism of Martin Luther King so

12. Solís, *Pedro Menéndez,* pp. 255 ff.

vividly as they understood the demands of Black Power. Always, Florida has been the passionate state. It is passionate still, and somehow the modern Yankees streaming into St. Petersburg and Miami have caught the contagion. Florida is their Valhalla; but they do not announce this modestly. They shout it, with a din that beats at the rest of the continent in an insistent fury worthy of loot-seeking Spanish soldiers of fortune. In the Land of Flowers, blood pulses strongly, and beliefs do not assert, but rage.

Florida had exactly twenty years of being British. This was not enough to give it anything in common with the thirteen colonies to the north. At the history of Virginia Dare, contemporary Floridians smile: many a Spanish wife in the time of Menéndez de Aviles had borne white children in St. Augustine. Florida drinks Kentucky bourbon these days, but it is also still plentifully stocked with Jamaican and Puerto Rican rum and also with pungent Mexican tequila. If tourist festivals pay tribute to early governors and missionaries, the festivals are most enthusiatic when they are celebrating pirates. The promoters of such festivals are even, as in Tampa, capable of inventing pirates themselves. José Gaspar, scourge of the Gulf, was born in a west-coast bar. From alcoholic fable, he quickly ascended to the distinction of being a patron saint. And where Benjamin Franklin and other Founding Fathers would be hopelessly incongruous, José Gaspar is right at home.

3

Sitting Out the
Spirit of '76

*O*VER a treaty table in winter-misted Paris, in February
1763, shivering British and Spanish diplomats in powdered wigs
reached an agreement: the distant Land of Flowers would be
traded to Britain in exchange for the bustling port of Havana,
which the British had conquered in 1762 in one of the American
forays of the Old World's Seven Years War. (To Virginia, it
was the French and Indian War.) Florida's new British owners
had reason to be elated: their country now extended over frigid
Canada, all of French Louisiana and its bayous east of the
coffee-colored Mississippi—excepting "the isle and City of
New Orleans"—and all of a mysteriously Spanish Florida, so
far undescribed in English journals. No longer did the banner of
León and Castille ripple in the wind over the vast stone fortress
the Spanish had built in St. Augustine. Spanish armor no longer
glittered hot-gold in the Florida sun, for no more Spanish troops
drilled in the light of that sun. Florida's Indians, Timucuas and
Calusas and smaller groups, who had held the peninsula in the
time of Ponce de León, had by this time been all but wiped
from the face of the earth. Such diseases as diphtheria and
syphilis had done their work, aided by the relentless British
guerillas based in Georgia and the Carolinas. Gone were most
of the Spanish missions. The lips of red men no longer mouthed

Franciscan prayers by dutiful rote; friars' brown robes no longer flapped in humid winds under the palms. Spanish Florida—what was left of it—watched doubtfully as two new breeds of men moved in: the smartly red-coated British army, and the sophisticated and aggressive Creek Nation of Indians. The Creeks were sophisticated because they had seen two centuries of white incursion with its attendant technology and cultural proselytizing.

The Creeks had originally controlled much of Alabama and nearly all of Georgia. They were divided into Upper and Lower towns, and their territory was full of war and peace villages and long council houses where they held the ceremony of the Black Drink, brewed from a variety of holly. Under the disciplined Creeks, the rural South was not so different from a much later South existing up to the time of World War II. Where Creeks had drunk the Black Drink, subsequent white Southerners swore by a tonic called Black Draught. Where the Creeks had played a particularly murderous kind of ball game, the latter-day South had and has its football rivalries, some attended by copious troops of on-duty police. Instead of Creek Council houses, white Southerners built frame courthouses; and in place of Creek temples, they constructed Protestant churches—the construction, much of the time, performed by blacks. Even as earlier Florida Indians had played host to red visitors from as far north as Ohio and Wisconsin, later rural Floridians were destined to play host to tourists of another kind. The continuity of Southern traditions is long, and it antedates Ponce de León by centuries.

The Creeks had come to Florida under pressure from burgeoning British settlements north of them. The first Creeks who made the journey from their Upper and Lower towns into the deepest South of sand beaches and feathery palms were called, by Creeks back home, *Siminoli,* wanderers. The Spanish, and afterwards the British, soon turned this into *Seminole.* By the date of the Treaty of Paris in 1763, north Florida had many Seminoles, as well as Creeks who maintained social and governmental ties with parent Georgia and Alabama villages, as the Seminoles did not. Creeks and Seminoles were as much invaders as the Spanish in their time had been; the issue of their coming would spark the bitter controversies of the First and Second Seminole wars, when a young United States contended that it had as much right to colonize Florida as the Creeks had ever had. Creek and Seminole villages were also augmented by another strain: black slaves frequently escaped Carolina and Georgia and Alabama masters to flee into Florida's shimmering longleaf forests and bay-filled swamps. The Indians also considered the black fugitives slaves, but the yoke of slavery they imposed was light: a small yearly tribute of crops to a Seminole master. Black refugees enjoyed life among the red men. With the advent of the British, many of them rose to positions of power in Indian villages, for they could speak English. They became interpreters, and it was often upon black understanding of red and white syntax that Florida treaties hinged. Blacks and Seminoles intermarried. Conservative Creeks considered their Seminole brothers "wild men," and the contrast between Creeks and Seminoles was enhanced as Seminole skins darkened. Many Creeks to the north had done racial mingling of their own with the Scottish traders sent them by Britain to offer such tempting conveniences as metal cookware—and then exact payment in land. There were many Creeks, by 1763, with blond hair and Scottish blue eyes. A ruling Creek family was called McGillivray, and there were plenty of McIntoshes, McCormicks, Farquharsons, and McGehees. Little Lachlans and Geordies ran in and out of Creek *chikees* while their mothers ground corn and stirred steaming cauldrons of cornmeal mush, *sofkee.* Today, most people are unaware that there are Creeks still living in north Florida: Indians with blue eyes? Even at powwows, there is skepticism; the Creeks, understandably irate, have to issue periodic statements that they are the genuine article. Among the Seminoles, by 1763, there were dark children called Cuffee and Abraham who watched their mothers stirring *sofkee* of their own. Seminole wives also made bread out of the roots of the slender-fronded zamia plant.

Already, then, Florida was an exotic mix. In St. Augustine, there were dark-haired, pale-skinned citizens who boasted of Castilian and Andalusian ancestry. On the lower southwest coast, there were former Cubans who mined the Gulf of fish and also sat long hours in the nearly tropical sun mending their nets. Scottish traders had left their mark on Indians, as had runaway blacks. The British, as they moved in, began to wonder what on earth they had acquired in this territorial outpost where cock-fights and an ethos of *mañana* were the rule, but afternoon tea with hot buttered scones was not, not ever. The Scottish traders had been businessmen, not housewives.

Since Florida was unwieldy in British eyes, its new owners divided it into two provinces, East and West Florida. The Pan-handle's Apalachicola River was fixed as the boundary line. As East Florida had St. Augustine, West had the intimidating set-tlement of Pensacola, a favorite resort of pirates and prostitutes, as well as of visiting Indians on whiskey-inspired sprees. Towns such as these were no prim Methodist enclaves, as were those in Georgia. They were not the proudly (if casually) Anglican set-tlements of Carolina planters. Florida was rough, and London lords wanted descriptions of it to assist them in their judgments. Since the British intention was to colonize the Floridas, English readers hungrily devoured treatises like those of the English Surveyor-General, de Brahm, who noted that St. Augustine houses were of masonry and shells and had wide piazzas "sup-ported by Tuscan pillars" and that the governor's house had also "a Belvidere and a grand portico decorated with Doric pillars and entablatures." [1] Perhaps; but no self-respecting Eng-lish peer would have confused it with the humblest of manor houses.

"I cannot help," wrote another observer, the naturalist Ber-nard Romans, who was addressing himself to the Earl of Hills-borough, back home

> taking notice of a remark which I have read some where . . . which is that dampness or discoloring of plaister and wainscot, the soon moulding of bread, moistness of spunge, dissolution of loaf sugar, rusting of metals and rotting of furniture, are certain marks of a bad air; now, every one of these marks . . . is more to be seen in St.

1. W. T. Cash, *The Story of Florida* (New York: American Historical Society, Inc., 1938), pp. 139–140.

Augustine than in any place I ever was at, and yet I do not think, that on all the continent, there is a more healthy spot; burials have been less frequent here than any where else . . . the Spanish inhabitants live here to a great age.[2]

Romans knew nothing about the actinic therapy of the sun, but Florida had acquired a promoter.

On the St. Mark's River, in the northern part of East Florida, there was a ramshackle stone fort falling into ruin, San Marcos de Apalache. Pensacola, said a British agent, boasted forty thatched huts along with a garrison that housed (more or less) three or four hundred inhabitants. In Pensacola, there were no darkly evergreen orange groves, fragrant in spring with drifts of creamy bloom. There were no sprawling fig trees such as those Spanish pioneers had brought to their first capital; nobody grew any grapes or tended any herb gardens. Grapes and herbs were in the woods, for the taking. What Pensacola had in common with St. Augustine was mostly the presence of alligators with red eyes and sinister teeth.

"The soil of many parts of Florida is remarkably fertile and may be cultivated to great advantage," the *Gentlemen's Magazine* of London informed its subscribers in November 1763. "On the shore oysters abound in plenty and the bays abound with fish. The inland country is plentifully flocked with cattle, whose hair is so fine that with a proper mixture of furr or wool it is capable of being manufactured into hats or cloth." [3] West Florida, predicted the article's author, would "soon be numbered among our most flourishing colonies." This, of course, was whistling in the dark; but lyrical Florida propaganda had begun. When British Governor Johnstone reached Pensacola in 1764, he tried not to see its "huddle of huts" but its geographical similarities to "Tyre, Sidon, Carthage, Colchos, Palmyra, Amsterdam, Venice, and Genoa." It was "the most pleasant place in the New World." [4]

---

2. Bernard Romans, *A Concise Natural History of East and West Florida* (1775; reprint edition, New Orleans: Pelican Publishing Co., 1961), p. 6.

3. Cash, *Story of Florida,* p. 142.

4. Cash, *Story of Florida,* p. 142.

But the British knew that poetry alone did not build thriving colonies. While their officials tolerated Florida's Latin Roman Catholics, some of whom were departing, they offered substantial lures for emigrants of their own kind. Large tracts of land went to Englishmen agreeing to come across the Atlantic, and bounties were promised for crops such as sugar, indigo, and rice. In 1764, Denys Rolle, a Londoner of substance, attempted to found a colony near modern Palatka, with indentured laborers. When he could not attract them, he turned to "vagrants, beggars, and debtors" from London's gutters. Unfortunately, the vagrants, beggars, and debtors began dreaming of tidy farms of their own in Florida, and when they had fled Rolle's colony, he was forced to use slave labor like that of Georgia and the Carolinas. Dr. Andrew Turnbull, a Scotsman, had the bright idea of bringing to Florida the natives of Mediterranean countries, where subtropical crops had long been grown. Surely, he reasoned, these people would know what to do with Florida soil, as the British did not always know. Turnbull's first choice was Greeks, but he was soon swelling their ranks with Italians from Leghorn and "a large company of starving Minorcans." [5] The strangers in paradise, however, could not get along. Knives glittered, and the Greeks and Italians staged a revolt. In Turnbull's colony of New Smyrna, the Minorcans emerged triumphant, until they decided that they had had enough of Turnbull's hot-tempered overseers and migrated north to the fleshpots of St. Augustine, where their descendants flourish today. Under the British, the Floridas were becoming not less heterogeneous, but more.

Few things united the provinces: not religion, not a common cultural tradition, not politics. The Floridas were far-flung and their people—polyglot black, polyglot red, and polyglot white—were often isolated. The Floridas were not fertile soil for the cogent political debates of such temperate climates as Virginia and New Jersey, where solid bourgeois citizens with related if not common national origins wanted representation in

5. Kathryn T. Abbey Hanna, *Florida: Land of Change* (Chapel Hill: University of North Carolina Press, 1948), p. 80.

London governing councils. A Minorcan suffering from malaria in St. Augustine and trying to build up a livelihood in figs was not likely to think in such abstractions as Liberty and Justice. Most of them were unaware that Caesar had had his Brutus, Charles I his Cromwell, and that George III could profit from their example. As unconcerned were the merchant princes of Indian trade, such as William Panton, a South Carolinian who came to West Florida and established the house of Panton, Leslie and Company, which was soon controlling Indian trade everywhere south of the Tennessee River. Panton was a dedicated Tory.

There was no reason, therefore, for Britain to fear contagion in Florida from the thirteen colonies to the north. The British Floridas were small. Commercially, they were insignificant. The cost of government was being borne, not by the colonists, but by the mother country, on whom the colonists depended for virtually every need. The American Loyalists who began arriving in East Florida swelled a small population. They were welcome. Back in London, the Colonial Secretary, the shrewd and seasoned Earl of Hillsborough, declared more than once that Florida was his favorite colony. Floridians were true-blue; they didn't cause any trouble.

Spain had difficulty making up her mind how she felt about the American Revolution, when it came. If England were defeated, Spain could find ways in which to profit from such a defeat. But what of the example of the rebellious erstwhile colonies? Grandees grew uneasy when they considered what might happen in the rest of Spanish America. Spain played a game of extreme caution at first. She gave money, under the table, to the French, who she knew would help the revolting colonies with it. It was regrettable, but Spain's hatred of the British went deep. Nobody, in the land of red-tiled roofs and olive groves that had bred conquistadores, could forget what had happened two hundred years earlier, when the Spanish Armada had been sent to invade England.

But then France grew indiscreet. On February 6, 1778, the French concluded treaties of commerce and political alliance with the *soi-disant* United States. Spain did not put pen to paper. She even tried, clumsily, to reconcile the rebels with their London antagonists by offering to serve as a mediator. Yet when the Spanish knew there could be no reconciliation, they finally brought themselves to sign a secret alliance with France in the spring of 1779. Spain cared nothing for the upstart colonies. She was still thinking about the Armada, and about the possibility of getting Florida back into the fold of her austerely Catholic possessions.

However, Spain had agreed formally to nothing in 1777, when Button Gwinnett, the elusive signer of the Declaration of Independence whose rare autograph now commands a small fortune, was appointed commander-in-chief of the forces of Georgia by the state's Council of Safety. Gwinnett had been enchanted with the rhetoric of his fellow Founding Fathers, and such was his innocence that he reasoned that the English and Spanish and Cubans in the Floridas merely awaited the sight of the American flag whipping smartly over the great fort at St. Augustine. He had proclamations distributed by emissaries who crossed the East Florida boundary at the St. Mary's River. Gwinnett waited confidently for East Floridians to rise against Britain. When no such rising occurred, he decided to send in soldiers. If the Floridians were lunatic enough to prefer George III to George Washington, they must be taught a lesson. A Colonel James Baker was ordered to march by land with a company of volunteer militia. Colonel Elbert, with four hundred Continentals in tow, was to rendezvous with Baker at a place called Sawpit, twelve miles from the mouth of the St. Johns River. Baker's volunteers soon showed themselves to be cowards interested only in their pay. In East Florida, many of them deserted outright, leaving Baker to handle incensed Seminoles who wanted no land-grabbing Americans in their midst. But Baker persevered, and at the appointed time, he got to Sawpit. The palmettos rustled, mockingbirds were singing from the swamps, and already the wild azaleas had flowered and then shed their orange petals. There was no Elbert. The colonel had got as far as the islands at the mouth of the St. Johns, but there he saw an assemblage of the British navy. "Heart of oak are our ships," Britons were fond of singing, "heart of oak are our men." There was a full complement of oaken hearts waiting at the mouth of the St. Johns, and Elbert ingloriously retreated to Georgia. Later that year, Button Gwinnett was killed in a duel with a hotheaded Scot named Lachlan McIntosh, and Georgia's Florida adventure was over.

If East Florida remained peaceful, with its nautical sentinels ready to frighten off would-be conquerors from the north, West Florida was another story. Spain still controlled New Orleans and the whole valley west of the Mississippi. Blue and yellow Spanish tiles were set into the houses of the city's erstwhile French Quarter, and the streets bore the names of Spanish princes. The governor of Louisiana was young Bernardo de Gálvez, whose father was a Spanish viceroy in South America and whose uncle was a Minister of the Indies. Gálvez was not a man in the lackadaisical tradition of most Spanish frontier officials. He quickly addressed himself to the business of making friends with the Creek Indians. One of them was Alexander McGillivray, not yet twenty-one, whose Loyalist father, a trader named Lachlan McGillivray, had had property in Georgia confiscated by the Americans. Lachlan McGillivray had returned to Scotland; his son Alexander, who had been getting a classical education in Charleston, South Carolina, returned to West Florida. Gálvez began playing an ingenious double role. He also offered a refuge to Americans who wanted to trade in his province. He began recruiting troops and drilling them, and he cocked a keen ear for diplomatic news.

When it came, with the intelligence that Spain had declared war on England on June 21, 1779, Gálvez moved swiftly. The British in West Florida had not yet heard. He marched into the town of Natchez, on the east bank of the Father of Waters, and summarily wrested it from British control. Then he proceeded to conquer all other British settlements on the river's east bank. By now, there was no doubt in the minds of British colonists that Gálvez meant business. On his part, he was determined to forestall any attack on New Orleans. When he was unable to persuade the Spanish captain-general of Cuba that further action was necessary, he shrugged off the timidity of officialdom and began making his own unauthorized military plans. In January 1780, he left New Orleans with 11 ships and 745 men for an attack on Mobile.

A norther was blowing on the Gulf. It made mountains of waves, and steel-grey rain slashed into the sailors' faces. On shore, a chill wind keened in the pines and tall rosemary bushes. Gálvez and his ships tossed in the Gulf until mid-February, when he sailed at last into Mobile Bay and began landing troops and cannons. His plan was to besiege Mobile. Ten days after he had arrived, 567 reinforcements came from Cuba; the captain-general had had a change of heart. There were 300 British in the tiny fort. Their food supplies were low. When the brown-eyed soldiers of Bernardo de Gálvez breached the fort wall in two places, the British surrendered.

Pensacola would be more difficult to take than Mobile, Gálvez knew. He sailed for Havana, and there he began readying an expedition of sixty-four ships and four thousand troops and their equipment. Five hundred men were sent to reinforce Mobile further. Gálvez and his Spanish ships of the line began entering Pensacola Bay on March 8, 1781. Soon soldiers were assembling on the rosemary-covered shores of Santa Rosa Island, where the spring light was so strong that the edge of the horizon shimmered a brilliant white. The commander of British Fort George, with about two thousand men, sent the message that he had no intention of surrendering. His food supply was better than Mobile's had been. At the end of March, a thousand fresh troops arrived from Havana; by May, the forces of Gálvez had fired Fort George's powder magazine, killing eighty-five English defenders. Then Spaniards began climbing over the fort's walls. As their fellows marched in triumphantly when they had opened the gates, they crushed beneath their feet the hopes of Great Britain to retain West Florida. Again, this part of the Floridas was Spanish. But East Florida was not entirely so. It had begun to fill with refugee Loyalists. Charleston and Savannah were evacuated, and five thousand Tories crossed the border on the St. Mary's and made for the safety of St. Augustine. There were not enough crops in East Florida to feed them, and great suffering resulted. America was now boasting that she, France, and Spain would clear the southeast of the British forever. But America had not reckoned on Spanish ambivalence. Fight Britain? By all means. Help revolting colonies? Never.

It was in the hazy warmth of a Tidewater Virginia autumn that the unthinkable—both to Britain and to Spain—happened. Lord Cornwallis surrendered; the fighting was over. America existed officially, as well as emotionally. By the spring of 1782, Patrick Tonyn, governor of East Florida, was wondering whether he and all his Loyalists should not sail home to the mother country. The Loyalists shrieked in protest, and began bombarding him with petitions. He reconsidered, but then he learned that the British cause in Florida was hopeless. The preliminaries of the peace negotiations called for the cession of East Florida to Spain. Already the Spanish had taken back their own in West Florida. What place was there in this godforsaken, backward, once more Latin Catholic outpost for British Protestants? St. Augustine settlers sent petitions to the king of Spain concerning their property rights and His Majesty loftily ignored them all. By February 1784, cession was a reality, and the British prepared to evacuate. Some decided to return to America. Those who wished to remain British might find a refuge in Nova Scotia, but the climate there was so raw that slaveowners feared the loss of their human property. Most of the British elected the Bahamas and the West Indies, and a share of them crossed the Mississippi into the howling wilderness beyond. Thirteen thousand persons, all told, black and white, moved out of Florida. In the environs of St. Augustine, plantations began to be overgrown; villages fell apart, and so did land values. Bandits began roaming the pinewoods and were still at it when the Spanish governor, Zespédes, arrived in June. Florida's Spanish and Cubans rejoiced; her Indians were fatalistic. Once more, Florida was a wild place where pines sang in the wind and warm waters washed inviolate shores against a background of dazzling blue sky and blue-green oceans that sparkled like diamonds in the sun. Once more Florida was out of the English-speaking American mainstream. The British interlude, the American War of Independence, began to assume dreamlike proportions in the minds of what was left of Florida's citizenry. Roman Catholic bells tolled once more in St. Augustine. Spanish who had left when the British had come began to return, and human aspirations in Florida were still unconcerned with the concepts of freedom and representation. Latin Floridians instead concerned themselves with the state of their souls and probable future time in purgatory. It is more than ironic that Florida's respite from despotism had been British; in the thirteen colonies, it was the British who had been excoriated as the despots. Spain had nominally been enlisted in the American cause. Now, ignoring the unsavory rebels of mainland America, she began claiming her own in the Land of Flowers. King and clergy ruled there once more, and Spain tried shutting her eyes to the columns of emigrants arriving from the north in the belief that the United States of America could eventually seize what a Spain in decline would not be able to hold. What, asked Spain, did Florida have to do with the poison of democracy? In the heart of the Earl of Hillsborough, living in retirement on his Irish estates in County Down, there was a poignant regret. His "favorite colony" was lost. Floridians were so easily governed, in spite of their barbarism, it was a pity.

4

Old Hickory
and Sir Walter

EITHER of the two principal molders of Florida in the nineteenth—and even, arguably, the twentieth—century was native to the state. Andrew Jackson, who brought the Territory its first institutional puritanism, was a back-country Carolinian who, at the time of his conquest of Florida, was based on his Tennessee plantation, the Hermitage, near Nashville. Architectural replicas of the Hermitage abound in modern Florida. Sir Walter Scott never laid eyes on the American South, but his writings gave it its code of honor, chivalry, and high romance. When a teen-age Baptist girl dreams of being Tallahassee's May Queen, she is paying homage to Jackson's Protestant ethic and Scott's tradition of winsome heroines. Even the now-cosmopolitan actress Faye Dunaway was a runner-up in her Tallahassee youth.

Florida never had quite the social cachet of South Carolina, which was likened to China because its denizens ate rice and worshipped their ancestors. Florida was equally addicted to ancestor-worship, but feasted on humbler grits. And where a Charlestonian of standing could point to staid Huguenot forebears (Ravenels and Manigaults), Floridian ancestors were often poor and sometimes downright unrespectable. By the time the United States acquired Florida from Spain in 1821, more than

46

one outlaw had roved into the land of high pines and shimmering palms. The average pioneer Floridian had become a species like the gloriously various animals to whom veterinarians, tactfully, refer as Mixed Breed.

Not all modern Floridians revere Andrew Jackson. The Creeks of contemporary Florida have good reason to call him "The Devil," which they do; they also call him *Jacksa Chula Harjo,* "Jackson—old and fierce," for, in 1814, he vanquished a Creek rebellion decisively at Horseshoe Bend on the Tallapoosa River in Alabama, then the Territory of Mississippi. The Creeks never recovered their former glory, at its zenith under Alexander McGillivray, who read Homer and Vergil in the original. Not only did Jackson conquer the Creeks; as president of the United States, he shipped a major part of the tribe out to the Indian Territory (later Oklahoma). The Creeks who stayed were mostly blue-eyed blonds not identifiable as Indians. At least fifteen hundred Creek households in north Florida today are their descendants.

Jackson was a man of the people, the first in the White House. The associates of George Washington and James Madison, attired in knee breeches, had danced minuets; Jackson's inauguration in 1829 was attended by a gaggle of roistering backwoodsmen in coonskin caps who climbed onto White House tables and triumphantly roared. But Jackson never approved of rebellions against the authority of the United States; his rebellion was reserved for Britain and Spain. In 1816, he blew up a disused British fort inhabited by runaway Negroes on the Apalachicola River and killed 270 fugitive blacks who had sought refuge from slavery there. They were American property. Sixty-one blacks were wounded; three escaped unhurt. Jackson believed of the Indians that the only good ones were dead ones; he had seen scalping victims in his frontier youth. That was why he swept down on Florida to punish its red men for daring to object to American squatters. In a series of forays in East Florida, he slew chiefs and imprisoned British traders as outside agitators. Never mind that Florida was Spanish. President James Monroe was trying to purchase it, and Jackson thought he could help his chief executive by making the market a buyer's. The whole of East Florida, he wrote Monroe in 1818, ought to be "seized and held as an indemnity for the outrages of Spain upon the property of our citizens." [1] Had not Spain failed to chastise sufficiently the "ruthless savages" who inhabited the land? He could take Florida in sixty days, he boasted. When Monroe received the letter he was sick in bed, and after reading two lines, about routine matters, he gave it to a subordinate. The subordinate didn't report back on Jackson's plans to conquer Spanish territory. Monroe learned of them only when Jackson, commander in chief of a campaign against resentful Seminoles refusing to vacate Florida for white newcomers, began the First Seminole War. Jackson attacked the Creek village of Fowltown, just north of the Georgia line, near today's Bainbridge. The Creeks fled south into Florida, where Jackson pursued them in the name of "peace and security." At a Seminole settlement on the Suwanee, Jackson seized the micco—the civil chief—and later had him hanged. Two luckless British traders on the scene were sent to Fort St. Mark's, on Apalachee Bay, and executed on the grounds that they were friendly to Creeks and Seminoles. Washington diplomats were appalled. Negotiations with Spain were delicate. But Spain understood Jackson's policy as James Monroe could not; Spain was no democracy. For five million U.S. dollars, she parted with the Land of Flowers, because she knew she could not hold it. John Quincy Adams, Monroe's Secretary of State, signed the treaty on behalf of the United States, and splendidly representing Spain was the Most Excellent Lord Don Luis de Onís, Gonzales, Lopez y Vara, Lord of the Town of Rayaces, Perpetual Regidor of the Corporation of the City of Salamanca, Knight Grand Cross of the Royal Vendee, and various other things. Ferdinand of Spain, restored to his throne after the ravages and relatives of Napoleon, ceded East and West Florida, all forts and buildings therein not private property, and the archives and documents pertaining to titles to the land. The boundary between Spain and America was fixed at the Sabine River, in what is now Texas, jogged across

1. John Spencer Bassett, *The Life of Andrew Jackson,* 2 vols. (Garden City, N.Y.: Doubleday, Page and Co., 1911), 1:245.

the Red River and then followed the south bank of the Arkansas. Surveyors were ordered to mark the exact boundaries. The United States had formally to guarantee freedom of religion to her new citizens; Spain in turn promised to withdraw all Spanish troops. The crucial clause of the Adams-Onís treaty, as far as Floridians were concerned, was that which provided that all land grants made by Spain before January 24, 1818, were to be ratified and confirmed to the persons in possession of the lands. All grants made after January 24, 1818, were now null and void. The shock to Americans who had bought Spanish land from impoverished Spanish noblemen after January 24, 1818, was profound. Some of those Americans instigated litigation in United States courts that would drag on for nearly a century.

Andrew Jackson marched into Pensacola in 1821, as Florida's first American governor. With him was his wife Rachel. He found Pensacola's forts "filthy and disgusting," and Rachel wrote a friend that she was in "a vast howling wilderness." The Spanish of Pensacola were heathens; on Sundays, their little bazaars were open for business, and the citizenry danced if they wanted to. "Make the Sabbath the market day for thy Soul," Rachel admonished, and her husband shut down Sunday business and merriment. He also quarreled with the retiring Spanish governor, Callava, and locked him in the calaboose. Callava was visited by a countryman there, and the two Spaniards got merrily drunk. But Spanish Pensacolians whispered—not about the spree, but at the tempestuous governor, Don Andrew Jackson.

For two months, Jackson raged through Pensacola while Rachel prayed for deliverance from her "Babylonish captivity." Then the Jacksons departed for the Hermitage, and bazaars were soon doing a brisk Sabbath trade again. Languid Sundays echoed with the strumming of Spanish guitars. Americans, arguing self-defense, took to killing Indians on the Escambia River. The Indians retaliated. Pensacola was used to vicissitudes; thirteen times, the city had seesawed between Spanish and French and British ownership. But this time Spain did not intervene. Gonzalezes and Morenos realized that they were Americans, whether they liked it or not. White Anglo-Saxon

Protestants who worshipped Old Hickory poured into Florida like a tidal wave. Spanish emporiums were shut once more, and no guitars echoed in sandy village streets on the Lord's Day. This time the change of owners was permanent.

Florida was a frontier for the common man, and the common man of the 1820s and 1830s was likely to be a fundamentalist. Protestant sects flourished, with shouting of proverbs and speaking in tongues. In Florida, church was drama as well as obligation. Pinewoods rang with the fulminations of evangelists; congregations went berserk with joy and/or fear. Railroads came to Florida in the 1830s, and the chief officer of one of them proclaimed truthfully that Pensacola was a healthful place, except during epidemics. There was as yet very little of the Wild West, but the Wild South was teeming. When American settlers inevitably began marrying señoritas, the señoritas usually converted to the prevailing austerities. In St. Augustine, the stately cathedral was still Roman Catholic, but it had competitors. Minorcans began turning into Methodists. The pressure on the existing Indian population was extreme. In 1824, two commissioners trying to find a territorial capital site that wasn't swamp, midway between Pensacola and St. Augustine, fixed on the village of the Creek chief Neamathla. It was called Old Fields; Seminoles had preceded Creeks on its site. Tallahassee was not created out of a vacuum; but the beaten Neamathla, who loved it for its live oaks and rich, russet hills, had to leave it. At the Cow Ford on the St. Johns River, a man named Isaiah D. Hart began laying out sites for the future city of Jacksonville. White Floridians began making treaties with outnumbered Seminoles, pushing the Indians down into the heart of the peninsula, where the heat was so bad and the mosquitoes so enterprising that north Floridians believed it could never be settled. Let the Indians have the trackless swamps; Andy Jackson was soon going to ship all of them west into the Arkansas Territory, anyhow. The process of Indian removal began not long before the Baldwin locomotive steamed into Florida's pinelands and skirted, where it could, the swamps.

Gradually, the Seminoles began melting into the fastnesses of the immense Green Swamp, north and east of Tampa Bay, a densely wooded place of blooming tree-orchids and clouds of white crinum lilies. The Americans built forts from which to control them; Fort Brooke, at the mouth of the Hillsborough River on Tampa Bay; Fort King, on the site of modern Ocala. The country of Hirrihigua and Mocoso now echoed with the forthright march of military boots. Elder American statesman John Randolph of Roanoke declared that, if he were given a choice between hell and Florida, he would opt for hell. United States infantrymen agreed with him heartily, as they battled malaria, dysentery, and apathy. Nervously, at night, when Indians could move so noiselessly through swamps and forests, the soldiers played cards and drank, hoping the Indians would not rise to murder them.

Meanwhile, northern Florida flourished. A grateful United States Congress made a gift of part of it to the Marquis de Lafayette, who dreamed of establishing a model community not dependent on slavery. Unfortunately, when French peasants arrived to try to grow French grapes, they battled heat and streaming rain and then left in disgust for Tallahassee, where they settled a part of the city soon christened Frenchtown. Lafayette's intended example of free labor proved unprofitable. He never came to Tallahassee, but another exotic visitor did. He was Prince Achille Murat, son of the King of Naples and nephew of Napoleon Bonaparte. The prince married a grand-niece of George Washington and started a series of plantations all doomed to disappoint. He was no farmer. It is a romantic story, that alliance of Bonapartes with Washingtons, until one learns that the prince had a habit of chewing tobacco—and spitting—and his wife Catherine made him take along a St. Bernard dog whose fur could receive the royal chaws. The prince was venturesome. However, according to a Tallahassee anecdote, after he had cooked and tasted a vulture, he pronounced: "Turkey buzzard, he no good."

Into northern Florida came also a number of blue bloods from the American South, among them the grandson of Thomas Jefferson, Francis Eppes. With them came slavery and an ethic of chivalry to white women. Episcopal churches were built for the prayers of the genteel. Jacksonville, St. Augustine, and Pensacola learned the liturgies of Archbishop Cranmer, and in Tallahassee the Episcopalians built their own cemetery to avoid contamination with the remains of backwoods riffraff.

The planters called it Middle Florida, their world of cotton fields and horse racing and long estate drives canopied by mossy oaks and bright with magenta crape myrtles as pointillist as a Seurat canvas. It was middle because it lay between St. Augustine on the east and Pensacola on the west. Everybody knew that the southern part of the state was uninhabitable. Middle Floridians who had no aristocratic ancestors diligently concealed the fact; signers of the Magna Charta were held in particularly high genealogical favor.

Jews who began coming down from the Carolinas were of proudly Sephardic stock; in Spain, their ancestors had been poets, financiers, and counselors to kings before their banishment. Florida is remarkable today for a phenomenon also remarkable in the nineteenth century: anti-Semitism does not flourish, and did not, then. After becoming a state, in 1845, Florida sent as her first senator to Washington a man named David Levy, who numbered among his antecedents a prime minister of Morocco named Yulee. Levy later changed his name to Levy Yulee; his wife was a social arbiter in Tallahassee. It may be that the Florida Christian's esteem for Jews derived from the same source that gave the area the rituals of knightly tournaments and its worship of the past. Sir Walter Scott was oblivious of Florida, but his Waverly novels gave the Bible stiff competition in fledgling Middle Florida bookstores. And in *Ivanhoe,* Sir Walter had created Isaac of York and his beautiful daughter Rebecca, both of whom made many of the crudely bigoted Christian characters in the novel look like oafs.

Sir Walter, who died at sixty-one in 1832, was an Episcopalian. Sir Walter worshipped the dashing Bonnie Prince Charlie. He disapproved of "fire-brands" who tried to upset the social applecart. He painted many lower-class characters movingly, and he believed the humble were usually to be trusted, but he enjoyed his title and the sprawling baronial manor of Abbotsford, which he filled with antique weapons. He was a High Tory. He sang of heroes. His Jeannie Deans, in *The Heart of*

Midlothian, could not tell a lie. Ivanhoe was dedicated to glory "which gilds our sepulchre and embalms our name . . . Chivalry! . . . she is the nurse of pure and high affection—the stay of the oppressed, the redressor of grievances, the curb of the power of the tyrant—Nobility were but an empty name without her, and liberty finds the best protection in her lance and in her sword." [2] Many things in Florida were born at Scott's imaginary tournament of Ashby-de-la-Zouche, in which Ivanhoe tilted with the sinister Brian de Bois-Guilbert.

Chivalry and Ashby-de-la-Zouche were especially important in Tallahassee, whose historian Susan Bradford Eppes in 1926 recalled her antebellum girlhood at Pine Hill Plantation. "The greater part of the South was composed of men of wealth and often of distinction as well. With abundant means and leisure for study, the men and women of the Old South stood unequalled in education, accomplishments, and mental ability." Every spring Tallahassee staged its own tournament, complete with a Queen of Love and Beauty, like Scott's Lady Rowena. There was also an Unknown Knight who, "clad in gleaming armor, sits on a magnificent charger; his cap is on, his visor down . . . on every tongue is the question, 'Who can it be?' " The romance of one particular knight was sullied when his mother, sitting with Princess Murat in her landau, got so excited that she screamed, "It's Phil—just Phil—nobody but Phil!" [3]

The writings of Mrs. Eppes are cloyingly heavy with the clichés of magnolias and southern moons. They present, too, the doctrine of states' rights as enunciated by John C. Calhoun, Old Hickory's vice-president. According to Mrs. Eppes, states' rights, soon to be "disregarded by the fanatical Abolitionists," guaranteed "personal liberty except to criminals . . . marriage laws were held sacred and divorces were rare and when these did take place the parties to such divorces were looked upon with suspicion and mistrust . . . Business houses held to a cer-

2. Edgar Johnson, *Sir Walter Scott: The Great Unknown*, 2 vols. (New York: Macmillan Co., 1970), 1:739.
3. Susan Bradford Eppes, *Through Some Eventful Years* (1926; facsimile reproduction, with introduction and index by Joseph D. Cushman, Jr., Gainesville: University of Florida Press, 1968), pp. 11, 21.

tain code of honor . . . and when a man wilfully defrauded his creditors he could not hold up his head and be recognized as the equal of honest men.'' Despite these comments on liberty, the same woman could write in her diary that, as a child, "I have a Christmas present three days before Christmas. It is a baby. Aunt Dinah gave it to me; she says the rabbits brought it to her and she thought right away, 'I'll gie dis chile ter Susie.' . . . I can have it to play with whenever I want.'' [4]

Toward another race of humans, that of the Creeks and the Seminoles, the prevailing attitude was one of terror and contempt. In 1830, Congress passed a Removal Act that would rid Florida of the savages who periodically raided the white settlements that had replaced their own. Many of the Creeks went west; but it was different with the Seminoles. They vowed to fight removal to the last man, and in the huge, misty fortress of the Green Swamp, where owls hooted and leopard frogs croaked, their war canoes glided noiselessly through labyrinthine, tannin-stained waters. The Seminoles were storing up ammunition. One of them, Osceola, shouted at an Indian commissioner over a treaty table: "The only treaty I will ever make is this!'' [5]—and fiercely, Osceola plunged his knife into the table's wood. Andrew Jackson had won the First Seminole War, but the second, now in the making, would dwarf its predecessor into a series of skirmishes. Osceola's war was one of blood and passion, and on its outcome depended the survival of his people, the Wanderers. South of Florida lay not land but ocean. The Seminoles could not move down an endless peninsula away from white planters and white deceit. As the principles of Sir Walter Scott did not apply to blacks, they applied even less to Indians.

4. Eppes, *Eventful Years*, pp. 44, 53.
5. Traditional in Tallahassee.

5

On the Banks of the
We-wa-thlock-o

*T*WENTIETH-CENTURY America, in post-Watergate shock, has no monopoly on moral calamities. One of the worst in the nation's history reached its bloody zenith in Florida during the 1830s and 1840s. The Second Seminole War cost Washington forty million dollars and numberless red, white, and black lives. It was a war with which a sizable segment of the population was not in sympathy. It was a ruthless drain on the nation's taxpayers and a recession followed it. Most of the soldiers saw no point to the conflict: how could you fight opponents who melted into unexplored swamps? There are impressive parallels between the Second Seminole War and Vietnam; they need no laboring. The moral calamity that prompted the Indian conflict, in the first place, was Andrew Jackson's policy of Indian removal. Old Hickory hated Indians: they drank and scalped; they had to go—it was that simple. And nobody realized that the real leadership of the Seminoles of Florida would soon pass from alcoholic old titular chief Micanopy to upstart Asi-Yaholo, "Crier of the Black Drink," whom the whites would call Osceola.

The prevailing white argument for Indian removal was that the Indians were hunters, not tillers of the soil: tillers, paler and nobler, surely deserved the earth, as beings who lived by the chase did not. In point of fact, southern America was alarmed by the rapidity with which Creeks, Choctaws, Chickasaws, Cherokees, and Seminoles were learning white ways. They were building prosperous farms. A mighty howl went up; white men needed those farms! The Indians were damned if they hunted and damned if they didn't. Over the dream of their extinction in a western wilderness, Old Hickory presided like a grim fury. Indians' rights to the soil were said to be "imperfect." The United States had jurisdiction over such lands. Naturally, the same argument did not apply to white squatters, frontiersmen who worshipped Jackson as much as the Indians despised him.

One of the largest wetlands in America was—and still is—the Green Swamp of central Florida. Lying northeast of Tampa, it covers nine hundred square miles full of tannin-stained water, snowy egrets, white ibises, and great blue herons. Lumbering alligators bellow on spring nights heavy with the odor of swamp gases. Towering trees are festooned with Spanish moss, wild orchids, trumpet creepers, and jasmine. Leopard frogs croak in the swamp's depths, and rain crows call on cloudy days, when it is a world of shadows. The Green Swamp is not so famous as the Everglades, but it is even wilder. Highways run along its edges, never in its interior. It is not so much talked about as the 'Glades, because it is less known. Some of it is inaccessible; even airboats cannot penetrate jungles of vines and crowded pond cypresses.

Five rivers begin in the Green Swamp: the Kissimmee and Peace, which flow southward; the Ocklawaha, which flows north; the Hillsborough, which empties into Tampa Bay; and entering the Gulf of Yankeetown, the Withlacoochee, which the Seminoles called We-wa-thlock-o—Little River. It was their fortress and their refuge, and on its lily-carpeted banks the terrible drama of their fight to keep Florida was played out until they surrendered, almost one by one, because they were starving, and soldiers had destroyed their crops.

The Removal Law, passed in 1830, was plain-speaking enough. The country's Indians east of the Mississippi were ordered to start packing for an uninhabited (the administration

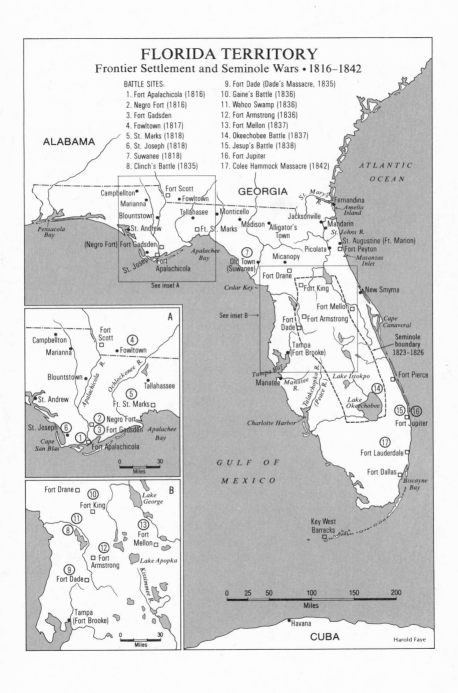

FLORIDA TERRITORY
Frontier Settlement and Seminole Wars • 1816–1842

BATTLE SITES:
1. Fort Apalachicola (1816)
2. Negro Fort (1816)
3. Fort Gadsden
4. Fowltown (1817)
5. St. Marks (1818)
6. St. Joseph (1818)
7. Suwanee (1818)
8. Clinch's Battle (1835)
9. Fort Dade (Dade's Massacre, 1835)
10. Gaine's Battle (1836)
11. Wahoo Swamp (1836)
12. Fort Armstrong (1836)
13. Fort Mellon (1837)
14. Okeechobee Battle (1837)
15. Jesup's Battle (1838)
16. Fort Jupiter
17. Colee Hammock Massacre (1842)

ALABAMA

GEORGIA

ATLANTIC OCEAN

Campbellton
Marianna
Blountstown
Fort Scott
Fowltown
Tallahasee
St. Andrew
Pensacola Bay
(Negro Fort) Fort Gadsden
St. Joseph
Fort Apalachicola
Apalachee Bay
Monticello
Ft. St. Marks
Madison
Alligator's Town
St. Mary's R.
Fernandina
Amelia Island
Jacksonville
Mandarin
St. Johns R.
St. Augustine (Ft. Marion)
Fort Peyton
Picolata
Old Town (Suwanee)
Micanopy
Matanzas Inlet

See inset A

Cedar Key
See inset B

Fort Drane
Fort King
Fort Mellon
Fort Armstrong
Fort Dade
New Smyrna
Cape Canaveral

Tampa (Fort Brooke)
Manatee
Manatee R.
Tampa Bay
Lake Istokpo
Lake Okeechobee

Seminole boundary 1823–1826
Fort Pierce

Charlotte Harbor

Fort Jupiter
Fort Lauderdale
Fort Dallas
Biscayne Bay

GULF OF MEXICO

Key West Barracks

Havana

CUBA

ATLANTIC OCEAN

A

Campbellton
Marianna
Fort Scott
Fowltown
Blountstown
Tallahassee
Ft. St. Marks
St. Andrew
St. Joseph
Negro Fort
Fort Gadsden
Apalachee Bay
Fort Apalachicola
Cape San Blas
Apalachicola R.
Ochlockonee R.

0   30
Miles

B

Fort Drane
Lake George
Fort King
Fort Mellon
Fort Armstrong
Lake Apopka
Fort Dade
Tampa (Fort Brooke)
Kissimmee R.

0   30
Miles

0   25   50   100   150   200
Miles

Harold Faye

said) portion of the Arkansas Territory. The law did not define the constitutional rights of any exiled tribe, nor did it tell Congress that it had to spend money on Indians if Congress wanted to spend it on something else. The law gave no instructions on how the red men were to be moved, nor did it mention the fact that, on the proposed Indian lands in the west, there were already squatters with removal ideas that didn't include the Arkansas Territory.

The federal government made the Treaty of Payne's Landing with the Seminoles in 1832. The scene was the edge of the wide Alachua Savannah that botanist William Bartram had tramped forty years earlier and then recalled in print. The Alachua Savannah, then as now, was full of sinkholes and of rivers that emerged from the earth and then sank underground again. It was—is—a surpassingly beautiful place; and, to the Seminoles, it was sacred.

At Payne's Landing, the Seminoles were curtly told that if they refused to move west the annuities they were receiving under earlier treaties would be handed over to more docile tribes. A delegation might go by way of Little Rock to Fort Gibson, in what is now Oklahoma. If "they," said the treaty, referring to the entire Seminole nation, liked what the delegation told them of the Arkansas Territory, they would agree to move. There was no provision for delegates not satisfied at all. When the group went to Fort Gibson, they were presented with a slightly altered treaty. "Should they be satisfied" was changed to "should this delegation be satisfied"; it was a nice distinction. The exploring party, which signed what it could not understand, consisted of Jumper, Coee Harjo, Tsali Emathla—whom Irish-born Americans persistently called Charley O'Mathla—his brother Holata Emathla, Yaharjo and John Hicks, and Nehathloco. With them went their black interpreter, Abraham, technically a slave, but in actuality a valued friend on whom they depended. Abraham was no rhetorician; he did not observe the revised wording from "they" to "this delegation." Soon enough, the Seminoles were escorted by some exiled Creeks on a tour of the western prairies. There they saw marauding Indians for whom the warpath was a way of life and who resented the presence of others. The Kiowas, Comanches, and Sioux were horse-stealers, protested Jumper; did the government think Seminoles were also thieves? He did not approve of this new land at all. It was unfortunate, countered the government, since he had just put his **X** on the Treaty of Fort Gibson. Now the Seminoles must get out of Florida.

The Indian policy of the United States, especially its policy toward the Seminoles, was hardly defensible. But it would not have been so bad had the government said forthrightly, "The land goes to the conquerors. We are those conquerors." Instead, it posed as the Great Father who was doing everything for the good of his red children. On the one hand, the government accused the Indians of being drunks; on the other, it footed large liquor bills before treaties were signed. Like most other Indians, the Seminoles were not a devious people. They could not understand hypocrisy. The task of fighting back fell, they believed, to them. They had swamps, as Georgia's pressured Cherokees did not.

When the delegation returned from Fort Gibson, Osceola was enraged. Fairly and squarely, he warned American authorities of the forthcoming war: "When I make up my mind, I act. If I speak, what I say I will do. If the hail rattles, let the flowers be crushed. The oak of the forest will lift up its head to the sky and the storm, towering and unscathed." [1] Astonishingly, the Indian agent at Fort King, modern Ocala, not only failed to take the warning seriously, but in his innocence and in admiration of Osceola's majesty, he bought the young chief a rifle. "I will use it well," said Osceola briefly. The agent, a career officer named Wiley Thompson, was happy that Florida was soon to be "relieved of Indians." His happiness was short-lived; Osceola shot him, one wet evening, near the stockades of Fort King and then severed his head to take back to the Green Swamp as a trophy.

In death, Wiley Thompson had a macabre revenge. The doctor attending Osceola after his capture was Thompson's brother-in-law, and when Osceola had played out the epic of his mortal-

1. William Hartley and Ellen Hartley, *Osceola* (New York: Hawthorn Books, 1973), p. 114.

ity in full regalia, the doctor cut off the chief's head and took it home, where naughty children were punished by being locked in a bedroom with the head impaled on one of the bedposts. The nineteenth century in America was no era of dainty Victorian lace. It reeked with slaughter and rang with violence.

In Florida, there are still miles between the values of white men and of red. Few Indians are acquisitive; they regard hospitality as an obligation, not a favor; they are unconcerned with status, because they already know who they are. When they scalped, it was because they had to, in order to defend the homeland given them by the Master of Breath for their sustenance. These days, Florida's Indians, like others in America, are bemused by a radical change: they are seeing white youngsters adopt their dress and dance at their powwows. There is a sudden premium on medicine men, beloved by white and black health-food devotees. Some of the older medicine men cannot believe in the miracle; those who can, deliver speeches and work with academic researchers. The Florida State University campus in Tallahassee is graced with recently built Osceola Hall. It was not always thus. Osceola Hall is a privately owned dormitory, and the sign in front of it asks, "Why spend your life looking? Spend it living!" That, of course, is exactly what Osceola wanted to do. He had no need to look to the wilds of the Arkansas Territory; he had Florida. He wanted to live in it, but if necessary he would forfeit his own life that others might remain.

The most dramatic episode of the Second Seminole War was the Dade Massacre that began it. In 1835, handsome Maj. Francis Langhorne Dade, scion of a First Family of Virginia, was stationed on Tampa Bay at Fort Brooke, not yet Tampa. On his horse Richard III, which he raced in peacetime, he set out with a large contingent from Fort Brooke to augment the force at Fort King, where Wiley Thompson was based (too late, as it happened: Osceola had already murdered Thompson). The men spent two days crossing the Big and Little Hillsborough rivers with their artillery. The Indians Jumper and Alligator watched from the sheltering forest. They and their band could have attacked Dade on the Hillsborough, but preferred to play cat-and-mouse. When they finally descended on Dade's troops, they swiftly gunned the bluecoats to extinction in a clatter of shot and war whoops and a haze of smoke. Only one man survived, a bleeding wreck who half-crawled back to Fort Brooke to tell what had happened.

It was the start of long years of war. Commanders came and went, each boasting at first that he would exterminate the Seminoles in short order, and each, in the end, retiring in disgust. Gen. Winfield Scott, whom his men called "Old Fuss and Feathers," arrived in Florida with a military band, "marquees of furniture," and a stock of French wines. He soon found that the Seminoles had no intention of leaving their refuge in the Cove of the Withlacoochee, present-day Lake Tsala Apopka. Scott was succeeded by Maj. Gen. Edmund Pendleton Gaines, possessed of a terrible temper and a hatred of Indians that had not been mitigated by the Black Hawk War in Illinois and Wisconsin in which he had served in 1832. Gaines lasted until Osceola and Jumper and Alligator sent word that they would end their warfare if the Seminoles might remain where they were. Gaines reported this to his superiors in Washington, who relieved him of his command for the impertinence. Gaines was succeeded by Gen. Duncan Clinch, who had once blown up an entire fortress of runaway blacks in northern Florida. Still the Seminoles kept to their swamps between raids. After Clinch, Richard Keith Call took over, and when he too failed to lure the Indians from the Withlacoochee so that European military tactics might be practiced on them, he relinquished his command to Thomas Sidney Jesup.

Jesup was wily. His orders led to the capture of Osceola under flag of truce; for the Seminoles, it was the beginning of the end. Jesup drove his men into the swamps after the Indians; he sharpened their eyes and ears. He ordered Seminole crops destroyed wherever they were found. The Seminole Nation grew hungry. And while Jesup stalked his prey without letup, Americans were reading in their newspapers the eloquent words of Seminole chiefs.

Jesup threw Osceola into prison. When he died there, of acute tonsillitis and a broken heart, white America was profoundly troubled. After reading newspaper reports, Walt Whitman told the nation how it had been:

When his hour for death had come,
He slowly raised himself from the bed on the floor,
Drew on his war-dress, shirt, leggings, and girdled the belt around
 his waist,
Call'd for vermillion paint (his looking glass was held before him),
Painted half his face and neck, his wrists, and back-hands,
Put the scalp-knife carefully in his belt—then lying down, resting a
 moment,
Rose again, half-sitting, smiled, gave in silence his extended hand
 to each and all,
Sank faintly low to the floor (tightly grasping the tomahawk
 handle,)
Fixed his look on wife and little children—the last:
(And here a line in memory of his name and death).[2]

After that, in the vision of many Americans, Andrew Jackson and his successors stood less tall.

In martyrdom, Osceola achieved what he had not been able to achieve in life: the sympathy of his oppressors. Straggling bands of Seminoles started to surrender themselves. Broken, as Osceola had been broken, they were taken to Fort Brooke, where they were penned in a stockade like so many cattle before they were driven onto steamers bound for New Orleans, the Arkansas River, and faraway Fort Gibson in the Arkansas Territory. The first group of Seminoles to arrive in Oklahoma learned that, as usual, the Great Father in Washington had not been entirely truthful.

It was one of the war's ironies that the man who badgered Washington into sending food and tools west was none other than Thomas Sidney Jesup. With his own money, Jesup bought a rifle for the hungry chief. He had had no scruples about violating a truce, but what had that violation been for, if not to insure that the Seminoles would go west and live in remote prosperity? Jesup kept his command until May 1838; several times he pro-

2. Walt Whitman, *Leaves of Grass,* edited by Malcolm Cowley (New York: Funk and Wagnalls, 1968), p. 463.

claimed the end of the war when a Micco or Tustenuggee surrendered.

When Jesup retired to another arena, Zachary Taylor took over: Old Rough and Ready. Old Rough and Ready and Richard Keith Call had a brainstorm. Why not use bloodhounds? They sent to Cuba for the dogs, an island specialty. The bloodhounds were not cheap. Each one cost $151.75, but Taylor and Call paid the price when the Cubans threw in five specialists in tracking. The dogs were attached to the troops, as were also the calves whose meat they ravenously consumed.

It was too much for John Quincy Adams, up in Congress. He submitted a recommendation:

> That the Secretary of War be directed to report to this House, the natural, political, and martial history of the bloodhounds, showing the peculiar fitness of that class of warriors to be the associates of the gallant army of the United States, specifying the nice discrimination of his scent between the blood of the freeman and the blood of the slave . . . between the blood of savage Seminoles and that of the Anglo-Saxon pious Christian . . . Also, whether a further importation of the same heroic race into the state of Maine, to await the contingency of a contested Northeastern Boundary question, is contemplated . . . Whether measures have been taken to secure to ourselves exclusively the employment of this auxiliary force, and whether he deems it expedient to extend the said bloodhounds and their posterity the benefits of the pension laws.[3]

Adams was only too correct. The dogs tracked everything in sight, especially the soldiers of Zachary Taylor.

If there was macabre humor in the war, there was also pathos. A traveling Shakespeare company visiting the Territory of Florida left their baggage unwatched one evening, and a band of roving Seminoles stole it. Coacoochee, the Wildcat, Osceola's successor, requested a parley; his people were famished. When he came into the camp, it was in the plumed turban of Hamlet, Prince of Denmark. Richard III, "judging from his royal purple and ermine," was in the rear, and beside him "a faithful friend

---

3. John K. Mahon, *History of the Second Seminole War* (Gainesville: University of Florida, 1967), p. 267.

wound up in the simple garb of Horatio." King Lear was represented, as was Caliban. The Indians were decked in spangles,
paste necklaces, and crimson vests. They took obvious delight
in their new clothes. This event marked the beginning of the
Seminole costume as it exists today. The cloak of Richard III
became the seminole woman's cape, and the headgear of Hamlet the badge of the tribe's medicine men.

Coacoochee's speech was moving. The Great Spirit, he said,
had given him legs to walk over the earth,

> hands to aid myself; eyes to see its ponds, rivers, forests, and game;
> then a head with which I think. The sun . . . shines to warm us and
> bring forth our crops, and the moon brings back the spirits of our
> warriors, our fathers, wives, and children. The white man comes;
> he grows pale and sick. Why cannot we live here in peace? I have
> said I am the enemy of the white man. I could live in peace with
> him, but they first steal our cattle and horses, cheat us, and take our
> lands. The white men are as thick as the leaves in the hammock;
> they come upon us thicker every year. They may shoot us, drive our
> women and children night and day; they may chain our hands and
> feet, but the red man's heart will always be free.[4]

Zachary Taylor was followed by General Armistead, who dis-
covered that he hated Florida. After Armistead arrived forthright
William Jenkins Worth, whose lieutenant, William Tecumseh
Sherman, captured a large number of Indians in southern
Florida. Halleck Tustenuggee, like Osceola, was captured under
a flag of truce. American citizens grew irate at the war's finan-
cial drain. One chief who did not surrender was stocky Billy
Bowlegs—Boleck—who conducted his people so deep into the
heart of the Everglades that no one could ever find them. In
March 1842, three thousand Seminoles had been shipped west.
It was not then the majority of the tribe. When Pascofa became
the last chief to surrender—hunted down on the Ochlockonee
River in north Florida—the country decided it had had enough.
It was prudent to forget Billy Bowlegs, to whom one white referred formally as Mr. William B. Legs. No one wanted ex-
treme south Florida; he would do no harm.

---

4. John T. Sprague, *The Origin, Progress and Conclusion of the Florida War* (New
York: D. Appleton Co., 1848), p. 260.

The Seminoles are still there, in the network of streams and sawgrass prairies and mangrove swamps and hammocks that comprise the Everglades. These Indians have never signed a peace treaty with the United States. In their *chikees* and compounds along the Tamiami Trail, from Naples east to Miami, they have set up shop for the benefit of Florida tourism; they are a silent people whose glance is often one of profound distrust. The tourists may take their pictures, but must pay for the privilege. In 1970, the Seminoles in Florida and Oklahoma were offered twelve million dollars—which they turned down as too little by far—as reparations for twenty-nine million acres of Florida land. In 1976, they accepted sixteen million dollars— fifty cents an acre—because they feared they could get no more. The descendants of Billy Bowlegs's band have begun to emerge from the 'Glades to raise cattle and study animal husbandry and aquaculture. They are guides in the Everglades, where they run airboats, a spine-shattering and noisy means of travel over the sharp grass. They wrestle alligators in front of admiring Yankees. Their women are following careers in public health. Under Joe Dan Osceola and Buffalo Tiger, the tribe has taken long steps into the twentieth century. It has even elected a woman as chairman of its Tribal Council. The transition to participation in contemporary American life has not been easy. Betty Mae Jumper, the current tribal chief, recalls how she begged her parents for the chance to go to school. Her grandmother opposed the idea, but with her mother's consent she eventually managed to finish nurse's training—not without having older people in the tribe throw mud at her for wearing white men's clothes when she came home on visits. Old Seminoles still do not trust their white American brothers; they have every reason not to. But the younger Indians want a share in Florida's economy.

Many Seminole children drop out of school—from discouragement, from the slings and arrows of racial prejudice, and from poverty. Infant mortality among the Seminoles in Florida is three and a half times the national rate; death from diabetes is four times; from pneumonia, twice. The suicide rate among teenagers is ten times greater than the national average, and the average life expectancy of a Florida Seminole is forty-four years. It is ironic that all this is happening in the very shadow of Miami Beach skyscrapers, where platinum-haired ladies employed by night, though not by day, wear mink-trimmed cashmere sweaters, and the neon jungle of bars is never empty after dark. The Seminoles have among them many alcoholics, for obvious reasons of frustration. Floridians say it is a "racial susceptibility to drink," which is biological nonsense. The alcoholics in Miami Beach are better supplied and less visible. Alcoholism is not an Indian monopoly.

Today the tribes of the southeast are uniting in an attempt to break off the shackles of their long oppression. The Coalition of Eastern Native Americans is growing in strength and resolution. There are no easy solutions to the problems of the Seminoles, but they are being squarely faced; and in the current wave of American enthusiasm for everything Indian, the average white and black Floridian is becoming more aware of the inequities. There are at least three thousand Seminoles in Florida; not all are bilingual. But some have begun to buy air-conditioning units paid for by jobs in agriculture and tourism. They attend classes on nutrition and modern medicine. If they prosper, they live in concrete block ranch houses. The Seminoles have medical secrets of their own; they have steadfastly refused to sell to a large pharmaceutical company the formula for their traditional and highly effective tranquilizer.

In the last analysis, the Seminoles are indeed the cliché of the Mysterious Indian. If they know you, they will laugh and joke and exchange ideas. But just as you have decided that they are beings like yourself, you see elderly medicine men like Josie Billie, garbed in elaborate multicolored piecework clothing and the high feathered turban of his office. Josie Billie does not talk much; his wisdom is ageless and ancient. At a recent Florida Folk Festival in White Springs, on the Suwanee River, a hush fell over the crowd when he mounted the platform to address the audience. In his venerable regality and almost mystical remoteness, he was a vision of bygone Seminole splendors, and black and white America knew it. His speech was very soft; the silence of the crowd was utter. They knew they were in the presence of history.

6

The American Revolution
That Came Too Late

*W*HEN Florida emerged from the bloodletting of the Second Seminole War, the Territory could hardly have been described as appealing. It was in the throes of a depression, brought on by the failure of the Union Bank of Tallahassee in 1837 in the wake of massacre panic. (The Union Bank of Tallahassee is still a Florida problem; the decaying little building has been moved from its original downtown Tallahassee location on Adams Street near the old police station to a ruthlessly visible spot on the broad Apalachee Parkway to the east, in the shadow of the capitol. Legislators swear they want the Union Bank razed because it looks seedy, and preservationists counter that some day they will manage to find the money to restore it; as the first bank in Florida, it must be kept. Meanwhile it sits, cracking and forlorn, with visible sign remnants of its last occupation by bail bondsmen.)

After the war with the Indians was over, and Osceola slept his long sleep and Coacoochee the Wildcat was doggedly plowing alien acres in Oklahoma before his eventual self-imposed exile in Mexico, Florida was full of half-cleared fields covered with rank weeds. Girdled trees stripped of their foilage stood ''like masts of ships,'' as Richard Keith Call's daughter Ellen was later to recall. It was also full of ''boom towns no longer

booming, rail fences rotting to earth, houses abandoned in process of construction, clambering wild vines half-hiding some
task given up, devastated and deserted plantations, the desolate
ashes of squatters' cabins, and the new graves of the massacred
in the gloom of the primeval wilderness."[1] The massacred, of
course, were both white and red, and occasionally black.

Florida attractive to immigrants? Hardly. And yet they came,
in carriages and—in the case of the squatters—in buckboard
wagons full of pitifully few possessions. Axes, plows, and
cookware were the essentials; women's dresses were not. The
poor of the Appalachian mountains were streaming in, pallid in
gamy buckskins and faded calicoes. In 1845, the population of
Florida reached fifty-eight thousand, depression notwithstand-
ing. The Territory was now eligible for statehood, which it got,
along with Iowa, because Congress still vainly imagined that
slave soil could be balanced with free soil and Americans would
continue happy with the arrangement. When the beleaguered
Cherokee Indians had asked the Great Father in Washington to
help them in their impasse with the state of Georgia, which
wanted them out, Andrew Jackson had told their chief he would
not interfere with states' rights: "I will not go to war for you,
John Ross. It's too damned late."[2]

The slaveholding states were naturally the most vocal about
states' rights; they had the most to lose if Emancipation ever became the law of the land. South Carolina called the vetoing of
Washington's less popular economic decrees, such as protective
tariffs, "nullification." A century later, in the civil rights strug-
gles of Alabama and Virginia, such vetoing of federal power
became "interposition"; the state interposed itself between its
people and the government. The problem is a continuing American ill, and nowhere is it better exemplified than in the history
of stubborn Florida. Antebellum state politics quickly became
immersed in discussions of slavery and industry-biased tariffs
and the ubiquitous states' rights.

In the counties east of the Suwanee River, the Democrats

1. Ellen Call Long, *Florida Breezes* (Jacksonville: Ashmead Brothers, 1882),
p. 209.
2. Margaret Coit, "The Presidency of Andrew Jackson," MS, p. 3.

were in control, and central and west Florida were run by an oligarchy of Whig planters. But despite their differences, Democrats and Whigs were both agreed that slavery was vital to Florida's future. Where whites did not own slaves—and the majority did not—it was only because they didn't have enough money to buy them. By 1850, the population of Florida was 87,445, up 30,000 from five years before. Thirty-nine thousand were black slaves. More than half of these lived in the sandy "quarters" of Middle Florida plantations, where yellow fever was rife and typhoid the order of the day. There were not more than three thousand slaveholders in the entire state. Florida had cotton, turpentine, and lumber. Just about everything else but vegetables, pasture grasses, and corn meal was imported. Jobbers bought household goods in northern and western states and then resold them to the planters. Kentucky provided an especially steady supply of mules and horses. The great Gulf ports were Pensacola, St. Mark's, and Apalachicola. When the oceangoing ships bearing Florida cotton and naval stores—turpentine products—to Europe had sailed, it was the signal for a round of festivity among the planters. "Cotton fields were many and large, and factories few and small." [3] The factories that existed were usually sawmills in Santa Rosa County, in the environs of Pensacola. Rhett Butler's observation to Scarlett O'Hara, in *Gone with the Wind,* that the South was the only country in history to go to war without a cannon factory was particularly true of the Land of Flowers. It did not have even a Tredegar Iron Works, such as Virginia had. North Florida is still noteworthy for its few large-scale manufacturing plants, a condition that appeals to conservationists and enrages economists. Will beautiful, fragrantly dim vistas of palms and pines provide lunch boxes with the niacin and protein needed to combat pellagra? Clinical pellagra and beriberi are things of the past in Florida, but among the poor they still exist subclinically: in other words, bad, but not bad enough instantly to be recognized by a doctor.

The expansion of Florida's population before the catastrophe

3. William Watson Davis, *The Civil War and Reconstruction in Florida,* Floridiana Facsimile and Reprint Series (Gainesville: University of Florida, 1964), p. 33.

of Fort Sumter in turn created more expansion. This spawned boom conditions in the postdepression 1850s, during which 380 miles of railway were hammered out to crisscross the state. Senator David Levy Yulee ran a line from Jacksonville down to Cedar Key. Tallahassee cotton planters had their own railroad to St. Mark's; an engine affectionately known as "Puffing Billy" transported their fleecy white bales to the Gulf, there to await shipment north and abroad. Small farmers gradually learned that Florida agriculture was not even Georgia's. Sandy soil, alternate conditions of drought and inundation and a numberless array of insect pests and subtropical diseases made Florida special. The fertile, red-clay Georgia hills end just below Tallahassee. At a place called the Cody Scarp, near the North Florida State Fairgrounds, the observer can see the beginning of a universe of flat, sandy pinelands that stretches out to the Gulf. South of Tallahassee, there are few hills in Florida and much less of the cold weather so necessary for revitalizing plant formation. Someone has named a thirty-foot rise in peninsular Florida *Alpine;* the individual may have been serious. South of Tallahassee, newcomers found that roses wilted in summer and apples failed year round. Florida squatters who planted corn in June found it stunted and laden with useless miniature cobs by July. There were new techniques to learn, and the labor was backbreaking.

It is not surprising that anybody who could afford a slave acquired one—and another, and another. Abolitionism became a dangerous word in Florida, and anti-Northern sentiment increased when several plantation governesses from New York and Massachusetts and Connecticut were discovered to be holding abolitionist meetings in slave quarters by night.

By 1850, national division over slavery and tariff policies was already keenly felt in Florida. Floridians formed Southern Rights Associations. On successive July Fourths, they orated against federal America; and in mass pinewoods meetings, they read to planters and poor whites alike the Holy Bible, fundamentalist prayers, and the venerable Declaration of Independence. What had been done before could be done again. Revolt! said the pinewoods messiahs. The American Revolution had bypassed Florida, but her people and her conditions had so

changed that now she was hotly praising the Declaration because she wanted independence of her own; the document was a
precedent. "May peace be our motto till war is inevitable!"
Democrats toasted each other. Wiser spirits such as Richard
Keith Call were strongly proslavery and against high tariffs, but
also profoundly disturbed. Was another American Revolution
possible? Could the South go it alone and survive? Call did not
think so. He had stood by his erstwhile chief, Andrew Jackson,
in the nullification controversy with South Carolina; he was still
a nationalist, and "strove to assemble the people here and
there." At first they shouted him down. Then they closed their
doors to him entirely, and also the news of their meetings. In
1860, when the national Democratic party's nearly fatal divi-
sions over the slavery issue had become evident in its South
Carolina convention, Florida delegates returned to spread the
news. Torches flared in crisp nights; mass meetings assembled
in a loud rumble of protest in front of the courthouses which
had long since replaced Creek council houses. The green countryside rang with fulsome speeches and with off-key town bands
that accompanied triumphal secession parades.

On May 15, 1860, when the heady summer heat had set in,
Democrats meeting in Jacksonville passed a resolution that

> regardless of who may be elected President, if it appear from such
> election that a majority of the people or the states of this Union
> deny to the South the amplest protection and security to slave prop-
> erty . . . then we are of the opinion that the rights of the citizens of
> Florida are no longer safe in the Union and we think she should
> raise the banner of secession and invite her Southern sisters to join
> her. [4]

Florida's response to John Brown's raid at Harpers Ferry,
West Virginia, was to create vigilante committees and Minute
Men like those being created in South Carolina, traditionally an
admired Florida example. On a steaming night in July 1860,
Dr. William Hollingworth of Bradford County, who opposed
slavery on moral grounds, was attacked in his house by a mob
of these roughnecks, whooping as they shot through Holling-

4 Davis, *Civil War*, p. 42.

worth's windows and doors. The doctor and his son fought back, but the elder Hollingworth was severely wounded. East Florida had bands of "whippers," who doted on passwords and vengeance-laden oaths. The whippers specialized in taking antislavery advocates from their beds at night into the woods and lashing them. One victim was whipped in the presence of his sick wife. Another got his head shaved; then he was driven out of Florida, though without the lash at his back. Jesse Durden, an antislavery farmer in west Florida's Calhoun County, was visited by a roving band on a late October night. Under an orange moon, he was brutally murdered; then the vigilantes proceeded down a country road to kill two of his friends. Intimates and kin of the slain men rose to avenge them, and soon Calhoun County was "in a state of insurrectionary war" worthy of a brigade of state militia. The militia made twenty-seven arrests, but the county still smoldered with the quasi-Corsican passions of a blood feud less celebrated than that of the Hatfields and McCoys, but nearly as tragic.

By November, when sweating, deliberate mules were grinding Florida's cane, and the wild scuppernong grapes festooning high trees were turning yellow in the hammocks, the state's newspapers were editorializing in the vein of Fernandina's *East Floridian:*

> The time has come—Lincoln is elected—The curtain has risen and the first act of the dark drama of Black Republicanism has been represented—The issue has been boldly made—Throw doubt and indecision to the winds—The requisite steps should be taken at once for the arming and equipment of every able-bodied man—The irrepressible conflict has commenced—We must meet it manfully and bravely—Florida will secede.[5]

Minute Men took to burning Lincoln in effigy. Senator David Levy Yulee decided "joyfully to return home" if Florida seceded, and Richard Keith Call, on his dreaming plantation of Orchard Pond north of Tallahassee, openly wept. Florida, he said, would never recover from secession. He was very nearly correct. Recovery was to take a century.

5. Davis, *Civil War*, p. 47.

Slavery was not the only issue, of course. It was not even, perhaps, the principal one. The Tariff Act of 1857 had benefited Southern planters and lessened the profits of Northern industrialists. The Yankees were mad, and they retaliated with abolitionist enthusiasms. Loss of profits was an issue closer to home in the North than the moral question of slavery, but the morality and its axioms had a nice ring to them. Many Northerners joined the Republican party because it promised them a protective tariff in the future. Money made better sense to manufacturers than *Uncle Tom's Cabin* ever would.

Also, Floridians had severe misconceptions about Abraham Lincoln. He was opposed to the extension of slavery to new territories, but he had no plan to abolish it where it existed. That came later, as it did with the far more obscure emancipation proclamation of Judah P. Benjamin, the Confederate Secretary of State. Lincoln favored enforcement of the Fugitive Slave Law and opposed abolition in the District of Columbia. But Floridians did not know these things. They believed the North envied the South its prosperity and well-being and wanted to unleash a horde of black barbarians on Southern gentility. The horde of barbarians were the same men and women who were house servants, often greatly esteemed, and field hands. In their plantation capacities, they were held to be civilized.

Florida called a Secession Convention in Tallahassee on January 3, 1861. By January 10, the delegates had voted to take Florida out of the Union. Paradoxically, many of the delegates were not from slaveholding areas. Late in January, the Confederate Army seized the United States Arsenal at Chattahoochee. They also took Pensacola forts Barrancas and McRee and the Pensacola Navy Yard. Fort Clinch fell to them in Fernandina, and Fort Marion, once the Castillo de San Marcos, in St. Augustine. Fort Pickens, on Santa Rosa Island, and the forts at Key West and the Dry Tortugas were left to the Union. (In Fort Jefferson, in the Tortugas, the physician who set the broken leg of Lincoln's assassin was one day to be confined. Dr. Samuel Mudd was to react to this harsh treatment by forgiving and heroic work in a yellow fever epidemic on the island.)

In 1861, Florida troops removed the lenses from the state's

lighthouses, an action that would hamper and exasperate the U.S. Navy. The doomsday of Fort Sumter came in April, but the fighting in Florida did not become anything more serious than skirmishing until 1864, when Confederate and Union forces clashed head-on at Ocean Pond, near Olustee, in the northern part of the state west of Jacksonville. Yet Jacksonville had already known suffering; Confederate troops had burned eight sawmills and more than four million feet of lumber; they had razed a foundry to prevent its falling into Union hands, destroyed a ship in the harbor and torn up railroad tracks as far west of Jacksonville as Baldwin. The Confederate control over Pensacolians was iron. Colonel Samuel Jones issued an ultimatum:

> There are certain lounging worthless people, white as well as black, who frequent the neighborhood of Pensacola and have no observable occupation; their intention may be honest, but the Colonel Commanding does not believe the fact, and as he has no use for their presence they are warned to leave, or the consequences rest on their own heads—the gallows is erected in Pensacola and will be in constant use after the 3rd day of April, 1862—the town is under complete martial law.[6]

But Jacksonville and Pensacola both eventually fell; by the time Union forces reached Pensacola, they found only ten men, thirty women, and thirty children still living in it. Jacksonville seesawed between North and South. On February 7, 1864, the Union brought fresh contingents into Jacksonville. Gen. Joseph Finegan gathered Confederate forces at Olustee, where they entrenched themselves along the shore of sparkling Ocean Pond with its slender, vaulting cypresses. On Saturday, February 20, the fighting began, as the Northern army advanced west from Jacksonville. Five thousand men on each side shot each other until Ocean Pond lay under a canopy of smoke and 300 soldiers had died in agony. The victory was Finegan's; his men killed 203 Yankees and wounded 1,152; 506 were missing in action. Finegan captured five Union cannons, 1,600 small arms, 400

6. Charlton W. Tebeau, *A History of Florida* (Coral Gables: University of Miami, 1971), p. 210.

accoutrements (soldiers' equipment other than clothing and
weapons), and 130,000 rounds of small arms ammunition. The
Confederacy and Florida could not prevent Union landings in
coastal areas, but the Southerners were ready to fight, inland.
Yet on September 18, Union Gen. Alexander Asboth collected
700 mounted men from a coastal stronghold and raided the
inland town of Marianna, in Jackson County, whose 500 inhabitants had put together a defense they dubbed the Cradle and
Grave Company. Augmented only by Confederate soldiers
home on sick leave, the company could do nothing against the
numbers of General Asboth. Marianna surrendered, and he
made off with 200 horses and mules and 400 cattle.

The most moving episode of the Civil War in Florida—at
least in retrospect—was the Battle of Natural Bridge in southern
Leon County a few miles from Tallahassee. Natural Bridge was
the last Confederate victory of the war. In Florida folklore, its
heroes are the teenage boys and old men who defended Tallahassee there; in plain fact, the Union navy's error in thinking its
ships could navigate the oyster bars of the St. Mark's River was
responsible for the Federals' rout.

John Newton, the Union general in charge at Key West,
decided that Florida morale had fallen sufficiently low after the
high point of Ocean Pond to make coastal Florida vulnerable,
more vulnerable than usual. On February 27, 1865, he ordered a
major named Weeks to board the vessel *Magnolia*—the irony of
the name was probably not lost on some of the men—with
Companies C, D, and E of the Second Florida Union Cavalry
and three companies of the Second U.S. Colored Infantry. In
darkness, the *Magnolia* made a rendezvous with the Federal
ships blockading the Gulf several miles out on shallow Apalachee Bay. The Northerners were in luck; a dense fog settled
on the bay, and they were able to gather schooners, transports, a
converted New York ferryboat equipped as the *Fort Henry,* and
several steamers. Newton himself arrived to supervise the
operation. The plan was for seamen and army troops to land and
destroy railroad bridges over the St. Mark's and Ochlockonee
and Aucilla rivers. They would break up the railroad from St.
Mark's to Tallahassee. The naval force would capture the Con-

federate battery at the St. Mark's light. There were five hundred seamen scheduled to cover the land expedition when it debarked at Port Leon, once a busy cotton port whose docks had been slowly rebuilt after a disastrous hurricane razed the town in the 1840s.

To hoodwink any Confederate scouts who might be keen-eyed in fog, the navy put out to sea on March 3. Promptly the ships were raked by sweeping gales and Weeks's men, without any seamen or troops of Newton's, had to row their way to the sea-myrtle-studded shore in the storm. The seamen and soldiers under the command of Newton did not reach Port Leon until the following day, when the troops tried to haul howitzers through Florida swamps. When Weeks saw a column of smoke to the east, he decided Confederate troops were burning the Newport bridge over the St. Mark's, and he marched there to meet a blaze of Confederate gunfire. It was no use to cross the river at Newport, he reasoned; the crossing would have to be made farther upstream, where a natural bridge had been formed by the St. Mark's River going underground and then rising again. Weeks and a task force stayed in the environs to prevent the Confederates from crossing the river. General Newton marched the rest of his men on a heavily canopied sand road toward Natural Bridge. By this time, even Tallahassee was aware of the Northern invasion and was busily digging trenches on the Houstoun plantation south of the capitol building.

When Newton arrived at Natural Bridge, he found Gen. William Miller and a company that included the Fifth Florida, Gamble's Battery, Dunham's Light Artillery, the First Florida Reserves, the Gadsden Greys, Love's Militia, and a group of cadets from the Seminary West of the Suwanee (today Florida State University). "The Baby Corps," Tallahasseans had christened the little contingent of schoolboys ready to risk their lives. Miller, his men, and the Baby Corps knew the pinewoods and swamps as General Newton did not. Newton was repulsed on the bridge three times; reinforcements of Confederate artillery arrived, and Newton's howitzers roared back, but his soldiers, black and white, were fast falling. When he retreated at last toward the Gulf, Miller chased him for twelve miles. The Baby Corps was unharmed. In a jubilant Tallahassee—the only Southern capital east of the Mississippi that remained unconquered until Appomattox—young bucks invited Susan Bradford, of Pine Hill plantation, to go on a picnic to the battle site and see all the blood and the corpses. "How awful!" she told them. "I do not understand such curiosity." [7] General Miller had reported the black dead were so many that in places they lay in piles, and the river itself was covered with floating dark corpses over which clouds of flies were buzzing with gleaming blue-black wings.

On April 1, Florida's governor, John Milton, killed himself; he could see Appomattox coming in spite of the Baby Corps's rescue of his capital. After Lee had surrendered, Federal detachments arrived in Tallahassee without incident, and the era of proud families bankrupted by investing in Confederate bonds had begun. So had Reconstruction.

The Civil War had strong effects on Florida, as it did on other Southern states. This was particularly so in north Florida, which was and is Southern in population and culture. There were concentrated the stinging bitterness, the Ku Klux Klan, the lynch mobs and racism and sweat that were all over the South. It is a profound emotional experience to stand today in Tallahassee's Old Fort Park, where the Houstoun plantation's trenches remain. Here indeed are marks of war, and Tallahassee has kept those trenches hollowed to remind its citizens. They were a conquered people; many, even in this decade, will tell you this, if you are a Northerner. There are matriarchs who are proud of never having read *Uncle Tom's Cabin,* innocent of the fact that the book has not aged well as literature and would probably make them yawn with boredom.

But the picture in all of Florida was not quite so desperate as that in Alabama and Georgia and the Carolinas and Virginia. Once again, Florida's climate saved her. It was such hell that Northern governors and officials who came were dedicated men willing to sacrifice health in order to help the black man and deal justly with the white. Carpetbaggers in numbers did not like torrid summers, malaria, paratyphoid, and dengue fever. Then the winter climate began drawing Northern tourists, who

7. Eppes, *Eventful Years,* p. 281.

discovered the charm of Jacksonville on the wide St. Johns, St. Augustine with its fort and ancient Spanish buildings, quail in the meadows, turkeys in the woods, and fish in the rivers and oceans. Tourists brought money, and it was badly needed. By the 1870s Tallahassee even gave a party for Harriet Beecher Stowe when she paid the city a visit: weren't her Florida travel articles bringing well-heeled visitors to the state? The Northerners pushed ever southward toward the Everglades, where Billy Bowlegs's Seminoles lived in their sanctuary. Since the tourists and Northern settlers liked warm winters, they increasingly favored southern Florida and left Tallahassee to its inhabitants, though they remained partial also to Jacksonville. In the summer, they fled North.

What ended the Civil War in Tallahassee was not Appomattox, but the Civil Rights Law of 1964 and the Black-Is-Beautiful movement. At first, the city was aghast. But those who claim that social change cannot be legislated have not seen what has happened in Florida's capital. Now, more than a decade after the law's passage, there is an increasing number of mixed marriages, including that of a very Southern local public relations man to a black woman—which event made, not the news, but the society pages of the *Tallahassee Democrat*. This does not mean that blacks and whites are losing their identities, and there is still much informal segregation. There is still the sprawling, unlovely slum of Frenchtown, long since abandoned by Lafayette's French grape-growers to former slaves and their descendants. There are the little country churches where black men and women in white robes gather to wade into rivers for "baptizings." But there is also sufficient sophistication among whites to view the racist as a redneck, a bigot, and nobody wants to be one. Tallahassee has elected a black mayor, and during the recent school-busing troubles in Boston, most of the town's citizens thought Massachusetts Yankees were behaving unrespectably. Wags suggested offering Southern troops to Washington to man Boston defense lines and insure the admission of black children to classrooms. "What's the *matter* with them, up there in Boston?" asked a very white and very Southern lady. "Don't they know segregation is wrong?"

7

Sons and Daughters
of Bras Coupé

*T*HE legend of Bras Coupé was old in the South before George Washington Cable ever gave it literary form and sent it to the *Atlantic Monthly,* which refused it on the grounds that it was "unmitigatedly distressful." It forms the core of Cable's novel of Louisiana planters, *The Grandissimes,* which is full of Creole violence and black passion. Bras Coupé was an African chief, captured and enslaved. His name literally meant "arm-cut-off," because, when a man lost his freedom, it was as if he had lost the power of an arm. Before his capture by slave raiders in Africa, Bras Coupé had been a prince of the Wolof tribe. When he was led off in chains to the slave ship, he assumed the name *Mioko-Koanga,* which is Wolof for the Louisiana French term *Bras Coupé.* "The arm which may no longer shake the spear or swing the wooden sword is no better than a useless stump," he said.[1]

The legend was not peculiar to Louisiana. It was all over Florida, as well. When visiting young English composer Frederick Delius heard it in the environs of St. Augustine in the 1880s, he turned it into *Koanga,* the first black opera ever writ-

1. George Washington Cable, *The Grandissimes,* edited with an introduction by Arvin Newton (New York: Sagamore Press, 1957), pp. ix, 171.

79

ten. It made stirring theater: the enslaved chief who strikes
down his white master in a fury of resentment; the manhunt that
follows in the swamp; the love between Koanga and Palmyra,
the quadroon he teaches to value her African heritage. Koanga-
Bras Coupé has long been a spiritual ancestor of both Florida
and Louisiana blacks. (Jazzman Sidney Bechet, in his autobiography *Treat It Gentle,* announced that Bras Coupé was really his
grandfather.) Bras Coupé is the incarnation of the long martyrdom and humiliation of slavery, and of the black man's eventual
spiritual and emotional survival. Bras Coupé is even a truer
symbol today for black Florida than he was in the nineteenth
and early twentieth centuries, for not all blacks were proud of
Africa before the modern black renaissance. They bought skin-
whiteners and hair-straighteners; many became "white folks'
niggers"; some turned to violence and drink. Slavery maimed
everyone concerned with it: owners, traffickers, and slaves
alike. It is no accident that America premiered the opera
Koanga in 1970, when its composer had been dead for thirty-six
years. The country's interest in black pride is not an ancient
one.

In November 1865, seven months after Appomattox, the federal government had deposed Florida's "rebel governor" Allison, who had succeeded Milton after the latter's suicide. David
Levy Yulee was in prison and so was Stephen Mallory, a Floridian and one-time Secretary of the Confederate Navy. So was
Allison himself. Provisional Governor William Marvin thought
this was a bit much, and wrote President Andrew Johnson for
clemency; Yulee's railroad needed him, and the damp prison air
aggravated Mallory's gout. Allison was not a bad man. But it
was several months before the trio were freed. Meanwhile, the
Union marched into Florida. They forced clergy to pray for
Andrew Johnson at Sunday services, and they brought in black
troops, an act meant to show Florida how thorough was the
social revolution that had been wrought. But Florida was already in no doubt of that.

When the nearly seventy thousand blacks in the state learned
they were free, they began streaming into Federal military
camps and towns by the thousands. The Union army hadn't

thought about this. In Marianna, Governor Marvin himself spoke to assembled blacks:

> There has been a story circulated in Middle Florida that on the first day of January next the land and mules will be taken from your former owners and divided among you. Such a story, I suppose, you have all heard. Have you? Speak out if you have and tell me. (''I'se hearn it! I'se hearn it!'' say all.) Well, who told you so? (An answer: "the soldiers"). . . I want you to understand me. The President will not give you one foot of land, nor a mule, nor a hog, nor a cow, nor even a knife or fork or spoon. (A voice: "Dar, ole man, you hear dat!'') [2]

Washington had had moral principles of emancipation, but only a vague idea of what was going to happen to the emancipated. In Florida, many returned to their old plantations, where there were at least food and security—provided the former owner had managed to keep his land. Others turned to United States marshals and the Freedmen's Bureau.

The design of the Freedmen's Bureau was grand:

> The work of the Bureau will be the promotion of productive industry, the settlement of those so lately slaves in homes of their own; the guarantee of their absolute freedom and their right to justice before the law . . . the dissemination of virtuous intelligence; and to aid in permanently establishing peace and securing property. [3]

What the Bureau soon understood it must actually do was to issue rations to the hungry—black and also white. It cared for a few orphans, for the sick and insane. It vaccinated blacks in droves for smallpox. It conducted sewing schools for black women. But trouble was brewing in Florida that no sewing school could cure, and the Bureau's agents knew it. They hoped the military would stay. "I would have no fear of the intelligent planters," wrote one from Tallahassee,

> but there are the bar-room loafers, previously slave drivers and overseers, and who are called "piney-woods men"—men who, as the old settlers have said to me, have escaped justice in other states

2. Davis, *Civil War*, p. 359.
3. Davis, *Civil War*, p. 377.

and have settled here. Then there is a class of boys of nineteen or twenty years of age, who would put a bowie-knife or a bullet through a Northern man as they would through a mad dog.[4]

The government in Tallahassee also made it clear that its plans for having the black man enfranchised were going to start very modestly. Legislatures of several Southern states, Florida among them, drew up laws that came popularly to be known as the Black Code, since they were designed to regulate the activities of former slaves. In Florida, these laws provided, among other things, the death penalty for "the inciting of insurrection among any portion of the population," for the rape of a white female, and for burglary. Freedmen's Bureau agent I. M. Hobbs, a Pennsylvanian based in Tallahassee, made the criticism that the object of the Black Code was to "put the black in a position inferior to the white: 'White citizens would resist any legislation that would appear to put freedmen on equality with whites.' " The arm of Bras Coupé was still effectively cut off. But conditions in Florida were better in general for blacks than they were elsewhere in the South. Southern newspapers began to intone the facts of immigration like a grim litany: "The tide of immigration is unprecedented . . . A thousand freedmen have passed through this city during the past week on their way to Florida . . . Nearly every day brings trains and wagons to Tallahassee from South Carolina." The *New York Times* reported that fifty thousand blacks had left South Carolina and a large share of them had gone to Florida.[5]

A. J. Peeler, a former slaveholder, toured the state, making speeches. In tiny, whitewashed Monticello, seat of Jefferson County in Middle Florida, he addressed himself to an elderly black:

"Uncle, who is Governor of Florida?" . . . "Don't know, sir." "Who is President of the United States?" (Many voices: "Don't speak.") "Yes, speak and answer the question." "Don't know,

4. Davis, *Civil War*, p. 399.
5. Davis, *Civil War*, pp. 421, 450.

sir." "Have you registered?" "Yes, sir." "Going to vote?" "Yes, sir." [6]

The point was impressive.

Yet, in 1868, one of the delegates to Florida's Constitutional Convention was a black man whom white observers called "the most cultured member of the Convention." Jonathan Gibbs was tall and light-colored, a native of Philadelphia. He had been educated at Dartmouth and at Princeton Theological Seminary, where he took a degree as a Presbyterian minister. He could orate with skill and passion. He had come to Florida for philanthropic work among blacks. Unfortunately, the other black delegates to the Convention included a semiliterate shoemaker and a mulatto whose white father had been his master, and who insisted on making rambling speeches at every opportunity. The fastidious Gibbs must have shuddered. He eventually became Superintendent of Public Instruction for the state, and such was the esteem he managed to win even among die-hard white rebels that Tallahassee named a street after him, Gibbs Drive, in a white section of the city.

After the Constitutional Convention of 1868 had pushed through a radical regime, Gibbs had to report to the legislature that the Ku Klux Klan was turning up everywhere. The year 1868 brought not only the radical Constitution, but an outbreak of vigilante lawlessness that has come to be the American cliché of the Reconstruction era. "Regulators" with guns on their saddlebows rode by night to "regulate" unwary blacks and Northern sympathizers into submission. Tension was especially high in Marianna (until the recent past a favorite lynching resort), where murders ravaged the countryside. Samuel Fleishman, a Jewish merchant, was called before a committee of citizens and told that he must leave the state because he had openly doubted white supremacy. He had lived in Marianna for twenty years. "They gave me two hours to arrange my affairs and get out of the town," he said. "I told them that if I had committed a crime I was willing to be tried and punished for it . . . but

6. Davis, *Civil War*, p. 485.

that I would rather die than leave. They informed me that they would take me off at sundown, willing or unwilling." [7] A week later, his corpse was found, twenty miles from town; it was matted with blood from gunshot wounds.

In Jacksonville, a squad of Federal soldiers was ambushed by a roving band of blacks; one of the soldiers was killed. To get revenge, the soldiers, under their officer, "shot up" the black section of Jacksonville, La Villa, killing a black boy and wounding two black men as well as a white man on the scene. "They whipped me from the crown of my head to the soles of my feet," said a woman who had been beaten by what she called the "True Klux," the Ku Klux Klan. "I was just raw. The blood oozed out through my frock, all around my waist, clean through." [8] The Klan were sexually conservative where white women were concerned; they did not undress these victims, since it would have been improper.

Reconstruction careened on and on, its radicals making things worse for the very blacks they sought to bring into the political mainstream, its die-hard rednecks terrorizing fields and forests and swamps and dim, canopied cut-roads, and its former patricians bitter in the depth of their humiliation. Radical Republicans also discovered a fatal occupation: in-fighting. The rednecks were not in-fighting. They knew only too clearly what they wanted: the utter and complete surrender of cowed blacks. And so the Republican party headed swiftly for disaster, and Florida blacks headed, not for enfranchisement, but segregation, in which the use of a public drinking fountain became a criminal act. The savagery continued until the presidential campaign of 1876 between Samuel Jones Tilden, Democrat, and Rutherford B. Hayes, Republican. Then Florida's returns became the critical pivot on which the national election turned. National Republicans executed a horse-trade: if the state went for Hayes, the Yankees would pull out and Reconstruction would be over. Florida incontestably voted for Tilden; but when the electors

7. Davis, *Civil War,* p. 576.
8. Davis, *Civil War,* p. 581.

met, their votes went to Hayes, and an era was ended. Now the sorrows of the blacks in the state began in earnest. Jim Crow cars appeared on railway trains. Hotels and eating establishments shut their doors against blacks. On every side, the black man faced degradation as bad as slavery had been. It went on for nearly a hundred years, when Southerner Lyndon B. Johnson came to the black's legal rescue with the Civil Rights Act of 1964.

Physically, blacks had built Florida; they had worked her fields and fired the bricks for her plantation houses; they had given Florida their music and their humor, humor which under the circumstances was gallantry; their African recipes, plus Spanish holdovers and such homely Appalachian staples as corn-meal mush, had given Florida her distinctive cuisine. Southern-fried is African-fried. And even while the white state went on turning a blind eye to these legacies, blacks produced men and women of distinction.

One of them was Mary McLeod Bethune, though she was a native of South Carolina. Her parents had been slaves; in her mother's veins ran the blood of African princes. Mary McLeod was determined to learn to read. Her chance came when the Missions Board of the Presbyterian Church sent a black teacher to Sumter County; Mary walked five miles each way daily to that school. After the mission school came Scotia Seminary in North Carolina, and a two-year stint at the fundamentalist Moody Bible Institute of Chicago. Mary wanted to be a missionary. But she took an assignment as an instructor at a black school in Georgia, where she married Albertus Bethune. The Bethunes were nomadic; they landed in Palatka, Florida, where their son Albert was born in 1899. The marriage was not happy. Mary said later: "Mr. Bethune was never interested in education, although himself a teacher. He could not understand that my soul was on fire to do things for my people." [9]

Bethune disappeared, and Mary headed for Daytona Beach,

---

9. Leedell W. Neyland, *Twelve Black Floridians* (Tallahassee: Florida Agricultural and Mechanical University Foundation, Inc., 1970), p. 17.

where the tracks of Henry Morrison Flagler's East Coast Railway were being laid. She had exactly a dollar and a half, and when she saw the conditions under which Flagler's black laborers were living, she was determined to stay. She began a ceaseless round of lectures, open begging from community leaders, and door-to-door canvassing. On October 3, 1904, she opened a school, with six pupils who paid tuition of fifty cents a week. In two years, enrollment had grown to two hundred. Teachers and students cleared the old shack that housed the school, mended broken crockery, stuffed burlap bags with Spanish moss to serve as mattresses, and mashed pokeberries to substitute for costly ink. Two white benefactors appeared: Thomas White, manufacturer of the White Sewing Machine, and James Gamble, a soap manufacturer, provided funds for building the Bethune school, which was soon merged with the Cookman Institute in Jacksonville. Cookman transferred to Daytona, and Bethune-Cookman had become a reality. National attention came, young blacks flocked to the campus, and Mrs. Bethune's fame spread abroad.

She went to Europe and was feted by Nancy, Viscountess Astor, at Cliveden, with a mammoth garden party; she was entertained in Scotland by Lady McLeod, a relative of the Carolinians who had owned Mary's parents. A dashing Italian exclaimed in greeting, "Ah, princess! Kissed by the sun!" Another man proposed to her and chased her all over Germany before he had to take her refusal seriously. Florida had never been like this! But, doggedly, she returned, the tinkling of Lady Astor's crystal goblets at Cliveden an improbable memory. In Florida, Mary McLeod Bethune could not legally use a public drinking fountain.

Bethune-Cookman was now valued at a million dollars. Mrs. Bethune's organization, the National Council of Negro Women, needed a headquarters in Washington and she paid a call on Marshall Field III. She walked out with $10,000, leaving a bemused Field to murmur, "I don't know of anyone else who could have done that." Nothing spoiled her. When she was eighty, she said contentedly, "Here I sit with my feet on deep carpet, bathed in light and wrapped in soft raiment, having the good things of life. Thank you, Lord.'' [10] The original dollar and a half had gone a long way.

The history of another important Florida institution of black education began even earlier than Bethune-Cookman's. In the early 1880s, black illiteracy was the rule. ''We must educate the rising generation,'' said white Governor William Dunnington Bloxham, himself a graduate of William and Mary in Virginia. ''There is no subject more important than public education . . . Universal suffrage demands universal education as its protector, for while the ballot is a most potent weapon, when wielded by ignorance, there is none more dangerous to free government.'' [11] In 1884, a ''normal school'' for the training of teachers was founded for blacks in Tallahassee. In 1887, the legislature authorized a State Normal College for Colored Students; responsible for introducing the resolution was Thomas Van Renssalaer Gibbs, son of Jonathan.

Thomas Gibbs was a former West Pointer who had become active in Jacksonville and Duval County politics. His power was to last just until the supporters of Samuel Tilden made their deal with those of Rutherford B. Hayes in the election of 1876. Reconstruction was over. Blacks were soon being intimidated at the polls by white ruffians; it must have saddened the urbane, moderate Thomas Gibbs profoundly. When his career was cut short by death in 1898, he was vice-president of the State Normal and Industrial College, Tallahassee, the institution whose founding resolution he had introduced in the legislature. It became successively Florida Agricultural and Mechanical College for Negroes, and, finally, Florida Agricultural and Mechanical University. Today it is fighting for its life, fiercely beloved by its alumni and by football fans, weakened by the integration that opened new doors for black teachers in white schools, and reminded repeatedly by the U.S. Department of Health, Education, and Welfare that Florida A & M had better become vastly more integrated in its student body—soon.

10. Neyland, *Black Floridians,* pp. 23–24.
11. Leedell W. Neyland, *A History of Florida Agricultural and Mechanical University* (Gainesville: University of Florida Press, 1965), p. 1.

The dilemma of Florida A & M is a rich reflection of black history in Florida. It rose in a time of optimism; it took students who did not know who Rembrandt was and graduated them with backgrounds which in many cases admitted them to graduate schools elsewhere. Of necessity, its admission standards were low. Then came the stirring Civil Rights crusades of the 1960s. For the first time, black students could eat in downtown Tallahassee. Then something strange happened: these young blacks wanted the right to eat anywhere and the right to decent jobs, but they discovered that they did not, for the most part, care for the after-hours society of whites.

The tightrope act of Dr. George W. Gore, president of Florida A & M in the 'sixties, was awesome to watch: he was responsible to white segregationists, responsible for black activists, and chronically in need of funds to expand his university programs. There are now a few white students at Florida A & M, but they hold no power of significance. There are white faculty, including as visiting professors such improbable people as Paul Hemphill, authority on the rural southern white and the country music that white Nashville, Tennessee, creates, and Czech composer Vaclav Nelhybel, who divides his time between the classics and listening to the football band. And everywhere, everyone, black and white, knows that Florida A & M is duplicating other services and programs in the university system of Florida, and that this is not good for state bank accounts.

The black experience in Florida has ranged from hell to euphoria. Slaves were driven by the whip. In Reconstruction, the black man had hope held out to him, only to have it withdrawn. The crippling effects of prejudice and segregation included Uncle Tomism, in many cases and emotionally devastated neurotics in others. In all this, Florida was on the side of her sister southern states. But there were differences.

Again, one of them was the climate. Blacks poured in from the upper South because they liked the warmth, and they established solid communities where men and women had identities, no matter how their white detractors might try to debase them. The middle-class black rose to power among his own and sometimes to wealth. Another difference was what can only be termed Florida's manic love of football. A white fan could wine and dine a black coach as a Mississippian could not: the reason why is a mystery, yet perhaps it is not irrelevant that Latin-rooted Florida is used to darker skins—Cubans, Spanish, Minorcan, Italian, Seminole—than Mississippi is. Anyone in Florida who ever threatened harm to Jake Gaither, celebrated retired head coach at Florida A & M, would be burned at the stake in Tallahassee—by whites.

When the final great change came in Florida in 1964 and the polls were opened to black citizens, it appeared to many observers that whites were weary of the struggle and relieved to have it over. Within a few years, predominantly white Tallahassee elected a black mayor whose picture appeared regularly on society pages as attending integrated Hawaiian patio parties. Citizens who denounced Mayor James Ford found fault, not with his political beliefs or his skin color, but with the fact that he was cautious about funding the local Animal Shelter, since he felt there were other priorities. Cat-lovers fulminated against him for his suggestion that felines ought to be licensed and vaccinated. More than one northern visitor reflected that, not only did Florida's capital, bastion of the Old South, have a black mayor: it had a socially popular black mayor who roused the strongest municipal emotions over the likes of Lassie and Morris.

Florida's capital has come far. Poverty there still is in black Florida—grinding poverty. The sight of windowless shacks on Gadsden County tobacco farms in the northern part of the state is a shocker. So is the sight of what goes on many black dinner tables where money is short—blackeyed peas and molasses. "These people don't want what we want," a white planter once genially explained to me. "They like their peas, and we don't give them windows because they're afraid of the ha'ants." My answer was: "If I go through that quarter with steak, champagne, and a glazier, do you think I will have no takers?" There might have been rural Alabamians or Mississippians who would have roared back an angry reply. The Florida planter merely looked me in the eye and then chuckled, "I reckon you've got a point."

That was what Florida reckoned—that its black citizens had a point. There was ugly violence in St. Augustine where Klan chief Hoss Manucy rode by night. (His ancestry was Minorcan.) There were stockade jailings, beatings, and white mobs being stood off courthouse steps by harried sheriffs trying to protect black prisoners. But then it all ended—so rapidly that Floridians blinked. Had segregation been so important? Segregation had defeated LeRoy Collins in a U.S. Senate race, because he had been converted to integration on ethical grounds. Now black fashion models appeared in department stores. Tensions—strong tensions—remain. So do bitter injustices. But Florida is well aware of the black role in her music (among others, James Weldon Johnson) and her art and her literature (among others, Zora Neale Hurston, novelist of rural Florida). Without her blacks, Florida would not be Florida. As she had sat out the Spirit of '76, she finally sat out white supremacy. Another thing that saved the blacks was tourism. Hoss Manucy didn't look very good to money-bearing Yankees; neither did the St. Augustine jailing of the elderly wife of Episcopal Bishop Endicott Peabody of Massachusetts. (Mrs. Peabody had knowingly sat down at the wrong lunch counter.) Race relations in Florida began in hypocrisy; they have continued with increasing courtesy. It is to be hoped the next step is real understanding, for the two cultures need not merge totally to smother the separate identities of either.

8

Remembering the *Maine*

THE years that followed the Hayes-Tilden compromise saw massive growth in Florida. Tycoon Henry Morrison Flagler began his Florida East Coast Railway down the Atlantic shoreline, and Henry Bradley Plant brought the Plant System with its attendant warehouses and freight yards to Tampa. For little Tampa, long a sleepy village drowsing in the shadow of Fort Brooke, Henry Plant meant a giant leap toward urban status. Both tycoons built hotels. In St. Augustine, where once Pedro Menéndez de Avilés had saluted the Spanish flag each sunset, Henry Flagler raised the massive pile of the Ponce de León. Its two Castilian towers dominated the red-roofed skyline. Acres of greensward and flowerbeds sheltered stone fountains where the Florida sunlight made rainbows in the spray. Magnolias bloomed creamily beside Moorish cloisters, Gothic niches sheltered crimson azaleas, and the gate to all this splendor was a medieval portcullis worthy of Ferdinand and Isabella. At night, the portcullis was lowered to exclude romancing couples. Inside, the Ponce de León had other splendors: "cardinals' chairs" in the lobby, a nine-foot concert grand piano, scutcheons bearing the arms of noble Spanish families, and treasures of marble, onyx, and silver in a decorative style correctly termed eclectic.

Northern society columnists were entranced, envisioning slim dons and dark-eyed señoritas. Actually, the señoritas were rheumatic dowagers in bombazine and the dons were their over-weight (and very rich) husbands, come south in search of the sun. Some of St. Augustine's year-round citizens were English-men pursuing a dream of endless wealth from flourishing citrus groves. It took them a long time to realize that frosts might not hit every year, but that, when they did, they were lethal.

Henry Plant wanted something even bigger than the Ponce de León. In Tampa, he began raising the Arabian-Nights mass of the Tampa Bay Hotel, for which he planned regal gardens, elec-tric launches, French *haute cuisine,* and various masterpieces in oils and wood and marble acquired from financially embarrassed European princes and dukes. Plant built a pavilion for orches-tras; he also built a swimming pool. The silver minarets began to rise above a venerable oak that Plant—constrained to come up with a worthy rival for Flagler's Fountain of Youth at St. Augustine—declared was the very tree under which Hernando de Soto had treated with the Timucua Indians. Everywhere ap-peared the horseshoe-and-crescent motif of Islam; had not the Moors once ruled Spain? There were also oriental rickshaws to transport the arthritic from magnificence to magnificence in-doors: a table, a sofa and two chairs that had belonged to Marie Antoinette; four armchairs lately owned by Louis Phillippe; and inlaid cabinets fresh from mysterious Japan. What the old world couldn't contribute, Grand Rapids, Michigan, could; its cabinet-makers were kept busy hammering out huge bedsteads and din-ing room tables for Henry Plant's Tampa Bay version of the Alhambra. Modern Florida hostelries lack the romance of those of Flagler and Plant, though they are furnished more scien-tifically. An education officer of the Florida Forest Service once explained to me how his department worked with Howard John-son, Inc., and the Holiday Inns of America. "Because," he said, "when you've got the possibility of a 300-pound drunk heaving himself across a bed, the wood had better be strong enough to take it, and that's where our knowledge can help." [1] Plant was scientific enough on his verandas; each wicker chair had been built to conform to the measurements of the world's

1. Personal conversation.

fattest man. His patrons were enjoined to eat; calorie charts and Ayds Reducing Candy had not yet appeared on the American scene, and the tranquilizers in use were low-proof alcoholic.

Long eclipsed by Tallahassee, Tampa now began to become a cosmopolitan city that made the state capital look like the country town it was. Tampa's fate was sealed, not only by the Plant System and the Tampa Bay Hotel, but by the humbler guava tree. The guavas brought Cubans; the Cubans built cigar factories; in the factories, the *lectores*—readers—droned of revolution against Spain's Cuban despotism; and in the ardor of revolt was born the Spanish-American War, bred in Tampa, Florida, and subsequently an American venture in imperialism.

Guavas had been brought to the hamlet of Sarasota, years before, by a farmer named Valentine Snell. Modern legend has it that guava seeds were carried to Tampa by mockingbirds. The tale is possible, though it is more logical that the trees were imported by guava-lovers who had been to Sarasota. In the summer of 1885, a Cuban guava planter named Bernardino Gargol invited to Tampa his friend Gavino Gutiérrez, a New Yorker. Gutiérrez found the guavas impressive, but even more impressive the eternal summer and lush vegetation of a city obviously on the march. Back in New York, Gutiérrez told friends who were cigar manufacturers about Tampa. In Key West, the small cigar factories had been plagued by labor troubles; in Tampa, he believed, the citizens wanted work too badly to cause trouble.

One of the cigar manufacturers who listened to Gavino Gutiérrez was Vicente Martinez Ybor, who had been discouraged by his Key West labor problems. Why not shift his operation to Tampa ? When he got in touch with the Tampa Board of Trade, they promised him special tax advantages. With his partner Eduard Manrara, he built the Ybor y Manrara plant and also an enclave at its doors to house the workers: Ybor City. New York cigar magnate Ignacio Haya was so impressed that he, too, decided to move to Tampa. So did the Cuestas, and Emilio Pons. Cuban refugees began pouring in, eager for a fresh start in a new land as warm as the old, and some Tampa citizens joined them. Tampa was soon the home of the "clear Havana," made by hand. The king of Spain put in a standing order. Independent of the larger factories were small operators called "buckeyes," who worked out of store fronts. Most of the hand-rolling in factories and most of the buckeyes have disappeared from modern Tampa, but the tradition of fine cigar-making lingers. Visiting dignitaries are presented with Tampa's best by the mayor, and the clock tower of the Standard Cigar Company is still a landmark in Ybor City. Ybor City has survived, as its neighboring district, the town of Fort Brooke, has not. The town of Fort Brooke boasted a vast array of brothels that horrified the Catholic Cubans; most notorious of the prostitutes was La Culebra, "the Serpent," a mulatto who plied her wares along Sixth Avenue near the border between the two zones. La Culebra and her sisters flourished into the era of the War with Spain, but eventually vocal evangelists forced them underground.

In its heyday, Ybor City was full of fascination and color. On religious feast days, Vicente Martinez Ybor sent wagons into the streets laden with gifts of suckling pigs and confections for his families. Cockfights flourished in dim arenas. The Spaniards and Cubans built clubs: *El Centro Español* and *El Liceo Cubano* and *El Centro Asturiano*. The smell of thick black coffee issued from club doors, with the laughter of families at Saturday night dances. On long, close summer afternoons, old men played checkers out in front. There were frequent parades, with Cuban and Spanish gay blades costumed as Don Quixote and Sancho Panza. Ybor City was a Latin fastness that baffled white Anglo-Saxon Protestant Floridians—but also drew them like a magnet. Ybor City cafés served chicken and yellow rice, guava paste, and rich yellow cheese. Outsiders came to enjoy the delicacies and to buy the cigars of Ybor y Manrara, Cuesta, and Ignacio Haya. They mingled with the Cubans and Spanish to drink dry red Marques de Riscal wine and, predictably, the two groups began to intermarry. Not much, at first. The Cubans and Spanish were fiercely jealous of their women and of their religion. They were also hostile to the Italians who came to Ybor City to open grocery stores and bakeries. Italians might be Catholics, but it was still mixed marriage when an Italian married a Cuban. When gambling rackets grew rife, the Cubans blamed the Italians for them; the Italians, in turn, said the culprits were Cuban.

But here and there a señorita caught the eye of a former Confederate Tampan and nervously joined the Episcopal, Methodist, or Baptist Church. Two cultures, Latin and Protestant Floridian, fused in the city of Tampa.

By this time, Greek sponge divers had begun to arrive in Tarpon Springs, a few miles north, turning the little west-coast resort, almost overnight, to a city of Mediterranean shops and hawking merchants from Kalymnos and Halki and Delos. The main street was rechristened Dodecanese Boulevard, and everywhere *baklava* pastries and massive loaves of soft white Greek bread were sold. The Greeks built a cathedral; the orthodox maintained that the statue of the Virgin there wept for lost sponge divers, while skeptics pointed out that Florida humidity is high.

To go to Tarpon Springs is still to take a trip to mini-Europe. The Greek language flourishes, and every drugstore is laden with the works of Aristotle and Plato, which are read. Dodecanese Boulevard is a fascinating array of shops stocking imports from all over the world—Greece and Turkey, Hong Kong, Guatemala, and even the People's Republic of China, which manufactures the straw hats so essential for prolonged exposure to Florida sun. Tarpon Springs has kept its exoticism. Ybor City has kept only the shell of what it once was—for, when the Cubans and Italians prospered, they bought houses in parts of Tampa that did not savor of the ghetto. The buildings remain; many are being restored, and once again Ybor City holds fiestas and torchlight parades on feast days. But the Cubans and Italians, for the most part, come from other sections of the city to participate in them. The cigar factories have long since become mechanized, though here and there an independent buckeye proprietor still rolls his cigars by hand. The immigrants from Greece, Spain, and Cuba who first peopled Tarpon Springs and Ybor City gave Florida its steady diet of Greek salad and Spanish bean soup. The other staple, Key lime pie, came from the Bahamians who settled in Key West, the "Conchs."

Florida was headily different. Passions ran high among her Latins and Mediterraneans, proud Asturians who had crossed the ocean to work for Vicente Martinez Ybor, Greeks who bore with equanimity—mostly—the racial prejudice of unlettered Florida crackers. They knew who they were; they had produced Homer and Euclid and Aristophanes, and the knowledge sustained them.

The Cubans were aflame with a passion other than pride: liberty. A Tampa Cuban regarded as a brother his counterpart in Havana. Anglo-Saxons heard, with horror, that the cigar factory *lectores* often read from Charles Darwin and Karl Marx. Ybor City was becoming a hotbed of socialism, they fumed. They were partly correct, though the restraining influence of the Roman Catholic Church was a check on the excesses of revolution and freethinking.

In Cuba's Oriente province, a group of guerillas had proclaimed the country's independence from Spain in 1868. This began a Ten Years' War that drained Cuba nearly dry of money and food and vitality. One hundred and forty-seven men were few enough against the imperial might of Spain; but in a year they had become more than 25,000. Even after the war's end, by the 1880s, Cuban-language newspapers in Ybor City, *Cuba* and *El Mosquito,* kept the cigar workers informed of the latest developments. *El lector* read stirring hymns to freedom. Out of Ybor City started coming speeches and manifestos that were to plunge America into a war most of her population did not understand.

At the end of the Ten Years' War, when the rebel leader Gomez was forced to surrender to Spain because Cuba had lost two hundred thousand lives and seven hundred million dollars in the destruction of property, Cuba was a smoking shell. But to America she sent one of her most eloquent libertarians, José Martí, who organized Freedom Clubs from Key West to New York and urged the cigarmakers to give him a tenth of their profits. The Ignacio Agramonte Club, named for a rebel hero of the Ten Years' War, invited Martí to Tampa; every one of his speeches had been reported to Ybor City by the journalists Nestor and Eligio Carbonell, whose battle cry was *"Cuba Libre!"*

The night José Martí arrived at the tiny railway station in Ybor City was thick with rain. Lanterns swung giddily along the unpaved streets in the downpour. Martí's train was late; trees were down along the line. When he finally arrived, he saw the shivering spectacle of fifty Cuban men. In a triumphal procession through the subtropic storm, the Cubans conducted Martí to Rubiera's Hotel, where he turned to them on the steps: "I am happy to feel myself among warriors," he said.[2]

The next day the sun emerged from the clouds, and Ybor City feted Martí with a parade. Cuban flags whipped in the wind; lampposts had been wound in garlands of leaves. With Ramon Rivera, the *lector* of Ybor y Manrara, Martí entered the factory. Rivera's substitute stopped his reading abruptly. After a reverential silence, the cigarmakers rose and sharply tapped their leaf-folders on the tables before them in welcome.

That night, Martí spoke in a jammed *Liceo Cubano*. He pleaded for racial brotherhood; he told his audience to "cast aside the fear of going barefoot, which is now a very common way of going in Cuba," and he built his oration toward an eloquent climax: "Now! Form your ranks! Countries are not created by wishful thinking in the depths of the soul! . . . Let us rise so that liberty does not run any risk in its hour of triumph through disorder or indolence or impatience in its preparation. Let us rise for the real Republic!" When he had finished, the hall was alive with "Vivas!" [3]

In a second address at the *Liceo Cubano,* he gave the speech for which, perhaps, he is most famous. Describing the storm he had seen from his train on the way down to Tampa, he told them:

> Suddenly the sun broke through a clearing in the woods, and there in the dazzling of the unexpected light I saw above the yellowish grass proudly rising from among the black trunks of the falling trees the flourishing branches of new pines. That is what we are: new pines! [4]

José Martí's persuasiveness could not have come to America at a more opportune time. The country longed to forget the

2. Jorge Manach, *Martí,* translated by Coley Taylor (New York: Devia-Adair, 1950), pp. 269 ff.
3. Manach, *Martí,* p. 276.
4. Manach, *Martí,* p. 276.

lingering lesions of civil war. Northerners and southerners felt that they could unite in a holy crusade to liberate a comfortably distant people—distant, that is, from the rest of the nation, though not from Florida. Theodore Roosevelt, a politician the nation was watching with admiration, forthrightly proclaimed his mission to preach "with all the fervor and zeal I possess, our duty to intervene in Cuba and to take this opportunity of driving the Spaniard from the Western World." [5] When news came that José Martí had been set upon by a band of terrorists in Cuba and murdered, Ybor City cigar manufacturers—there were now ninety-seven of them—started a fund in Martí's memory. Cuban women arrived to seek jobs in the Tampa factories, while their husbands fought on. Dignitaries came, among them, Palma, who was to become president of the Republic of Cuba, and also the secretary of the revolutionary party and several revolutionary generals. Cuban organizations from all over America sent guns and ammunition to Tampa, to be dispatched to Cuba under cover of darkness. When the Spanish commandant in Havana threatened to stop shipping cigar tobacco to Tampa, Tampa was indignant. Before the embargo could take effect, steamers were sent to Havana to gather enough Cuban tobacco to keep Ybor City alive during the coming inevitable war. Tampa businessmen who were Poles and Germans and Jews and Scotch-Irish enlarged on the necessity of liberating their beloved bronze brothers of Cuba. The porch of the Tampa Bay Hotel was full of reporters waiting in their wide wicker chairs for something to happen. When it did, it happened in Havana Harbor. The U.S. battleship *Maine* was blown to bits under a canopy of West Indian stars, and now the war hawks had a slogan: "Remember the *Maine!*"

But when correspondents arrived in Cuba, to be on the scene when war was declared, they found an apparently peaceful capital, at odds with the reports José Martí had made. One of the correspondents was the artist Frederic Remington, who sent an impatient telegram to New York that everything was quiet, there

5. Theodore Roosevelt, *The Rough Riders* (New York: Charles Scribner's Sons, 1906), p. 1.

was no trouble, there would be no war. From New York the answer was prompt: William Randolph Hearst promised to furnish a war, in due time.

Hearst nagged at America's conscience and sense of national honor until Congress declared war on Spain late in April 1898. Adm. George Dewey steamed toward Manila Bay in the Spanish Philippines, where outmoded Spanish ships of the line were outmatched by his modern battleships. Dewey blew them as high as the *Maine* had been blown.

Riding triumphantly into Florida came the commanding general of the army the United States prepared to send into Cuba. He was William Rufus Shafter, and he weighed 320 pounds. No steed could hold him; he traveled in a buckboard wagon with heavy-duty springs, pulled by Percheron workhorses. No army cot could survive him, either; his aides unhinged doors wherever they happened to be and up-ended them to make a sufficiently sturdy bed. If General Shafter was not exactly a figure of romance, Theodore Roosevelt was. With Col. Leonard Wood, Roosevelt headed a group of volunteers that people had christened the Rough Riders. The Rough Riders came from the American west; they were cowboys and Indians and prospectors and law enforcement officers and others who didn't reveal their occupations. The Rough Riders also included four Methodist clergymen who saw Catholic Cuba as a Babylon in need of destruction. They waited happily in Catholic Tampa, oblivious of the inconsistency. Some of Roosevelt's company were former football heroes from eastern universities; some, like William Tiffany, were socialites. One, "Reggie" Ronalds, was a drinking companion of Edward, Prince of Wales, whose aging mother Victoria still ruled England with dignity and iron.

Now fresh reporters came to wait at the Tampa Bay Hotel. One of them, all the way from London, was young Winston Churchill. Clara Barton, founder of the American Red Cross, arrived to set up hospital operations. When the rainy season began, supplies of beef and hardtack moldered in poorly ventilated warehouses. Ybor City was now full of U.S. soldiers waiting to be shipped out; some passed out in the heat, and Cuban women moved among them with pitchers of cooling water. In the town of Fort Brooke, Tampa's fancy ladies conducted a brisk trade. Florida's climate was hell, believed Yankee volunteers, but Tampa was alive with humanity and elation. It was also not without humor. The prostitutes who set up shop at the Tampa docks christened their thoroughfare Last Chance Street. By the middle of June, Tampa Bay was full of U.S. Navy transports and General Shafter was—slowly—pacing the deck of his leading ship. There had been confusion, as well as rotten rations. There had not, for instance, been room enough for the horses of the Rough Riders, who in spite of their sobriquet would have to become inglorious infantry. Only Lieutenant Colonel Roosevelt had his mount. The voyage to Cuba would take six days—if they were lucky and encountered no hurricanes. Floridians flocked to the shores of Tampa Bay as the navy finally swung away from Port Tampa docks. Tugboats whistled, winches creaked, and the huge anchors were raised. The troops were elated, spoiling to fight. They knew some of them would not return, but the war to save Cuba was one of glory and romance, a cradle of heroes. The fortunate would be coming back to ticker-tape welcomes at summer's end. (In Lieutenant Colonel Roosevelt's future was the charge up San Juan Hill, near the city of Santiago, and after it a charge on the White House.)

For Spain, it was the end of a new-world adventure begun nearly four hundred years before. Brigantines and caravels and pinnaces had sailed the main of Florida long before a United States of America existed. Spanish warriors had slain, and Spanish missionaries had prayed. Whole tribes of Indians had been exterminated. Spanish armor had flashed brightly in the Florida sun. Now that sun shone on the massive khaki bulk of William Rufus Shafter. Spain could not hold Cuba, as she had not been able to hold Florida. Ironically, the end of Spain in the western hemisphere was engineered from Tampa, Florida, where Hernando de Soto had landed. Tampa had made the United States go to war for the friends and relatives of its citizens.

Marti's statue, worn by sun and rainy seasons, stands in Tampa's Ybor City today in the small Park of the Friends of José

Martí. He wears a black arm band, for Tampa's Cubans excoriate the communism of Fidel Castro, also a rebel of Oriente Province. The *lectores* are only a memory now; they have been replaced by transistor radios playing pop music and baseball games. But still there is an enchantment in Ybor City difficult to define. Perhaps it is in the mellow fragrances of the cigar factories, perhaps in the seamed faces of aged Cuban cigarmakers working by hand in tiny storefront buckeyes. It is the rustling of *cocos plumosa* palms in the seawind, soft stars on cestrum-scented summer nights, the music of guitars that still pours out from *El Centro Español,* where the old men still play checkers. It is the rumbling of trains toward Hav-a-Tampa and Standard and Cuesta Rey, the saffron tang of Spanish yellow rice and bean soup, and the grave Cuban families whose men dress up on Sundays, no matter how high the temperature, in black suits and stiff white collars and decorous ties, while their rigidly corseted women in pastel taffetas fan themselves with palmetto fans in Cuervo's restaurant. It is the legacy of Martí's pleas for freedom, and the banjos and laughter of the blacks who moved into Ybor City as the Cubans moved out. But the Cubans always return: Cuervo's and the Columbia Restaurant with its potted palms and strolling serenaders draw them like a magnet.

The poet of Ybor City is writer José Yglesias; he has not remained, but from his desk in New York City, he remembers. Palms are once more rising in the city's old streets; buildings are being restored; and over it all, perhaps, presides the benevolent ghost of Vicente Martinez Ybor, whose fondness for Tampa, Florida, led to an entire nation's going to war. Again in Ybor City the oleanders bloom white and pink, and high banana leaves clatter in coastal breezes. There has been change, but the magic remains, as does the love of Florida's Cubans who grew up there.

The Tampa Cuban is a traditionalist; his story goes back, not to the downfall of Fulgencio Batista, but to the Ten Years' War. Miami's Cubans, on the other hand, are completely of the twentieth century. In Cuban hearts in Tampa, there linger the mellowness and grace of an earlier era. In a courtly gesture, Tampans have named a president of the United States as honorary *alcalde,* or mayor, of Ybor City. He was John Fitzgerald Kennedy, and in Tampa he rode in the last parade from which he would emerge alive; Dallas came three days later. And in the Italian Club and the *Centro Asturiano,* Latin families still speak of the triumphal parade as if it had happened yesterday. It, too, has become a part of the Ybor City legend; it, too, lends magic to the very stones of Ybor City streets. The *Maine* is not the only Ybor City link to the rest of America. What is remembered there is the proud tradition of craftsmanship; when an American man wants luxury, he still smokes an Ybor City cigar.

9

The Almighty Orange

$\mathcal{W}$HEN Americans think of Florida, they think inevitably of oranges. Furthermore, they think of oranges as a necessity for human survival. Oranges contain Vitamin C; oranges are delicious; oranges require a warm climate. These things have made Florida the citrus capital of the world. The United States produces more citrus fruit than any other nation, and Florida leads her sister warm states in such production, having not only the latitude for citrus culture, but a readily available water supply, as well. Irrigation, when needed, is uncomplicated: the grove owner merely taps the underground water resources of the Floridian Aquifer.

To stand atop the monolithic Citrus Tower, on Route 27 near Clermont in central Florida, is—to put it conservatively—a mind-boggling experience. In every direction, vast seas of rounded, dark-green trees stretch away on gentle, lake-studded hills toward the horizon. In spring, the trees are laden with white blossoms of such intense fragrance that ships' passengers off the Atlantic and Gulf coasts can smell it several miles out at sea.

The fruit season starts in autumn, and, in a bewildering succession of varieties, it continues until the following midsummer. All year round, the Florida Citrus Mutual spreads the gospel of health through citrus consumption. D. C. Jarvis, M.D., late purveyor of Vermont folk medicine, is not appreciated by citrus

103

people, since he advanced the argument that citrus was alkaline, and the body needed acid fruits such as apples—which thrive in frigid Vermont. Florida has its own host of folk-medicine sales-men; and among the orthodox, citrus is held to ward off heart attacks and strokes, prevent scurvy, aid in the control of diabe-tes, and vanquish the common cold. Dr. Linus Pauling and his megadoses of Vitamin C are well thought of. When Prin-cess Beatrix of the Netherlands produced her first offspring, Florida's governor, then Claude R. Kirk, Jr., immediately or-dered that the infant be supplied daily with complimentary Florida orange juice to ensure its survival and prosperity.

The journey of the fruits to Florida has been a long one. Probably they originated on the warm southern slopes of the Himalayas, in northeastern India and nearby Burma. In prehis-toric times, early forms of the orange, the shaddock (ancestor of the grapefruit), and some of the mandarin species crossed into western China and from there to Indo-China. Limes, lemons, and citrons spread into India and the Malay Peninsula. The only citrus originating in China seems to have been the trifoliate orange, *Poncirus,* and the kumquat, *Fortunella.* Today the sweet orange, like the shaddock, is unknown in the wild state. Agricultural historians believe it developed into something like its present form in eastern China. The first mention of oranges in literature appears in the *Shu-ching,* a Chinese book compiled in the sixth century B.C. Sanskrit literature of the eighth century B.C. mentions mandarins, the orange fruits like tangerines in which the peel separates readily from the interior pulp. These were first noted in Chinese literature in 200 B.C.

The Sanskrit name for the orange was *nagarunga.* In Persian, this became *naranj;* it was *aurantium* in Latin, *naranja* in Span-ish, and appeared in English as *orange.*

The earliest citrus fruit known in Europe was the citron, val-ued for its aromatic rind. Before the days of Alexander the Great, Greeks imported citrons from Persia. From Greece, cit-rons spread to Palestine, where one variety became a sacred food to be consumed during the Jewish Feast of Tabernacles. Formerly, the Jews had used the cone of the cedar tree in this ceremony. The Greek word for cedar was *kedros;* when citrons were substituted for cedar cones, Greek Palestinians called them cedar-apples (*kedromelon*). The Greek *kedrus* became *cedrus* in Latin, and by the time Pliny was writing his *Natural History,* the form *citrus* had evolved to refer to the citron.

Sweet oranges were enjoyed well before the birth of Christ. In the first century A.D., Romans were eating sweet oranges as "Indian Fruit." At length, they established groves from seed in southern Italy; these lasted until the Dark Ages; Goths and Vandals destroyed them. North Africa abounded in citrus, and from there it was brought into southern Spain by the Moors. When Vasco da Gama reached India in 1498, sweet oranges were already under cultivation back home in southern Europe, and Louis XI of France had become an avid consumer of sweet oranges from Provence. In 1493, on a second voyage to Hispaniola, Columbus brought orange, lemon, and citron seeds from the Canary Islands, and thirty years later, according to the Spanish historian Oviedo y Valdes, sweet-orange groves were abundant in the West Indies.

Pedro Menéndez de Avilés brought the sweet orange into Florida at St. Augustine in 1565. By 1579, Menéndez reported back to Spain that oranges were now abundant in Florida. From Spanish gardens and groves, Florida's Indians carried fruit into their villages; as they ate, they scattered the seeds. Some of the sweet-orange trees did not long survive in the northern locations, but the hardier, sour type of orange—the same type used in the making of Dundee and Cooper's Oxford Marmalade—did. Thickets of sour oranges are to be found today on the edge of many a Florida lake and stream. William Bartram, the great Philadelphia naturalist, found wild oranges in abundance in 1773 and was puzzled:

> Whether the orange tree is an exotick, brot in here by the Spaniards, or a Native to this country, is a question. I have inquired of some of the old Spaniards at St. Augustine, who tell me that they were first brot in by the Spaniards and spread over the country by the Indians.[1]

---

1. Louis W. Ziegler and Herbert S. Wolfe, *Citrus Growing in Florida* (Gainesville: University of Florida, 1961), p. 6.

The Spanish planted oranges for domestic use, not commerce. New Yorkers drank no orange juice until Spain ceded Florida to the British in 1763. Then enterprising traders started shipping the fruit north, extolling its health-giving benefits. Oranges came into their own in 1821, when Spain ceded Florida to the United States. The St. Johns River and its tributaries flowered with orange blossoms; ripe fruit was carried north by American steamers and soon it became a staple in New York and Boston diets. The arrival of the insect pest scale in 1838 slowed production, but never stopped it; by 1870, scale was waning as mysteriously as it had come, and Florida orange production virtually "exploded." Between 1874 and 1877, the eastern United States was annually importing about 200 million oranges with a value of more than $2 million dollars. Most of these oranges came from the Mediterranean; some were shipped in from the West Indies.

In the West Indies, a century before, a British East India captain named Shaddock had introduced the fruit that bears his name. The shaddock is, botanically, a variety of pommelo, and from it is descended the modern grapefruit. No one is sure whether grapefruits developed in the West Indies or in Florida. But when America tasted it, the grapefruit also became a favorite—not on so grand a scale as the orange, but grand enough.

Lemons and limes were also imported from the West Indies; but why not grow them in Florida? The state's vitality had been sapped by civil war; but the very Yankees who had conquered now arrived with orange and grapefruit and lemon and lime seeds. Gen. Henry S. Sanford, who had been Abraham Lincoln's ambassador to Belgium, now turned his attention to bringing into Florida every variety of citrus he could think of. Growers built railroads and packing houses; practiced scientific horticulture; learned that trifoliate citrus worked best as a stock in cooler parts of the state, and that rough lemon stock was best in the sandy midsection. Onto these stocks were grafted a wide array of citrus varieties, and growers worked constantly to develop superior strains.

The crowning touch of Florida's citrus expansion was provided when a thin, tubercular young man from North Adams, Massachusetts, arrived in the central Florida town of DeLand. Lue Gim Gong was Chinese, born in Canton. From China, he had made his way to New England; and when he developed tuberculosis, he read tourist literature that promised him relief in Florida. For Lue Gim Gong, the miracle worked; after coming to DeLand in 1886, he survived for thirty-nine years. During those years, he worked at hybridizing new varieties of tomatoes and grapefruit and—especially—oranges. In 1888 was born the cold-resistant Lue Gim Gong orange that hangs like a golden apple in the waxy, deep-green foliage of its tree for two years. Lue Gim Gong oranges were adopted by planters along the Indian River. Eventually, Lue Gim Gong received the U.S. Department of Agriculture's Wilder Medal. He never realized a fortune from his orange, but in DeLand citizens honored him and saw that his old age was passed in comfort. The Lue Gim Gong orange is still a factor in Florida's citrus industry.

The Florida orange production season runs from September until early August. Of major importance are the three "normal" varieties of orange: Valencia, Pineapple, and Hamlin. The Parson Brown and Lue Gim Gong are of secondary importance. Of minor importance are the Dream and Washington varieties, both navels; and the Ruby, a blood orange. The sour Jaffa has in recent years had a revival among home growers.

The grapefruit, developed in the middle of the eighteenth century, was called "the forbidden fruit or smaller shaddock." Grapefruits were introduced to Florida by Odet Phillippe, who settled near modern Safety Harbor on Tampa Bay in 1823. Phillippe, a native of Lyons, in France, had been a doctor in South Carolina. He had been lured to Florida by a band of ailing pirates he had treated successfully on the bounding main.

Odet Phillippe lived to a great age, a cigar-smoking citrus grower dressed immaculately in white linen. He owned the St. Helena groves, and, in the city of Tampa, two pool halls, a pair of bowling alleys, and an oyster house. He had brought the grapefruit to St. Helena from the Bahamas. Until 1885, it was a curiosity; then it caught on. Today, Florida produces 70 percent of all the grapefruit in the world. Originally, the flesh was a pale ivory yellow. Later mutants had pink and red flesh, and some were seedless. Those with seeds are tastier than the seedless varieties, but more bother. The oldest grapefruit variety still grown today is the Duncan, which is remarkably hardy to cold, but also possessed of thirty to fifty seeds.

Among the mandarins, the seedless, dark-orange, tangy-tasting satsumas are the hardiest to frost. King oranges are mandarins that were introduced from Saigon in 1882. Tangerine varieties of mandarins arrived in Florida about 1825; other varieties, from Italy, were subsequently introduced. The principal tangerine of commerical importance is the Dancy. The Honey Tangerine, or Murcott, is an attractive specialty fruit.

The true lemon came from Burma, made its way to the Near East, and was brought into Sicily by Moslem invaders. Columbus brought lemons to the West Indies, and from there the Spanish brought them to St. Augustine. Commercial lemon culture began in Florida in 1870. It suffered several setbacks, but after 1953, production increased by leaps and bounds: Americans began buying frozen lemonade. Florida lemons are huge, and they frighten some supermarket patrons used to smaller ones; their juice and acid content is high, and they have no unpleasant aftertaste. Villafranca and Ponderosa lemons are the most popular of the Florida fruits. The Meyer lemon, which possesses exceptional hardiness to cold, is not a true lemon at all. It looks like a large orange, and its peel tastes as bitter as gall. (It can be masked with the smooth peel oil of true lemon.)

True limes, small and highly acid, were reported plentiful in Haiti as early as 1520 by the Spanish historian Oviedo; they soon became naturalized in the Caribbean, and from there they spread to the Florida Keys. Today, Key limes are best known in Key lime pie; a dessert much like lemon meringue pie, it is served from one end of Florida to the other. The Persian lime, which originated not in Persia but in Tahiti, is a hybrid variety larger than the Key and is the most important variety grown in Florida. Tiny orange Calamondins are not true limes, though they taste like them and are popular with Florida gardeners. Kumquats, of the genus *Fortunella,* are a gift-crate staple.

All citrus species cross easily with each other, and citrus

species will cross with Fortunellas. The most important commercial hybrids in Florida today are the tangelo, a cross between tangerines and grapefruit, and the tangor, a hybrid of mandarin and sweet orange, of which the Temple variety is the best known.

Citrus cultivation involves many operations. Stocks such as rough lemon, sour orange, sweet orange, and the cold-hardy trifoliate orange must be budded with the scions growers select. Nursery row soils must approximate those of the actual groves for which the trees are destined. The grower begins a heroic battle with temperature, which must be neither too tropical nor too cold; rainfall, which in Florida ranges from drought to flood, depending on the month in question; and such hazards as root rot, nematodes, and a variety of viruses. Freezes are catastrophes when they occur; yet, where they do not, it is too hot to grow commercial oranges with any success because of the nature of the soil. Transplanting and spraying and pruning must be done according to carefully specified rules. Ants and fruit-flies must be vanquished. On the sandy soils of central Florida, copious fertilizing is necessary. Scale insects, white flies, mites and mealybugs and scab and greasy spot lie in wait. On frigid winter nights, the groves must be fired with smudge pots or other portable heaters. And when the grower has managed to produce his fruits, he must hire fruit pickers who, in turn, require government-specified standards of housing, wage negotiation, stout canvas bags, and plenty of wooden fruit boxes. There are market standards of size, acid content, and amount of juice. There are fees to packing houses, and to truckers and ships. When a fresh Florida orange, grapefruit, tangerine, lime, or lemon reaches its destined market, south or north, its cost may seem steep. Actually, it is selling cheaply, if one considers the uncertainty and sometimes downright agony in its production.

Of the several milestones in the Florida citrus industry, one was the organization in 1935 of the Florida Citrus Commission, composed of twelve members appointed by the governor for two-year terms. Members must be growers, grower-handlers, or grower-processors. The commission handles advertising for the

promotion of orange juice, and a mighty promotion it is: 10 percent of the value of the crop in the grove is spent on advertising.
The Citrus Commission also sets standards for maturity and
quality of fruit, as well as for containers, tags, and stamping. It
sponsors research—for instance, into the artificial coloration
that has become so common that American housewives usually
believe that all oranges are colored brightly orange instead of
the muddy green some of the fruit is. The research, which also
covers every other aspect of orange-growing and marketing, has
a budget approximately half that of advertising. Florida children, when told that the young of the Old World often receive
oranges as Christmas presents, stare in goggle-eyed disbelief.
Aren't there oranges everywhere for everybody all the time?

The Florida Citrus Mutual was founded in 1949; its activities
are wide-ranging. It sells and merchandises fruit, performs an
educational function, seeks to obtain favorable freight rates, and
conducts research in the production and harvesting and marketing of fruit. Its members are growers and they pay an annual fee
of five dollars.

The great revolution in Florida's citrus industry came after
World War II, when canned fruit assumed a greater importance
than it had had, and frozen concentrate was developed. Today,
approximately 19 percent of the total crop is represented by
fresh fruit. According to recent surveys, this is about twenty-
one and a half million boxes, of which five million stay in
Florida. The remaining 81 percent of the crop is divided among
various processing operations: canned juice and salad sections,
chilled juice in cartons and glass bottles, and frozen concentrate. Large food and beverage firms control these processing
operations; Coca Cola is the parent company of Minute-Maid,
and also represented on the Florida scene are such firms as
Salada, Libby, McNeil and Libby, and General Foods. There is
also a flourishing Florida citrus industry in the processing of by-
products—for instance, surplus peel, which can be converted
into cattle food.

At the close of World War II, Florida was producing just
under 180 million boxes of citrus per year. By 1970, the total
had risen to 280 million, at a total value of $315,882,000. The

inland central part of the state accounts for most of the crop. St. Johns County, with St. Augustine, is a northern citrus limit, and a chancy one, at that. Gainesville, in Alachua County, is another northern limit. The Indian River, a long lagoon on the lower east coast, produces its own choice fruit; the climate there is mild and breeze-stirred. South of Lake Okeechobee, citrus assumes less importance, until, with limes, on the Keys, it peters out altogether. The true citrus counties in central Florida, and Indian River and St. Lucie counties in the Indian River region, have more than a hundred thousand acres in citrus. The border counties have less than five thousand. Passionate gardeners on Florida's northern edge grow their calamondins and oranges in pots and depend heavily on satsumas and Meyer lemons for home consumption.

What of the future? As long as there is a demand for citrus by-products and for the processed fruit, and as long as the population of the United States goes on increasing or at least remains stable, the industry's health is assured. Agricultural economists estimate that, in the 1979–1980 season, state production will exceed 202 million boxes of Florida orange, Temple, and grapefruit alone. Orange and grapefruit cultivation are expected to increase, and Temple cultivation to remain essentially constant. Florida folk belief ascribes to grapefruit miraculous powers in the combat of diabetes. What is miraculous is the grapefruit's low calorie count; it is no nostrum for metabolic disorders, but it is a tasty way of keeping one's weight down. Seeress Jeane Dixon, in a 1975 visit to Tallahassee, had the courtesy to predict future cures with orange by-products.

The ambience of citrus in Florida is an obsessive preoccupation with health, health foods, causes of death, and the length of time a retiree can last if he's careful. It is also the power of such orange tycoons as former State Senator Ben Hill Griffin, Jr., who, if he wishes to survey his properties in central Florida, must do so by helicopter.

To the romantic, however, the impact of citrus in Florida is neither its commercial glory nor its political clout nor even its gossip: it is the clouds of pale orange-blossoms every year. It is the inland oceans of green in which golden oranges and yellow grapefruits are set like oversize pendants. It is the citrus lakes with their warm, low winds, and the high-pitched fatalistic laughter of black pickers in the orange and lemon groves. Most of the rest of America cannot grow citrus fruit; it is one more factor that has made Florida special.

10

Charlestons and Chimeras

EVEN with the wisdom of hindsight, it is difficult to pinpoint the exact historical hour in which Florida became a national Never-Never land. The state had its tradition—as it happened, not true—of Ponce de León's search for a Fountain of Youth. Moonstruck, or possibly sun-struck, conquistadores had come looking for gold. Prosaic Englishmen had sought and found live-oak groves to supply the British navy's shipbuilders. Acquisitive Americans had hailed their newest and hottest frontier, but they had soon found that frontier a scene of systemless and dragged-out slaughter that ended in the Trail of Tears and the Seminole flight into the Everglades. Then had come Reconstruction, with its fine intentions, its daily impracticalities, and its over-all incompetence. Subsequently, the Hayes-Tilden compromise had put an end to the worst—thus far—in Florida annals, and stirring times had begun. (Today, the status of Florida as a Never-Never-Land is official, for Disney World has imported Tinker Bell.)

The stirring times had been made more stirring still by Henry Morrison Flagler and Henry Bradley Plant, whose hotels dotted the state like improbable fantasies. The citrus boom, too, had contributed to Floridian euphoria; men like General Sanford had raided the world beyond in order to see what species would prosper at home. Florida legends had proliferated after the Civil War. *Florida for Tourists, Invalids, and Settlers* was a volume

113

among many similar others whose title aptly reflected what yonder America wanted of the Sunshine State. Tourists had long been coming to Jacksonville, where they promenaded down Bay Street along the St. Johns River waterfront and bought disinfected alligator teeth to send their cousins back home. Tourists were also a part of the Tampa Bay Hotel, whose interior vastness they explored in Mr. Plant's rickshaws. The invalids mentioned were mostly heart cases and the tubercular; some of both recovered, and some didn't. Settlers came to farm, to run groves, to build packing plants, to create cities, and to garner fortunes in speculative real estate. All these things launched the rocket that was the Florida Boom of the 1920s. There had never been a boom like it. There may never be again, though Florida's realtors and chambers of commerce keep on trying.

The Boom was never statewide. Tallahassee, still a quiet little Confederate bastion in 1920, made its own reveries beneath its canopy of live oaks and pines. It faithfully read Sir Walter Scott. Ladies left calling cards for each other and clung to the fashion of white gloves and parasols—a fashion still in evidence as recently as 1963. It was killed by the mini-skirt; why use the cover of a parasol when you had almost no bottom half to your costume? Nor did parasols look quite right with pantsuits. But garden-party hats are still far from obsolete.

The Boom of the 1920s belonged to south Florida. It belonged to such planned paradises as Boca Raton, north of Miami, where the Mizner brothers meditated on splendors to eclipse those of Flagler and Plant. It belonged to Miami Beach, where developer Carl Fisher dredged out Biscayne Bay to create a gaudy metropolis later delivered up to the Mafia, and still later rescued by grim-eyed grand juries. It belonged to George Merrick's Coral Gables, touted as an enclave of Spanish perfection (complete with Venetian waterways, an idea borrowed from Renaissance Italy) that would satisfy the most fastidious in their demands for earthly heaven. Most handsomely, the Boom belonged to St. Petersburg, the site of which, Pinellas Point, the American Medical Association had earlier decided was fit for a Health City. The proof of this was that what inhabitants there were on Pinellas Point all had ruddy cheeks—the result, said the doctors, of pure air. (No one seems to have thought of sunburn.) Pure air antedates actinic therapy by several decades in the Land of Flowers. Enterprising publishers arrived, after a Russian named Peter Demens, born Piotr Alexeitch Dementiev, had built his Orange Belt Railroad from the mainland to Pinellas Point. Its terminus became St. Petersburg, a name with a certain amount of Czarist glamor. The publishers published come-ons by the score. Trains were chartered for hacking and wheezing sufferers from the north; when they arrived, sniffles and all, St. Petersburg sent brass bands to the railroad station to welcome them. As the city paved its streets, its corners were rounded off, not with curbs, but with ramps that wheel chairs could negotiate. Mitchell the Sand Man, a real estate wizard who made capital of the sandy earth that possessed so little fertility along the Gulf, built benches for prospective lot buyers with tired feet. The benches were so popular that the aggregate of them was christened "Mitchell's Prayer Meeting." At first, the benches were orange; but the mayor of St. Petersburg didn't like orange, so the official color became green.

World War I put a crimp in the city's growth, but it didn't stop it. Americans traveled less, but they didn't cease traveling altogether, particularly the elderly, who equated sunshine with life. St. Petersburg entrepreneurs made sure that such tourists paid for what they got. "St. Pete," said some of the visitors, was like neither heaven nor hell, for in neither place did you need money and in St. Pete you needed it every hour. Mitchell the Sand Man kept advertising: "Man is made of sand. Dust settles. Be a man and buy sand!" [1] When the War to End Wars was over, the northern sons and daughters of St. Pete pilgrims suddenly discovered that their parents weren't limping with arthritis any more, but were playing shuffleboard, going fishing, and learning the intricacies of social dancing. The Sunshine City—for that was the label that ultimately stuck—not only bore with its oldsters, but recruited them. Sons and daughters and grandchildren came, too, and they liked the fact that the Sunshine City had no winter.

Henry Ford had given America the flivver, and the flivver

---

1. Carl Grismer, *The Story of St. Petersburg* (St. Petersburg, Fla.: P. K. Smith & Co., 1948), p. 201.

brought a generation of Tin-Can Tourists, so named because they carried their food supplies in the back seat. The Tin-Canners set up Tent Cities. And it was not long before the real estate promoters were courting even bigger fry. "The Sunshine City is the rooster's boots!" they said. Successful salesmen, in the vivid slang of the 'twenties, became "Lord High He-Buzzards." Florida was shaped like an automatic pistol "shooting to kill at the gloom and poverty of the north." One Good Investment beat a Lifetime of Toil. Florida was where you could "whack the bucks into a pile," and "Eternal Paradise where work is no more." These were heady promises. Dollars were "clams" and "simoleons," and could be had by all. Real estate men adopted a uniform of white knickers and bow-ties; the minions of these "knickerbocker boys" were the "bird dogs," who frequented the green benches and spread rumors of investments that would double in a month, provided one had the guidance of a mentor in plus-fours.

In 1920, young Walter Fuller of St. Petersburg was already a veteran of speculation in land. He and his father had made and lost three million dollars in several subdivisions: made the money because the subdivisions looked as promising as they would prove in the long run, lost it because both Fullers gambled on the fact that World War I would last only twelve months. Neither was daunted. Walter watched America for signs of a real estate revival. After the war was over, he noted increased industrial production, inflation, and "fevered prosperity." [2] But production soon caught up with demand. Factories therefore began curtailing their output. But the factories had paid well. Henry Ford's five-dollar-a-day minimum wage had been banked by workers who had taken no vacations. Now they jumped into their flivvers and came into St. Petersburg by the thousands. Mitchell the Sand Man was elected the city's mayor, though he soon had to resign, after a party in City Hall, where he became drunk and disorderly and on such charges was arrested. He never made it back to City Hall, but he did become a

2. Walter P. Fuller, *This Was Florida's Boom* (St. Petersburg, Fla.: St. Petersburg Times Publishing Company, 1954), p. 8.

Tent City czar, and he continued to hatch schemes for the sale of the sandy pineland that stretched along the Gulf Coast in a virtually empty infinity.

Walter Fuller thought he knew what was coming: wild years. For $45.27, he bought forty acres north of the city in Pinellas Park. He never bothered to go and look at his land. He merely cleared its title and sat back to wait. The waiting took four years. By then, he was able to sell his unseen forty acres to a Philadelphia lawyer for $40,000. Nine months later, the lawyer sold the forty acres for $60,000. For Walter Fuller, this was only the beginning. With Francis Burklew, a Tent City mayor, he plotted a selling program that started with a transaction involving $500 and ended in a torrent of multimillions. When land auctions were held, Noel Mitchell donned a silk stovepipe hat and took the bids of flivver dreamers who had decided to say farewell to factories forever, be men, and buy sand. Across from the principal Tent City, Fuller erected impressive signs: SEE FULLER.

"Who'n hell's Fuller?" the Tin-Canners wanted to know.

"Why," expanded Burklew, "he's a fine fellow. I know him quite well. In fact, I bought a couple lots from him the other day. Dirt cheap, too. Wanta go see them?"

A week later, Fuller had sold 326 lots. "No advertisements, no commissions, no showing, no expense. A clean 100 percent sale." [3]

The rapid buying and selling of vacant lots gave the Boom in St. Petersburg further leverage. Mule teams pulled up pine stumps and sweating black men dug up the tenacious root systems of saw palmettoes. The workmen earned the sum of a dollar and a half a day—provided they were "first class Negro labor." Fuller also offered his blacks a Christmas bonus of a hundred dollars. But he was visited by a deputation that told him, "Ifen you will be so kind as to give us fifty cents a day more and let us have it each Saturday night, we will excuse the bonus and be greatly obliged." [4] Jook joints proliferated on the

---

3. Fuller, *Boom*, p. 12.
4. Fuller, *Boom*, pp. 20 ff.

city's outskirts: the word probably derived from the West
African *dzugu,* meaning disorderly, and it was first given its
American currency by a young Florida reporter named Malcolm
Johnson, later editor of the *Tallahassee Democrat.*

While the black men drank and danced, knickerbocker boys
touted lots that might be anywhere from forty to a hundred feet
wide. Walter Fuller parlayed sale after sale into a six-figure
total, excluding mortgages worth millions. He bought and sold
in stunning rapidity. A couple named Taylor, Handsome Jack
and his "quite lovely" wife Evelyn, arrived in his office to
purchase an acreage for which Fuller had paid $50,000 in part-
nership with a Philadelphia investor. Fuller's asking price was
$270,000. The Taylors offered a down payment of $70,000,
which Fuller and his partner eagerly accepted.

"Well," said a witness, "I guess this is a deal if somebody
will kindly produce some money."

"Evelyn!" commanded Handsome Jack.

Evelyn asked if she might retire to a private office. This, said
Fuller and his colleagues, was it. With only a moment's hesita-
tion, Evelyn walked over to a corner, "turned her back, hiked
her skirt slightly and rolled down a sheer silk stocking (they
were powder blue.)" She proceeded to peel off seven ten-
thousand-dollar bills; nobody had noticed them around her
ankles because their color had blended so well with her hose.
There were many buyers in Boom days who distrusted banks.[5]

The Taylors lingered in the Sunshine City to build the sump-
tuous stucco-and-red-tiled Rolyat Hotel. They discarded their
Pierce-Arrow for a Daimler and ordered their clothes from Manhattan. On the grounds of the Rolyat, imported parrots chattered; in the pools, glittering goldfish swam. The Taylors provided a tiled wishing well for the sentimental who might fall
under the spell of all the pseudo-Iberian luxe. A Monkey Island
was duly populated with monkeys. In Sunshine City night
clubs, speculators blissfully defied prohibition and "drank whiskey and talked about lots, or just talked about lots." [6] Flamin-

5. Fuller, *Boom,* pp. 35 ff.
6. Fuller, *Boom,* p. 25.

goes with clipped wings arrived by freight-car loads for the intended dazzlement of golf course patrons. Walter Fuller bought a night club he christened the Gangplank and hired an exotic dancer named Paige (she pronounced it *Pay-Gee*) who did a tiger dance, complete with tiger skin. One night, the single strap on her skin gave way. She was naked as a jaybird underneath, but with aplomb she did a step or two and then walked calmly to her dressing room. Word got out that this was part of the act. The Gangplank was mobbed, and in a single night grossed more than four thousand dollars. The offending strap, however, had by then been mended.

The Florida Keys, that enchanted string of coconut-palm coral islands that stretches southwest of Miami toward the flaming purple bougainvilleas of Key West, were only mildly involved in the Boom. They had been opened to the land-buying public by Henry Morrison Flagler in 1912, when his Overseas Railroad from Jacksonville to Key West was completed. It was an engineering triumph of viaducts and stretching bridges; the longest of the bridges was seven miles. The Overseas Railroad had cost Mr. Flagler twenty million dollars in its Keys section alone. He had come riding into Key West on the first train; he was eighty-three, and he wore a frock coat and a tall silk hat shaded by an umbrella. Four months later, he was dead, but he had seen his dream come to fruition. Yet the Keys remained isolated enough. Rain provided their fresh water. It was possible to grow almost nothing in the grainy coral sand except native palms and related species and West Indian gumbo-limbos and mahoganies. Vegetables and meats came to the Keys on Flagler's freight cars and, later, on trucks.

What was destined to open the Keys to a frenzy of building activity was not the train, nor even the automobile, but the airplane. The earliest Americans in the Keys had relied on ships for their needs. Flagler's railroad was destroyed by a murderous hurricane in September 1935—ironically, it was Labor Day. A highway replaced the railroad, using many of the original bridges and trestles, and today that highway is heavily traveled, not only by tourists, but by produce and slaughterhouse trucks. The Overseas Highway survived even Hurricane Donna, in

1960. But the true highway to Key West is the air; the city is a quick jump from Miami. Key West was fortunate in escaping the hysteria of the Boom. The clapboarded, vine-clad simplicity was never spoiled by the architecture Floridians call "Boom Spanish." Key West kept its white walls and cupolas, its tin roofs and its thatched porches shaded by traveler palms. It kept, too, its tiny multicolored frame houses in the Cuban quarter, where descendants of pre-Tampa cigarmakers still live, though they work at a variety of trades. Key West retained one of its greatest treasures until the mid-1960s: the Elanon Ice Cream Parlor, where the flavors were soursop and sapodilla and mango and guava and where the thin metal chairs and white tiles symbolized an era of grace that antedated hot dog stands by decades. The Elanon vanished, leaving devotees who mourn it still, but much of its atmosphere has been captured in a series of remarkable woodcarvings by the folk artist Mario Sanchez; they are displayed in galleries and museums in the town.

If there was little action on the Keys during the Boom, there was a superabundance of it in Miami and on the long sandbar across Biscayne Bay to the east. At the beginning of World War I, realtor Edward Dammers had had a hard time selling Miami Beach waterfront lots for a thousand dollars apiece. Henry Flagler's railroad and the Boom changed all that. By the early 'twenties, the lower east coast was exploding, and its expertise in public relations amounted to virtuosity.

One sultry New York evening in August 1925, a young English newspaperman named Theyre Weigall was sitting in the stalls of the Ziegfeld Follies. A lady in black tights and a glittering green-sequin waistcoat was singing about the Bam-Bam-Bammy Shore. When she had finished, she was replaced by a "lime-lit drop scene" purporting to represent "Biscayne Bay, Florida—the Eternal Summer Paradise." Into this setting stepped a comedian named Will Rogers, whose broad grin was infectious. Weigall watched, entranced. Rogers was telling a string of jokes about the Florida Boom, "stories dealing with the fortunes that were being made in Florida and with his own laments that he was unable, by the force of domestic ties, to go there himself." Weigall was broke; he wasn't sure he knew exactly where Florida was, but it sounded too good to miss. As Weigall was strolling home from the Follies, he passed a realtor's window. In it was "the authenticated story of a young man who had made $500,000 in Florida in four weeks by a judicious judgment of land values. 'Say! YOU can do what George Cusack, Jr., did!' " Weigall stared at the inset photograph of George Cusack, Jr., and decided that the man looked half-witted. If *he* could make half a million dollars in one month, so could others—notably Theyre Weigall. Soon he went to the terminal of the Pennsylvania Railroad and bought a one-way ticket to Miami, the Magic City.[7]

Slowly the train inched its way down the east coast of America. By Savannah everyone was sweating profusely. Italian passengers were eating garlic sausages and depositing the skins underneath the seats of the train, and Italian babies were being sick of surfeit. Weigall was grateful for the sooty ice cream cone a vendor proffered. It was dark when the train reached Jacksonville, in whose terminal hundreds were rushing in all directions, carrying papers and shouting, while engines shook with blasts of escaping steam, and loudspeakers roared train schedules. After Jacksonville, the moon rose, and Weigall saw his first palm trees. In the morning, he saw the Florida sun glaring down on "dead-flat wastes" covered only with brown grass and slash pines. Occasionally, there was a white coral rock-house with a red-tiled roof, the incarnation of Boom Spanish. The tracks were running parallel to the Great Dixie Highway, now, and the road was covered with machines and humanity. There were Fords and Rolls Royces; there were bicycles; there were touring cars with camp beds and washstands lashed to the rear. There was also a bevy of parrots; the travelers had evidently provided themselves with tropical pets before the journey had been completed. Occasionally, Weigall saw large stone gateways leading (apparently) into nothing; in front there were likely to be small booths, and men in knickers seated at trestle tables from which they gesticulated earnestly at the inhabitants of cars that stopped to investigate. When the train reached

7. Theyre H. Weigall, *Boom in Paradise* (New York: Alfred H. King, 1932), p. 17.

Miami Central Station, Weigall was covered with soot, but a kindly taxicab driver took him to a small hotel with a vacancy and a bathtub. Afterwards Weigall

> wandered out into the blazing sunlight of that tropical afternoon into that bedlam that was Miami . . . Everywhere there was building going forward at express speed; and mingled with the perpetual screeching of the motor-horns a thousand automatic riveters poured out their deafening music, a thousand drills and hammers and winches added to the insane chorus. Everywhere there was dust. Hatless, coatless men rushed about the blazing streets, their arms full of papers, perspiration pouring from their foreheads. Every shop seemed to be combined with a real estate office; at every doorway crowds of young men were shouting and speechmaking, thrusting forward papers and proclaiming to heaven the unsurpassed chances they were offering to make a fortune . . . Everybody in Miami was real-estate mad. Towering office buildings, almost entirely occupied by "realtors," were the scenes of indescribable enthusiasm and confusion. Everywhere there was handshaking, backslapping, and general boosting. Everyone I saw seemed to be shaking hands, offering cigars, studying mysterious-looking diagrams of "desirable subdivisions." [8]

At Miami Beach, hotels and apartment houses and private residences had replaced marshes full of blue herons. Carl Fisher of Indianapolis was building his billion-dollar sandbar; so far—in those idyllic days before the Fontainebleau and Montmartre ("Mo-Mar") hotels, omnipresent social directors, and frenetic Miss Universe contests—the sandbar was a beautiful place full of green lawns and coconut palms and seagrapes. Hibiscus bushes bloomed red and salmon beside lakes and canals. Yellow allamanda vines climbed pillars at whose bases flowered red-blossomed ixora bushes. At night, the streets were lit with tall electric streetlights. This was the choice section of the Beach. Farther down the streetcar line were the honkytonks, blaring "Yessir, That's My Baby!" and boop-boop-a-doop music while cotton-clad flappers and their dates shook out Charlestons on postage-stamp-sized dance floors and teenagers

8. Weigall, *Paradise*, pp. 49–50.

licked puffy towers of pink cotton candy. The sea washed gently on the beach; white stars were out, though they were dimmed by the honky-tonks' marquees.

When Weigall made the rounds of Miami newspapers, he found that they were not in need of his talents. For a while—to keep himself in hot dogs, a newly discovered American delicacy that he adored—he drifted from salesman's job to salesman's job, presided over by wizards who invariably admitted to "talking big money. Yessir! I'm talking like J. Pierpont Rockerbilt!" After a few stints at manual labor, Weigall finally got a job publicizing Coral Gables. Soon he was escorting visiting notables like New York's Mayor James J. Walker over the Venetian bridges.

To Weigall and others like him, the Boom was never quite real. It was a romance, fanned by soft trade winds from the Atlantic and Gulf. Glittering hotels were strung out against a backdrop of dark sky illumined by the Milky Way. Echoes drifted from black dance halls, and there was laughter from the tiny roadhouses where prohibition had gone by the board and whiskey was three dollars a fifth. Fashionable orchestras played their music on the marble patios of country clubs, and everywhere the coconut and areca and date and traveler palms were spotlighted in red and green and yellow. Japanese lanterns hung in the trees, and always the slow waves washed across a coral beach not yet utterly destroyed. The germ of destruction was there, however. It was in the belief that Miami Beach must ultimately have enough hotels and resorts to house America.

Over in Tampa, Dave Davis and his dredges and bulldozers were building the Boom-born Davis Islands, "the eighth wonder of the world." Son of a Florida steamboat captain, Dave was adept at walking ships' rails when he was dared to do so. He had seen what was happening on Biscayne Bay and set out to duplicate it on the shores of the Bay that the Calusa had long ago called Tanpa. Dave borrowed money and built a yacht basin and an electric power plant and apartment buildings like the Palace of Florence, not far from the Palace of Venice. Up in St. Augustine, he borrowed more money and began Davis Shores. In the back of his mind was a project for Monaco, rock-

bound fortress of roulette; some day there would be Davis Islands in the Mediterranean, built on Florida profits. No doubt
the reigning Prince of Monaco would rejoice.

The frenzy went on. People bought lots on options. They all
juggled paper profits, and they knew that nothing could possibly
go wrong in the Land of Flowers, because how could the warm
sun stop shining? If America, in the 'twenties, was trusting,
Florida was more so. It was the very epitome of national home-
grown fairytale. And once again, it was also a piece of history
dominated by weather. Men had forgotten that, even as the sub-
tropics are heartbreakingly beautiful, they are far from the innocent haven they seem. All the palm-strewn loveliness is based
on the raw savagery of water and wind that sooner or later go
mad.

The madness began quietly enough in Tampa and St. Petersburg. On Monday, December 7, 1925, it started raining. It was
a cold rain, borne in on a frigid wind that gusted into the fronds
of cocos plumosa and areca palms and rattled the brittle
branches of jacaranda trees. Australian pines shivered as the
streams of rain kept falling. December 7 was also the first day
of the convention, in St. Petersburg, of the Investment Bankers'
Association of America. The bankers had been looking forward
to playing golf; instead, they were cooped up in their Boom
Spanish hotels, staring with melancholy faces through casement
windows at a scene of desolation. Bridge and backgammon
palled. What sort of Sunshine City was this, anyhow? On
Tuesday, the rain came down harder; by Wednesday, it was
pelting. Binder boys gathered gloomily in their jerry-built of-
fices and donned heavy sweaters. At night, the temperature sank
to near-freezing levels. At last, the irate bankers departed, to
announce to the country in general that the sunshine of the
Sunshine City was a myth, as far as they were concerned. And
the bankers had many friends who listened carefully.

All that summer and autumn, land sales—on paper—had
been rocketing to new totals. After the soggy bankers had left,
sales plummeted. In northern newspapers, there were daily
headlines about Florida's cold wave; other cold waves were
recalled. When the sun came out, temperatures fell lower. At

night, central Florida was gripped by frost, and oranges turned mushy on cracking branches in the groves. The Tin-Can Tourists headed for northern homes. Lumber companies caught with an overstock of wood were unable to sell it, because nobody was making the money to buy it. Finally, the lumbermen made a huge bonfire of their stock; in its flames the dreams of the Sunshine City also went up in smoke.

Banks held troubled audits. Unemployment statistics made gloomy reading. Landlords dropped their rents, but the tourists were not returning from the north. The snow they knew was better than the freezing rain they didn't. Land prices fell by the hour; nobody wanted the new bargains. Davis Islands landowners, in Tampa, weren't keeping up their payments. Up in St. Augustine, in order to meet his payroll at Davis Shores, Dave Davis had to borrow a quarter of a million dollars from a sanguine New York bank, which lent it on condition that he turn over the Davis Islands of Tampa to an Island Investment Company. Dave was shattered, and decided that what he needed was a sea voyage to Europe, where he would investigate the coastline of Monaco, though now his European Davis Islands would have to be delayed. Dave didn't want to stay in Florida. The rest of America, secure in the homely puritanism and maximlaced thrift of Calvin Coolidge, was still prosperous; Florida was becoming a shambles.

The summer of 1926 was a cooker. Pavements reflected shimmering waves of hot air. The sun beat down on the whiteness of Miami Beach, and at night it was so sultry that few people wanted to dance on lantern-lit patios. Air conditioning had been invented in Apalachicola, Florida, three-quarters of a century earlier, but it was not yet in general use, even in movie houses, which, in the 'thirties, would be displaying banners that read: "Twenty degrees cooler inside!" A few hospital operating theaters had the miracle, but in homes it was almost nonexistent. Zinnias in Miami gardens died of their own splendor. Palms browned. And then the hurricane came.

September, 1926: There was no hurricane-warning system in Florida then; hurricane warnings circulated by the local weather bureau office were largely ignored; and the gales and floods and rising seas took Miami Beach by catastrophic surprise. To Marjory Stoneman Douglas, daughter of editor Frank Stoneman of the *Miami Herald,* the storm's effects on Miami and Miami Beach real estate resembled

> the explosive force of a vast bomb. All night long the screaming of incredible winds of more than 125 miles an hour deafened the noises of falling trees, collapsing walls, breaking glass, torn-away roofs, as the driven tides burst over the bay front and the low grounds, driving ships aground, boats into houses, and leaving debris everywhere.[9]

When Miami and the Beach's wreckage lay unsuspecting in the calm that was the hurricane's eye, citizens wandered distracted in the streets, staring at rubble where there had been pseudo-Andalusian dash. They were trapped when the hurricane redoubled its force from another direction; they died, screaming, until their lungs were too full of water to produce sound. When it was all over, and the harbor was blocked by wrecked vessels, Miami and its sister city across Biscayne Bay started cleaning up. Men who had been real estate millionaires wielded brooms and pushed wheelbarrows. A dejected Theyre Weigall returned to his native England a wiser man. The contagion of despair had spread from Tampa and St. Petersburg down to the lower east coast, and from there it then fanned out over the entire state. Banks closed. Among the victims of Florida's collapse was the father of Ernest Hemingway. In St. Petersburg, the owner of the *St. Petersburg Times,* Paul Poynter, confronted a deflated and nearly penniless Walter Fuller, an entrepreneur of functioning companies no more.

"Walter, I have been hard up many a time and have had to sweat through many a deal, but this is the first time in my life I have been desperately in need of immediate cash. Here is the account of the Allen-Fuller Corporation. It is about $8,000. Can you pay something on account?"

"That's impossible," Fuller told him truthfully.

"How about this $1,100 due by Fuller-Hunter?"

---

9. Marjory Stoneman Douglas, *Florida: The Long Frontier* (New York and Evanston: Harper and Brothers, 1967), p. 266.

"You'll have to see Hunter about that. He has sole authority to pay out Fuller-Hunter money, and he's out of town."

"Well, Walter, here's your wife's personal account of nine dollars. Can you pay that?"

He could—not easily—and he did. But he was thinking to himself, You can't lick a Boom. "Next time you see one," he advised a friend, "grab your pocketbook and run, brother, run!" [10]

Dave Davis departed from Davis Islands and Davis Shores for Europe in October. One night, he was feeling feisty enough to accept a dare from fellow-passengers on his ship. "Walk the rail!" they challenged. Dave had grown up on a Tampa Bay steamer, hadn't he? He was confident of his balance, even though the sea was stormy and a cold equinoctial rain was falling. Nobody but the crew knew that the rail had been waxed. Dave began his act for an admiring and sodden audience; just then, a high wave engulfed the deck, and when it subsided D. P. Davis, the Florida land czar, had drowned in the Atlantic Ocean. Telegraph wires hummed with rumors of murder and suicide. But a fellow-voyager told the simple truth to the insurance company: "Dave was just walking the rail again, and this time he wasn't lucky." [11]

Walter Fuller was in New York soon afterwards, trying to inspire confidence in the Yankee bank officials he was seeing. He was having no luck. Lonesome, broke, discouraged, he was wandering down Broadway one night beneath the glittering theater marquees that illumined the pale fox furs of blond New York women elegant in finger waves and satin louis-heeled pumps as they stepped gingerly from their Cadillacs. In New York, boom times survived. Fuller was passed by a pair of nattily dressed male Broadwayites, and when he overheard them discussing his home state he strained to catch the words.

"You know what's the matter with Florida?" said one.

The other said, "Who cares?" [12]

10. Fuller, *Boom,* p. 64.

11. Carl Grismer, *Tampa* (St. Petersburg, Fla.: St. Petersburg Printing Co., 1950), p. 259.

12. Fuller, *Boom,* p. 39.

11

High Old Times in the Pork-Chop Latitudes

*T*HE Great Depression came to Florida three years before it gripped the rest of the nation. In central and south Florida, depression meant agonizing layoffs and debts. In north Florida, it often meant literally living off the land. Dreaming Yankees primed for quick profits and fine fishing off coconut-lined shores had been pulled south by the Boom. The Yankees had not tarried in the piney woods. North Florida now slumbered as it had not since the days of its humble thatch-roofed string of Spanish missions around which dying-out bands of Timucuas had huddled in settlements of the *chikees* Spanish priests called *bohios*. As of 1926, from Live Oak, in Suwanee County west of Jacksonville, to Pensacola, there was not a single paved road except for a nine-mile stretch east of the obscure lumber town of Milton. And when there was hardly a piece of pavement in four hundred miles, doughty explorers needed the toughest of Fords and Chevvies to brave the ruts and sandpiles and mud puddles. Not many did.

Pellagra was widespread in north Florida; talk to natives there today, and many will admit that their parents and grandparents suffered, not only from pellagra and beriberi, but from hookworms, a once almost universal ailment of the rural South. Often a family's most valuable investment was its pigs. The runty animals could feed on pine mast in the forests, and at slaughtering time they provided side-meat (bacon), backbone, spareribs, sausage, chitterlings (pronounced "chitlins," and meaning pigs' intestines), pork brains, liver, and lights (lungs) and—for festive occasions—hams and pork chops. Downstate Yankees had always preferred lamb chops, though lamb was not easily come by in the Depression. The northern and southern sections of the peninsula were eventually given the nicknames of the prevailing cuisine, probably by a Tampa newspaper. A pork-chopper hailed from the north, a lamb-chopper from the south. Since legislative districts in the state were mapped out by area, not by population, the pork-choppers had a stunning edge in the state capitol. In Liberty County, a state representative might come from a district with a population of less than ten persons per square mile. In Dade County, with Miami and Miami Beach, his lamb-chop counterpart would be representing population densities of nearly a thousand persons per square mile. Because of the area of north Florida, four hundred miles of it from east to west, it sent legions of pork-choppers to Tallahassee, where the lamb-choppers found their own voices feeble indeed. Thus it was that, during the Depression, a fine old Florida custom began: the appropriation of highway money for the pork-chop latitudes and the neglect of St. Petersburg and Miami. Gorgeously capacious roads were constructed from swamp to swamp; the one from Telogia Crossroads to Newport, a minuscule hamlet south of Tallahassee, remains especially impressive. The pork-choppers were thereby able to provide construction jobs for suffering cousins and friends. Mental hospitals were built—in areas that were all but inaccessible until the roads came. Stetson-hatted, red-faced, courtly to women (whom they called ladies), collectively bigoted against blacks en masse and individually often almost unbelievably loyal to black friends and retainers they fed out of their own pockets when the going was rough, the pork-choppers had style. To the lamb-choppers, most of whom had Yankee blood in their veins, the pork-choppers were anathema. Paradoxically, pork-choppers kept Florida feudal at the same time that they were building an educational system that later attracted the world-famous to its faculties:

Elena Nikolaidi, former *kammersängerin* of the Vienna State Opera; Sidney Fox, whose experiments with test-tube life sent shivers down pork-chop spines when their Baptist owners heard him lecture; painter Karl Zerbe, late of Munich and Boston, afterwards of Tallahassee, whose art few pork-choppers understood even when they were paying whopping sums for it; composer Ernst Von Dohnanyi, onetime friend of Johannes Brahms. Dohnanyi's death in 1960 threw north Florida—for he had charm—into an orgy of mourning even though his works had consistently baffled many of his new-found neighbors.

The depression was hard on Tallahassee; but Tallahassee had known hardship since the end of the Civil War. Young Mark Van Doren, arriving in the city in 1912 (he was just eighteen) to be best man at his brother Carl's wedding to Tallahassee belle Irita Bradford, noted the complete absence of paved streets, the presence of pigs and cattle on mud and sand roads, and the ambience of the Deep South: "Its heat . . . its elaborate and pretty manners . . . and its tall pecan trees which I forever wondered at."[1]

In the 1930s, Florida's capital hadn't changed much from the pre-World War I town Mark Van Doren had visited. Its people still had their hogs, melons, tomatoes, cucumbers, and squash to sustain them, and cane syrup to sweeten their chicory coffee. But they didn't have department stores—or riots. Urban Anglo-Cuban Tampa was in turmoil. Banks failed; former millionaires appeared on street corners with orange carts, instead of apples; cigar sales fell off nationally, and Ybor City mechanized its factories, to be able to dismiss workers. Socialist propaganda fell on fertile ground. The Ku Klux Klan appeared in Tampa, to kidnap known leftists by night and force them to drink castor oil when the kidnappers did not tar and feather them. Norman Thomas, the national leader of socialism, protested vigorously. Dave Sholtz, then governor, saw the promotion of race tracks as an answer to the state's financial maladies. The real answer, when it came, was of course the WPA. Some of Governor

---

1. Mark Van Doren, *The Autobiography of Mark Van Doren* (New York: Harcourt, Brace, 1958), p. 70.

Sholtz's innovations linger; it is usually a little startling to out-landers to experience a first Higher Education Night at the dog track.

Miami slept unquiet sleep. The Keys lay shining and thinly populated under their nearly tropical sun. Ernest Hemingway, of Key West, had money, but not many other citizens did. Tennessee Williams had not yet arrived there. Black cleaning women from St. Petersburg's Methodist Town were told they would no longer be needed, and they eked out a living for their families on collard greens, turnips, field peas, and crackling bread laced with molasses. Tourism was at its nadir. And yet, while Florida seemingly endured its standstill misery from one end of the state to the other, an empire was being silently built that, with pork-chop support, would become one of the most complex America has ever known. Its builder, who did the job almost single-handed, would be ultimately so powerful that the United States Congress would pass federal legislation directed specifically against him. Slowly, in the 1930s, Florida began to realize that she had an uncrowned king, aided and abetted in the rural northern districts from which the pork-choppers hailed.

The king was Edward Ball, a school dropout at thirteen in his native Virginia. In 1974, at eighty-six, Edward Ball flew more than 300,000 air miles in supervision of his worldwide holdings. He is on easy terms with the Shah of Iran, as well as with the state senators left in the postreapportionment Panhandle. Every night, in his suite in the Robert Meyer Hotel in downtown Jacksonville, "Mister Ed Ball" still offers a toast with his close associates as he raises a tall highball glass of Jack Daniel's bourbon and ginger ale: "Confusion to the enemy!" Down the decades, Ball has confused the enemy thoroughly, and it was his power, as much as the state system of districting, that made the pork-chop legislatures what they were. What they were was colorful, like "Mister Ed" himself.

Ball seldom changes his mind. It is significant that former U.S. Secretary of State James Byrnes autographed his picture for Ball with the legend, "To Ed Ball, who says what he means and means what he says." Ball is a man of almost incalculable wealth and also of such simple tastes that he often has a breakfast of cheap hot cocoa at a Jacksonville stand-up counter. He does not smoke; associates who do reportedly find that they do not advance in his organization. Edward Ball came in line for the kingship of Florida the day his unfashionably dressed sister Jessie Dew Ball married Alfred Irénée Du Pont, a member of the gunpowder dynasty who had strayed from Delaware to Jacksonville. Du Pont hired his bride's brother, who had variously sold law books and office furniture, to assist him in his business ventures at a salary of five thousand dollars a year. Du Pont knew a winner when he saw one; almost immediately, with Ball's canny advice, he began to acquire Florida banks. When Du Pont died in 1935, there were seven of them. In 1974, thanks to the activities of Edward Ball, trustee of the Du Pont estate, there were thirty-one. Du Pont owned 280,000 acres of Panhandle land valued at $1,087,776 when he departed Florida forever. In the 1960s, Ball testified before a U.S. Congressional commission that the Du Pont estate held 900,000 acres in north Florida and more than a million in other parts of the state and in Georgia. Ball, not Du Pont, acquired the Florida East Coast Railway that Henry Morrison Flagler had built, and also two sugar refineries dependent on it. During the 'twenties, on Du Pont's behalf, Ball bought miles of real estate for the St. Joe Paper Company, based at the small Gulf Coast port of St. Joe. The paper company was and is St. Joe; its reeking mill belches forth to its workers the odor of life, which they call "the smell of money." It is probably somewhat disingenuous for the city fathers of Port St. Joe to describe it as a Vacation Paradise. The St. Joe factory, as veteran political observer Leon Odell Griffith has noted, "is the tip of the iceberg of company property." [2]

Affiliated container corporations dot the United States: Baltimore; Chesapeake, Virginia; Birmingham; Charlotte; Louisville; Memphis; Northlake, Illinois; Mesquite, Texas; Houston; Reserve, Louisiana. What happens in Ball's Florida pinelands affects an impressive share of towns and cities in the rest of the United States of America. There is also an arresting symbolic

2. Leon Odell Griffith, *Ed Ball: Confusion to the Enemy* (Tampa: Trend House, 1975), p. 69.

significance in the fact that Ball is a connection of Mary Ball Washington, mother of the Father of His Country. Mary Ball Washington was born in the Ball family mansion of Epping Forest. When Jessie Dew Ball married Alfred Irénée Du Pont, she named his Jacksonville house Epping Forest. Ed Ball was born at Ball's Neck, Virginia. When the opportunity offered itself, he bought the concession at Mount Vernon, which he ran at a handy profit for more than forty years.

When the Du Ponts and Ed Ball went to Miami in 1924, they were agreed on one thing: the Boom was a mirage. There would be a panic. Subsequently, the knowledge of their rightness made Ball the most conservative of bank lenders. After the death of Alfred Du Pont, Jessie Ball Du Pont became a figure of mystery. She dressed more simply than ever; anonymously, she gave huge donations to charities. There were millions at her disposal, but when her brother testified in a U.S. Senate hearing to defend the amount the estate handed over annually to her, he practiced a form of oratory that the Deep South calls poormouthing:

> Mrs. Du Pont has been criticized for the income she gets, but most of these years she was in the 91 percent bracket and when you take 91 cents out of each dollar, it doesn't leave too much to give to charitable and education [*sic*] institutions which she has done. At times I have wondered how she was able to eat.[3]

Withal, she managed. Several years later, when Ball was again under federal investigation, former governor and Supreme Court Justice Millard Caldwell described Ball as simplicity itself, a man who didn't own an automobile. On his passport, Ball lists his occupation as agriculture (he grows pine trees). And while he may have no motor vehicle registered in his own name, his castle of Ballynahinch in northern Ireland commands a beautiful view of emerald downs. He shares the ownership of Ballynahinch with a group of favored investors; no property must be allowed to remain idle.

The trouble with Edward Ball, as J. A. Maloney, editor and

3. Griffith, *Ed Ball*, p. 28.

publisher of the *Apalachicola Times,* once remarked, is that he owns so irremediably many pine trees, and those pine trees can't vote. Florida's Panhandle, Maloney contended, could not develop economically because of Ball's "pine curtain." But it is for that same pine curtain that conservationists hail "Mister Ed" as a protector of wildlife. He owns the sanctuary of Wakulla Springs, a few miles south of Tallahassee, where herons and limpkins are so tame that they watch tourists, unfazed, from narrow shores. To protect his preserve, Ball put a fence across the Wakulla River. Howls of anguish went up; how could one man block a navigable waterway? A suit was brought against him; finally, a circuit judge ruled that he owned the river bottom. By this time, it was generally realized that the river was navigable only if the navigators in question got out of a shallow canoe and pushed it through tough mats of eelgrass. Formerly, Ball operated the sanctuary jointly with the Audubon Society; but he quarreled irretrievably with them when he wanted a jetport in the Everglades and the society didn't. He did not get it, which rankled.

Some of Ball's power was broken when the Eighty-Ninth Congress voted in a bill proposed by Representative Wright Patman of Texas and Senator Wayne Morse of Oregon. It struck the testamentary-estate exception from the Bank Holding Law in force in the United States. "The new law of the land," as Ball's biographer has noted, "affected a single American citizen: Ed Ball of Florida." Even so, the elder statesman continued irrepressible. Once, when he was driving above the speed limit in Wakulla County, a nervous passenger, Colonel Manuel of the Florida Turnpike Authority, asked him: "Mr. Ball, do you drive frequently?"

"Not as often as I did before my fourth coronary, Colonel." [4]

He has had his opponents. LeRoy Collins, termed by political journalist Robert Sherrill in 1965 "the last governor seriously active in behalf of the public," has been one. [5] Robert King

4. Griffith, *Ed Ball,* p. 65.

5. Robert Sherrill, "Florida's Legislature: The Pork-Chop State of Mind," *Harper's* 9 (November 1965): 82–97, 86.

High, the liberal mayor of Miami whose heart gave out after a losing race for the governor's mansion in Tallahassee, was another. The power of Ed Ball turned Senator Claude Denson Pepper, Florida's "Red-Hot Pepper" and also a liberal, into overtly humble U.S. Representative Claude Denson Pepper from Dade County. The vanquisher of Pepper, with Ball's blessing, was George Smathers, "Gorgeous George" to his deriders. One of Smathers's speeches in the anti-Pepper campaign is, in its own way, a masterpiece of Florida ingenuity. It was delivered to a rural audience:

> Are you aware that Claude Pepper is known all over Washington as a shameless extrovert? Not only that, but this man is reliably reported to practice nepotism with his sister-in-law, and he has a sister who was once a thespian in wicked New York. Worst of all, it is an established fact that Mr. Pepper, before his marriage, practiced celibacy.[6]

Aficionados of politics in the Land of Flowers claim that the speech was based upon another given by a forgotten victor in central Florida, who labeled his opponent "a known heterosexual and monogamist." Whatever the provenance of Mr. Smathers's observations, they amused their rural hearers, but did not altogether deceive them. But they voted against Claude Pepper, nonetheless; it was repeatedly brought home to them that he had attended the Harvard Law School "and so did Alger Hiss." The irony was that Edward Ball had once supported Pepper; now he was calling him "that buzzard," because the independent Pepper had opposed him on too many issues. Ball and Smathers were hand in glove, and though Smathers was, by residence, a lamb-chopper, he had sound pork-chop instincts.

It is difficult for many Floridians to denounce the pork-choppers, because they abounded in charm and fascination, even while they ignored worthy bills and passed others of doubtful benefit to the state's people as a whole. There was silver-haired Dilworth Clarke, of Monticello. Clarke had been the patriarch of the Florida Senate. When his district was abolished, he had the metal nameplate marking his assigned legislative parking

---

6. Robert Sherrill, *Gothic Politics in the Deep South* (New York: Grossman Publishers, 1968), p. 150.

space brought to stand proudly in front of his Monticello residence. There were passers-by who had some difficulty with tears when they saw it. His constituency, Jefferson County, had been the smallest in Florida. This had had its advantages. When a reapportionment session, the first of many, proposed to assign him Liberty County as well, he is supposed to have quipped with an engaging smile, "Give me Liberty, and you give me death." Charley Eugene Johns, a railroad conductor for more than a quarter of a century who ended up as Florida's acting governor in the 'fifties because the incumbent had died suddenly, had been a protegé of Clarke: "He's like a Daddy to me," he lamented at Clarke's departure. None of the most ancient pork-choppers done out of their districts lived long in retirement; death found easy and disheartened prey.[7]

Charley Johns, who survives, lent his own flavor to Florida in the pork-chop days. His campaign posters were pasted in a hundred peeling, steaming railroad depots: "Charley E. Johns knows what it is to work for his bread by the sweat of his brow!" His home town was Starke, population four thousand. Back in the legislature after his term in the mansion, Johns instituted the Johns Committee, which he intended to watch over Florida's morals. The committee declared an all-out war on homosexuals, yet the pickings were few. Then it hired a press agent who turned out a remarkable booklet to drum up interest: *Homosexuality and Citizenship in Florida*. Its contents included a gay glossary and graphic pictures, all to illustrate the Evil that Charley Eugene Johns was fighting so valiantly. Floridians were horrified; they said the booklet was obscene. The governor, Farris Bryant, refused to read it. In Miami (of all places), the booklet was condemned as "hard-core pornography." And Charley Johns's face was red, especially when a Washington pamphleteer reprinted the volume, and it became a collector's item.

Legislative vaudeville? Undoubtedly. Legislative injustice? Demonstrably. A pork-chop state senator once opposed an urban-renewal bill: "Don't you think we could make a good argument that we need some slums in America so people can re-

7. Sherrill, "Florida's Legislature," p. 87.

alize there is somewhere for them to work up to?'' [8] When the U.S. government wanted to buy some duck marshes for the state, it was accused of "socialistic rural renewal." The Federal Hand was feared as lying potentially too heavy on the quackers. In 1959, the Florida House of Representatives refused to grant county libraries $100,000 because "it is a good idea but we don't have money this year." [9] Then they set aside $500,000 for fighting the fire ant (a battle even now not won, and if you think of ants as innocuous, you don't know fire ants and their stings.) The lawmakers also gave several million dollars to the cause of eradicating the screwworm, which afflicts cows, and the burrowing nematode, which afflicts orange trees. In Gaines-ville, at the University of Florida, wondering spectators have noticed two separate buildings in entomology, one devoted to the study of bugs that attack man and one to bugs that don't. It all makes entertaining narrative—until one is reminded that Florida is very nearly tropical, and bugs can be a matter of life and death; until the present century, they were. And without the cattle and citrus industries, Florida couldn't make the humblest of contributions to the state library system.

Fuller Warren, who served as the state's governor from 1949 to 1951, was a pork-chopper among pork-choppers. He was, naturally, a Democrat; Republicanism had as yet made few inroads. Warren described himself as "a backwoods boy," and so he was, for Blountstown, in the Panhandle, was about as backwoodsy as you could get, in those days. The author of *Eruptions of Eloquence* and *Speaking of Speaking,* Warren developed into a model of pork-chop oratory. Cities were never cities, but "great cities." A sunset was not a sunset, but "a crimson phantasmagoria in the western skies." Mothers brought their babies to hear him speak, and according to Warren, the babies rarely cried. ("I do not mean to say that the infants in our audiences were interested, but I do record the fact that they appeared to be attentive.") [10]

Warren advised aspirants to high office,

8. Sherrill, "Florida's Legislature," p. 90.
9. Sherrill, "Florida's Legislature," p. 83.
10. Fuller Warren and Allen Morris, *How To Win in Politics* (Tallahassee: Peninsular Publishing Company, 1949), p. 21.

I recommend the use of many adjectives, a plethora of adjectives. Never use a lone adjective where ten can be crowded in. The goal of most orators is sound, not sense, and an array of euphonious, alliterative adjectives makes mightily for sound. For example, instead of saying an opponent is a "mean man," fulminate in stentorian tones, "he is a snarling, snapping, hissing monstrosity." And instead of saying a girl has a "sweet voice," intone that she has "a soft, susurrant, satisfying accent," or "a dulcet, melodious voice." Or, instead of calling a vicious man a cad, really swing out and castigate him as a "lying, libidinous, lecherous libertine." [11]

But Fuller Warren, for all his dash and verbosity, was a sound politician, thoroughly dedicated to the people of his state. There were times when his simplicity could not grasp fiscal complexities; there were also times when he spoke with great courage. In 1945, he came out for reapportionment; to defy its principles, he said, was a species of anarchy. He was against sales taxes, because they burdened people with low incomes. He did the North a favor when he ordered that shipment of unripe oranges be stopped and instituted the taste-testing of citrus. He began a massive reforestation program that put new life into Florida's economy. Also, he fenced in the state's pastures and got roaming cows off the highways. This last coup may seem trivial to the uninitiated, but driving in the Sunshine State was formidably risky when its bovines had a green open-range world to wander in unfettered. "You'd be driving at night, all of a sudden you'd hear a crash, and you'd wind up with no radiator and a pair of horns decorating your motor," a veteran of unfenced Florida used to say. Fuller Warren never lacked the ability to laugh at himself. A few years ago, a state newspaper asked a series of governors who had been the greatest Floridian. Most replied with grave constitutional and legal statements and cited the distinguished dead. Not Fuller Warren. Who had been the greatest Floridian? *He* had, he said: he was the man who got the cows off the highways.

He admired politicians who could take care of most situations. He was especially fond of citing Governor John W. Mar-

---

11. Warren and Morris, *How To Win*, p. 26.

tin (1924–1928), whose rival was a notorious anti-Catholic named Sidney Catts. Catts had charged that Catholics were storing weapons in the cellar of the Catholic cathedral in Tampa. They would use these weapons to conquer Florida. Wise men had already pointed out that there was as yet no Catholic cathedral in Tampa, and that no Catholic churches in Tampa had cellars. But it remained for Martin to put Catts out of office:

> My friends, you gave your support once to Catts on his promise to run the Pope out of business. Did he keep his promise? No! While he was Governor, mind you, and supposed to be looking after this promise he made you, one Pope died and he let them appoint another without raising a finger to stop it![12]

Fuller Warren was much more than the essence of Cracker Florida—which he also was, except for its racial and religious bigotry. He was cosmopolitan, under the folksy exterior, and he had the interests of common men at heart. Because he spoke a positively Elizabethan language, of richness they could not understand but only admire, they loved him. He wanted clean cities without slums. He wanted equality of representation in Florida. He wanted Florida to be admired by his country. And, all the while, in office and out of it, he wrote letters to the newspapers. Floridians were watching for them until September 1973, when Fuller Warren died a lonely death in modest circumstances in Miami at the age of sixty-eight. He had been married once, but the marriage had ended in divorce. He had wanted no fortune from high office. There were no children. He was buried in Blountstown, and, in the tiny cemetery, surviving Florida officials as well as Panhandle crackers wept. The secret of Fuller Warren's uniqueness, perhaps, had been an innocent and honorable joy that antedated the present era of country-club candidates for office and full-time ghost writers. No one could have ghostwritten a Warren stump speech; no one ever tried.

Between 1954 and 1961 LeRoy Collins was Florida's governor. It was still the pork-chop era, and Collins was a Tallahassean. But he was also a man of historical sophistication, dedi-

---

12. Warren and Morris, *How To Win*, p. 173.

cated to public service, and he brought Florida more than once into the national limelight with his progressive platform and his bid for tourism. What he was faced with was the Supreme Court desegregation decision of 1954. He knew Florida needed adjustments and relief from strife and disorder. He also approved legislation affecting the state's public education, child welfare, prisons, and mental health. Like Warren, he favored reapportionment. He advocated the development of a broader industrial base and educational development. Under his administration, Florida universities were integrated without fanfare. LeRoy Collins, born and bred in the Deep South, came to believe that segregation had to be destroyed.

Pork-chopism in Florida did not expire suddenly. Its death was prolonged and painful, for the 'chop legislators tried several halfhearted reapportionment plans upon which the federal government did not look with favor. "One man, one vote" was a slogan of disaster everywhere north of Orlando, a city as yet unravished by Mickey, Donald, and Goofy until the administration of Governor Haydon Burns in the mid-1960s. Burns invited the late Walt Disney to Tallahassee; there were conferences in the governor's mansion and some speedily passed tax laws with appropriate shelters. Cartoonists, after that, drew Burns in a Mouseketeer hat.

While reapportionment plans were being dreamed up and discarded or invalidated, Fidel Castro brought Florida sudden changes. Robert King High, mayor of Miami, watched successive waves of Cuban refugees land at the Miami airport. Many kissed the American earth as they left their planes. *"Viva Cuba Libre!"* shouted welcoming crowds in the language of José Martí. A quarter of a million new residents, many of whom could speak no English, created a metropolitan crisis. Mayor High took to radio and television, hoping they would be "a mass tranquilizing pill." He shuttled between Miami and Washington seeking federal aid. Doctors from Havana became busboys and cab drivers, but what began as a potential disaster for Miami turned into triumph, as the newcomers adapted to American language and life with stunning rapidity. Miami also started learning Spanish. High was catapulted into national and state news, and he decided to run for Florida's governorship. He was a liberal, like Claude Pepper, and an admirer of John Kennedy. "Easy morality," he quoted an article, "is the prevailing morality of the government of Florida." [13] His campaign slogan became "Integrity is the issue." He was not without naiveté. When he was riding in a campaign parade in Jacksonville, a member of the crowd shoved a strange man into his car. "You don't mind if one of your campaign workers rides with you, do you, Mayor?" The mayor didn't, and chatted affably with the intruder. Shortly thereafter an advertisement appeared in Florida newspapers:

> A man is known by the company he keeps . . . Above: Robert King High and his Jacksonville motorcade companion, convicted criminal X _____. Robert King High is shown with one of his associates in his Friday Jacksonville motorcade, none other than X _____. X _____ pleaded guilty for his part in the insurance-car repairing scandal . . . he was sentenced to serve eighteen months in jail in Division A, Criminal Court . . . Robert King High and convicted felon X _____: . . . are these the kind of buddies you want running Florida for the next four years? [14]

There were 'choppers who could play rough indeed. They also referred repeatedly to "the bloc vote," which was not technically racist, but efficiently suggestive. "Their candidate will win unless you vote!" north Florida billboards proclaimed. But the tactics backfired. High won the Democratic nomination. For the conservative two-party aggregate of Florida, however, his penchant for innovation was too much. He lost to Republican Claude R. Kirk, Jr., and the one-party system in Florida had been shaken, if not permanently damaged. A year later, High was dead of a heart attack. Kirk had his own style; he introduced his fiancée at his inaugural ball only as Madame X. Florida matrons endured agonies of social suspense until they learned she was an attractive German-born divorcée from South America, née Erika Mattfeld.

13. Faith High Barnebey, *Integrity Is the Issue: Campaign Life with Robert King High* (Miami: E. A. Seeman Publishing, Inc., 1971), p. 81.
14. Barnebey, *Integrity*, p. 148.

In the autumn of 1970, Pensacolian Democrat Reubin O'Donovan Askew began the first of two terms in office. Askew came from pork-chop territory, but there his link to the moribund political system ended. As a senator, he had battled for reapportionment. By 1972, he saw the reality happen. "One man, one vote" came officially to Florida. White-haired patriarchs retired to pillared white houses ringed with azalea hedges; north Florida is Greek Revival country architecturally. Miami arrived in force. There were fewer Stetsons on the streets, and a delicatessen appeared in the capitol's shadow, with chopped liver, knishes, and blintzes. Florida, which had had one of the worst-apportioned legislatures in the land, now had one of the best. Tallahassee acquired the bagel, and also lobbyists from Miami who spoke courteously to their representatives as "Señor Legislator."

Had the pork-choppers been all bad? They had not, lamb-choppers admitted. They had even differed among themselves, running the gamut from the progressive allegiances of Fuller Warren to the die-hard conservatism of Dilworth Clarke, who once genially pointed out that, in Monticello, "Nigger babies have been named after me." It was simply that pork-chop concerns had not been statewide, but regional. The pork-choppers' constituents had come first, and if a hamlet needed jobs, it got a mental hospital to which Miami and Tampa relatives would have to travel far to visit. Once at Cedar Key, where the mangrove shore of the west coast begins, a town official reminisced: "They did a lot, you know—the pork-chop gang. They gave us roads and schools and hospitals and kept the poor folks out this way from goin' hungry. Folks forget so much of what they did. Maybe they sold the cities short, but who else would've cared about *us?* They had hearts." [15]

Reapportionment has solved some of Florida's problems (for instance, the four-laning of downstate roads has proceeded apace), though it has not settled all of them. The woes of Florida's unemployed unskilled laborers and malnourished migrant workers have been compounded by a national recession

---

15. Jahoda, *The Other Florida*, p. 321.

that looks to a lot of Floridians like a depression. Only miles from Miami, Seminoles are dying of tuberculosis and alcoholism and hypertension. Not far from the plastic magnificence of Disney World, virulent typhoid fever has appeared in migrant camps. Public officials can be dedicated—and so can fruit and vegetable growers—but both can also be conscienceless. Kickbacks and government favors are not dead. "It's sort of embarrassing," people say in Jacksonville. "So many places in this city are named for people now in jail." The political morality of the state reflects that of the nation. There are signs, however, that some healthy puritanism is taking over. Governor Askew is so famous for his scrupulous honesty, piety, and teetotalism that the irreverent call him and his cabinet Snow White and the Seven Dwarfs. And there is comfort in the lampoon.

When the pork-chop era disappeared, so did a great deal of good southern copy. No longer did silver-tongued drawls dominate house and senate chambers. Fewer and fewer legislators looked and dressed like Colonel Sanders, the inventor of Kentucky Fried Chicken. Where there had been eccentricity, there was now homogeneity. The vividness of the nineteenth-century South was gone forever. As urbanites and liberals and moralists rejoice, it is perhaps pardonable that a few nostalgic souls with a poetic bent should weep, or at least sigh heavily. Florida, with its particular traditions, also reflects America's, though the traditions vary from section to section of the land. What the traditions have in common is romance, if not justice, and there are romances America will see no longer as she becomes worldly-wise and acquires mathematically correct political representation, and her women master the culinary techniques of Escoffier.

Edward Ball and other industrial giants may linger in America, but Fuller Warren will not pass our way again.

12

The Four Hundred,
More or Less

IT is a long journey from Fuller Warren's Blountstown to Palm Beach, that spotless enclave on Florida's lower Atlantic coast where the mansions of the super-rich play at being crosses between monasteries and museums and—lately—Far-Eastern temples. Geographically, the distance between Blountstown and Palm Beach is just under six hundred miles. Socially, and even experientially, those miles are Martian in extent. America has conquered the moon, but Blountstown has never even intimidated the Florida Gold Coast, much less invaded it. Yet there are links. Palm Beach has made forays into hinterlands only slightly to the east of Blountstown; it has done so in the persons of several members of the millionaire Phipps family, whose coffers were filled in late nineteenth-century America by the Bessemer process that converts pig iron into steel. Today it is not possible to drive far in the environs of the state capital without seeing legions of pine trees bearing identical signs: POSTED: JOHN H. PHIPPS.

Other Phippses have remained in Palm Beach; three generations of them have settled in comfortably, and, according to Cleveland Amory, they are "the beefsteak of the Palm Beach social menu." Sportsman Ogden Phipps has said this state of affairs was never intentional. "We never came here for business

144

purposes; we just kept trying to get away. The trouble was that Palm Beach kept catching up with us." [1]

Another Palm Beach social staple was Gerard B. Lambert, the Listerine magnate, who rode into his fortune on the wings of halitosis and the sad but compelling aphorism, "Even your best friend won't tell you."

Palm Beach, Florida, has given America the Palm Beach suit and the sport shirt. It has also given her a comic strip. In the 1920s, William J. Connors of Buffalo, New York, a bluff, self-made businessman, offered to build a toll road from the agricultural section of Palm Beach County to the coast. His wife loved the Beach's splendors, but he preferred fishing and hunting in rough-and-ready interior camps. While she paraded in her furs and diamonds, Connors was swapping stories with alligator hunters in the Everglades. To cartoonist George McManus, a Palm Beach visitor, the situation was irresistibly comic. "Bringing Up Father" was created on the spot, and Jiggs and Maggie wrangled their way quickly into the nation's affections.

To the American middle class, Palm Beach is glamor. It is the recklessly medieval Boom Spanish fantasies of architect Addison Mizner; it is the home of the Lilly dress and the Kennedy family. Its harbor is where the yachts lie at anchor, rocking and sparkling, at nightfall, and slender women in floating Leo Narducci gowns grace the crafts' saloons and laugh champagne-tinged laughter. Palm Beach is an unending Heart Fund gala; it is oil money and steel money and any kind of money originally created by northern hustlers and since mellowed into the treasure of third- and fourth-generation Harvard alumni who have come down to the palms and the Australian pines for a variety of reasons ranging from health to boredom. But Palm Beach does not stand high with the American social Old Guard. A headmaster of Groton preparatory school used to warn his charges, as he sped them off on their Easter vacations: "Do not go to Palm Beach—that den of iniquity!" [2]

1. Cleveland Amory, *The Last Resorts* (New York: Harper and Brothers, 1952), p. 389.

2. Amory, *Last Resorts*, p. 329.

The cruellest—and possibly truest—Palm Beach observations have been made by John Ney, a resident writer:

> Generally speaking, there is something askew in the background of almost everyone who lives in Palm Beach; it is just a bit more plastered over in the older residents. If the fatal flaw is not to be found in purely financial or social problems, it usually turns up in some sort of personal handicap. Two brothers of "impeccable" breeding may not have equal mental equipment. One takes over the family business, and the other drifts to Palm Beach. . . . In time, he may re-enter business in Florida. If such a venture is successful, and it often is, he has the last laugh. If it is not, he doesn't.[3]

The fatal flaw: crusty and stainless Newport, Rhode Island, has made much of it. The late Consuelo Vanderbilt Balsan (*her* fatal flaw was that she was an ex-duchess) came south for the sun, but in the privacy of her mansion, ten miles beyond Palm Beach, she eventually decided "the place is actually so dreadful I won't go near it. The only time I go to Palm Beach now is to get my hair washed and to get some money out of the bank." [4]

Palm Beach has always been a sort of rarefied mirror of its time. During the Boom, it boomed with cosmic largesse; and during the green years, when parlor psychiatrists were discovering Sigmund Freud, Palm Beach took to psychoanalyzing itself. Henry Morrison Flagler had built the Florida East Coast Railway that had made the city possible; little more than a decade after his death, Palm Beach was speculating that

> Flagler's exceptionally repressed libido burst open on first view of Florida, which he substituted for the Sadie Thompson he didn't as yet dare take on, and . . . he spent many years of solidly sublimated sexual effort in draping her (Florida, that is) in the best that money could buy.[5]

There were, nevertheless, Palm Beachers who believed Florida was less "a sublimated mistress" than "just sand with business possibilities." [6] If Florida was Flagler's sublimation, Palm

---

3. John Ney, *Palm Beach* (Boston: Little, Brown, 1966), pp. 109–110.

4. Amory, *Last Resorts*, p. 9.

5. Ney, *Palm Beach*, pp. 75–76.

6. Ney, *Palm Beach*, p. 76.

Beach itself, said the Freudians, was Paris Singer's. The son of sewing-machine czar Isaac Merritt Singer spent years in loving servitude to dancer Isadora Duncan. (In Palm Beach, they called her "Is-a-Bore When Drunken.") When Isadora left him, he sublimated *his* libido by becoming a social arbiter while his crony Addison Mizner was busy piling up hundred-roomed Boom Spanish testaments of tainted money, tropic vegetation, and the owners' yen to belong to a peerage—any peerage. The industrial rich also wanted a Brahmin privilege of exclusion; thus it was that, when the Kennedys arrived, eyebrows were raised because they were "so Oirish." It is one of the many fascinations of Palm Beach that its official county history, published in 1967, makes not one mention of the Kennedy family nor of the fact that a president of the United States maintained a Palm Beach residence. The First Federal Savings and Loan Association of Lake Worth, in Palm Beach County, sponsors of the volume, evidently decided that the Kennedys had no place in a history intended to be "an inspiring cultural treasure" and "a living relic of one of the most fabulous eras in the history of our country." Even Founding Father Joseph P. Kennedy is entirely absent, but not other vital facts, such as this one: "The smallest homestead claim in the United States was filed by John Haly for an island in Lake Worth which contained less than ½ acre (49/100 acre). This island was known as Haly's Island." [7]

Palm Beach likes to think its history began with Ponce de León; the island of Santa Marta to which he sailed from the future site of St. Augustine is modern Singer's Island, city and county chroniclers urge. It may be that the remains of a sour-orange grove between Delray Beach and Boca Raton are Spanish; it may also be that the grove and its nearby abandoned dwellings date from Florida's British period. At any rate, grove and buildings are the earliest structural evidence of European man in Palm Beach County. Before Ponce, it belonged to the Ais, a rather seedy Indian tribe that lived on fish and produced pottery mediocre when measured by the standards of any other North American native handiwork.

7. David Forshay, *Lure of the Sun* (Lake Worth, Fla.: First Federal Savings and Loan Association, 1967), p. 85.

Even the Ais had a characteristic that was later to belong to
Palm Beach's most celebrated habitués; they migrated from
town to town with the change of seasons—for even Palm Beach
has seasons, as has southern Florida, generally. They range
from the intense thunderstorm-laden heat of summer to the
windy dryness of autumn to the balmy liveability of winter to
the *déja-vu* windy dryness of spring. During fall and spring, the
parched Everglades are alive with fires; they always have been.
Calusas also came and went; after the Spanish and British
periods, American troops chased the Seminoles into Palm Beach
County. No white American thought the county worth settling
until the army built a lighthouse on the Loxahatchee in 1859.
Blockade-runners came with the Civil War, and so did "a population comprised mostly of Confederate deserters, renegades,
and riffraff." [8]

The first permanent nonmilitary settler in what was to become
the city of Palm Beach was a German horticulturist who was
also a draft dodger from the Union army. He planted lemons
and limes and figs and guavas, mangoes and bananas and avo-
cados and pineapples; probably it was he who introduced the red
poinsettia and blue plumbago flowers. From a narrow strip of
the beach, he dug a canal to freshwater Lake Worth; in swept
the Atlantic tides, and Lake Worth became salt water. A mid-
western family named Pierce arrived in 1873; before the turn of
the century, Palm Beachers were not Old South or New England, but downright former citizens of Michigan, Illinois,
Ohio, Iowa, and Wisconsin who hated snow and liked experi-
menting with plants. Already the "fatal flaw" had appeared in
Palm Beach; all the world knew there were no "old families"
hailing from American prairies. Old families lived on Beacon
Hill, in Tidewater Virgina, and on Carolina Low Country plantations, where darkies strummed away soft summer evenings on
what Thomas Jefferson had called "the banjore."

In 1878, a Spanish ship named *La Providencia* appeared on
Palm Beach—driven by a storm, some said; others avowed she
had a tipsy crew. The ship contained a cargo of coconuts and a

8. Forshay, *Lure,* p. 9.

vast quantity of wine, some of which could not be accounted for. The captain and his crew had a rousing frolic and gave the coconuts away to resident Palm Beachers. *La Providencia*— what was left of her—was sold at public auction for twenty dollars. The ship turned out to be worth far more than that to Palm Beach, for when Henry Flagler made his tour of inspection in the 1890s, he was impressed by the vast groves of coconut trees waving along the Atlantic shore. Here was an ideal spot for another Flagler wonder-hotel; the Florida East Coast Railway was extended south, replacing a tiny stretch of tracks that operated out of the hamlet of Juno to loading platforms named Mars and Venus; Palm Beach County harbored at least one classicist. A visitor had christened the line the Celestial Railroad; Flagler's was bigger and better, if not so poetic.

Already the oil tycoon was "the Father of Florida"; now he became the Father of Palm Beach, as well. He built one of the largest wooden buildings in the world, the Royal Poinciana Hotel. (For a man of his vision, it is odd that he never thought about the possibility of termites.) The Royal Poinciana was also the largest resort hotel in existence, and its patrons came in private railroad cars to its 1,150 rooms and 32 acres. Flagler had hired "the best artisans in the nation"; they had used 1,400 kegs of nails, 5,000,000 feet of lumber, 360,000 shingles, 4,000 barrels of lime, 500,000 bricks, and 240,000 gallons of paint. They had installed 1,200 windows and 1,300 doors, and they had done it all in nine months. The Poinciana was a wonder, not only of America, but of the planet Earth. In later years, two sprawling additions were built, doubling the hostelry's size. Some of the patrons had not only private railroad cars, but private trains; Harry Payne Whitney arrived one year with twenty-five guests and a trainful of servants to take over an entire floor.[9]

Great names were a staple at the Royal Poinciana: August Belmont, the Duke and Duchess of Manchester, Countess Boni de Castellane, Mrs. George Jay Gould, John Jacob Astor, Wan-

9. Theodore Pratt, *That Was Palm Beach* (St. Petersburg, Fla.: Great Outdoors Publishing Co., 1968), pp. 53 ff.

amakers, Stotesburys and Wideners arrived from Philadelphia; the North also gave the Royal Poinciana a room reservation from John Warne "Bet-a-Million" Gates. When the hotel's guests wished to make a tour of the city of Palm Beach (West Palm Beach was Flagler's "help city"), they were propelled by Afromobiles—two-seated wicker chairs pedalled by a bicycle mechanism driven by a deferential black. The going rate was two dollars an hour, fairly steep for the 1890s. At night, the Royal Poinciana reveled; from the ballroom to the bar, there was a secret passage called "Hypocrites' Row" for the use of drinkers who didn't want to be seen using the bar's main entrance.

One of the Royal Poinciana's institutions was Cakewalk Night. Clad in satins, feathers, and diamonds, the guests lined up in the ballroom, while Pinkerton detectives patrolled unobtrusively. On a long table, presided over by four judges selected from visiting celebrities, was set a tiered and sugared white cake, the prize for the best black dancing couple. Usually, there were six such couples to entertain the white audience. The male dancers wore red satin trousers and green coats and high top hats, and their women gyrated in chiffon and liberal quantities of rouge. These couples were the "cake-ists," and what they danced was ragtime as well as the cakewalk; afterwards, they bowed deeply for the attending millionaires. They also sang spirituals and popular tunes: "Georgia Camp Meeting," "Golden Slippers," and "Bill Bailey, Won't You Please Come Home?" Stotesburys, Vanderbilts, and Wanamakers were entranced. At the end of the evening, everybody joined in while the performers sang "Ta-Ra-Ra-*Boom*-De-Ay!" After Washington's birthday on February 22, all the tycoons and their fur-draped wives departed for the North, and the Royal Poinciana closed its doors. Palm Beach glittered for barely two months, but already it was an international legend. Flagler bought out all the Palm Beach pioneers, who retired gracefully to West Palm Beach, where they opened stores. He also gave away staggering sums of money to people in trouble with orange groves, people in trouble with coconut plantations, and simply people in trouble. A modern Palm Beach writer has compared him to Daddy Warbucks.[10]

But all was not well in the private life of Daddy Warbucks. One morning at the breakfast table, his wife serenely announced that she was engaged to be married to the czar of all the Russias. Flagler sent for a legion of doctors, but they told him what he already suspected; Mrs. Flagler was completely *non compos mentis* and must be taken to an institution. For several years after his wife's incarceration, Flagler maintained a discreet relationship with a woman of modest means named Mary Lily Kenan; her parents were dead, and she had been living with relatives. However, Mary Lily became increasingly sensitive to gossip and began insisting on marriage. In New York, divorces could not be granted on the grounds of a mate's insanity. Flagler then changed his residence to Florida and had a discussion with some legislators; the legislature obligingly passed the Flagler Divorce Law, by which rich men could get rid of mad wives; after Flagler had taken advantage of it, it was duly repealed, and Florida's marriage statutes returned to their former puritanism. Flagler and Mary Lily, his Little Orphan Annie, were married on August 24, 1901; he was seventy-one and she was thirty-four.

Mary Lily had a sweet singing voice; for this she was rewarded with "the finest residence you can think of," Palm Beach's Whitehall, pillared and marbled and heavy with gold. Mary Lily's rival, Mrs. E. T. Stotesbury, had gold bathroom fixtures. "They're very economical, you know," Mrs. Stotesbury always said, "You don't have to polish them." [11] Mary Lily did not concentrate on bathrooms; she wrought a Marble Hall in seven hues, with French and Chinese salons, the largest private pipe organ in the country, and sixteen suites of guest rooms. Unkind critics compared Whitehall to "a garish railroad car blown up into Palm Beach's historic palace." [12] There

10. Ney, *Palm Beach*, p. 12.
11. Amory, *Last Resorts*, p. 37.
12. Ney, *Palm Beach*, p. 78.

Mary Lily entertained on a gargantuan scale; she bought fifty complete dinner services and a wardrobe so large that she never wore anything twice. John Ney has observed,

> They were a sobering vision for the sympathetic visitor: Flagler staring glumly at the shimmering marble walls, saying sadly to an admirer, "I wish I could swap it for a little shack," repeating over and over again his Delphic credo, "Satisfaction and contentment are not synonymous"; and upstairs, Mary Lily throwing out the day's frocks.[13]

Daddy Warbucks's Little Orphan Annie was orphan no more. Yet, though her idyll was over its romance, it did not end until the day in 1913 that Flagler broke his hip on steep Whitehall stairs. Mary Lily outlived him by only four years. The previous Mrs. Flagler survived in a cottage on the grounds of a New York state sanitarium; she now painted her eyebrows with burnt cork and her cheeks with red dye, carried her Ouija board with her at all times, and debated constantly with herself out loud over the preparations for her imminent marriage to Nicholas of Russia.

Palm Beach institutions other than Whitehall were flourishing before World War I. One of them was Bradley's Beach Club, the founder of which, Edward Reilly Bradley, is possibly the only professional gambler in history who became, in death, commemorated by a park and a memorial plaque. Bradley's Beach Club was incorporated in 1899, and its proprietor was soon boasting that, next to Monte Carlo, his club was the most famous gambling establishment in the world. American Society and even various royal Europeans visited Bradley's to amuse themselves; they were required to wear evening dress after 7:00 P.M. They were not immune to being bounced for improper behavior, and Bradley, a Kentucky Colonel, also employed a hidden rifleman in charge of a fleet of armed guards. Gentlemen could not smoke in the roulette room. At first, Bradley's was not a success; then, to the scandalized astonishment of the Old Guard, insofar as it existed in Palm Beach, he admitted women.

13. Ney, *Palm Beach,* p. 78.

The ladies brought their husbands, and Bradley's boomed. No resident Floridian was allowed; Bradley did not want to be accused of tempting the locals to ruin. Migratory status and immense wealth were mandatory. Loud laughter was not permitted—a sign was posted to warn the patrons. Bradley was a generous man; "There are no pockets in a shroud," he was fond of saying.[14] He even rebuilt a hurricane-damaged church whose pastor had denounced him from the pulpit; between professional men, of whatever stripe, certain things were understood.

Once, Florida tried to close Bradley's. The governor sent a representative from Tallahassee to Palm Beach; this dignitary was detained long enough for Bradley to be tipped off. Hastily, all the gambling equipment was removed from the open and deposited in a hidden basement room under the trap door of the ballroom, which, according to veteran Florida writer Theodore Pratt, "had been built for such an emergency."[15] When the governor's aide entered Bradley's, he heard the serene sounds of an orchestra and saw a sedate clientele dining and dancing; clearly, the institution was simply social, as its charter stated.

Usually, Bradley was a shrewd judge of human nature. Once, however, he was bested. A comely young woman came to him in his private office one night, her eyes swimming in tears. She said she and her young bridegroom were in Palm Beach on their honeymoon, and he had just lost their entire savings of five thousand dollars. Bradley cogitated, and then opened the drawer of his desk and drew out five one-thousand-dollar bills. "I shall give you these on condition you promise me that neither you nor your husband will ever enter this club again." Sobbing, the bride agreed. Near the door, though unseen by those leaving, she pointed to her husband, who was just departing. Then she disappeared. The next night, Colonel Bradley was touring his tables and saw the same young man. Outraged, he sent for him. "You were told never to come here again!" he thundered. "You cannot afford that kind of money. Your wife agreed." The young man was astonished. "My *what?*" "Your wife,"

14. Pratt, *That Was Palm Beach*, p. 53.
15. Pratt, *That Was Palm Beach*, p. 54.

Bradley told him sternly. The young man smiled. "I am not married. As far as affording it, Colonel Bradley, I think I can. My name is Russell Firestone." [16] When Colonel Bradley died in 1946, one of his patrons, Joseph P. Kennedy, sadly announced of Palm Beach, "The zipperoo has gone out of the place." [17]

Nineteen seventeen was a historic year for Palm Beach. One winter morning, Paris Singer was sitting on the porch of the Royal Poinciana with a social and very sick fat man named Addison Mizner, who was suffering from necrosis, heart and lung symptoms, and "a general breakdown." [18] Singer was also dying—or so he thought. Both men were bored with dying, however, and fell into conversation. What would Mizner do, Singer asked, if he could do anything he wanted? Mizner looked up, down, and sideways, and answered: "I'd build something that wasn't made of wood, and I wouldn't paint it yellow." The father of Boom Spanish had spoken, and Singer resolved to finance him. A year later, the Everglades Club was a reality: a little bit, said a society reporter, "of Seville and the Alhambra, a dash of Madeira and Algiers, an Italian lagoon and Terraced Garden and the incomparable Florida sunshine and climate, combine to make of the club and its surroundings a wondrous combination of the Old World and the New." [19]

The Stotesburys said they wanted a cottage. Mizner designed them one. It sprawled from Lake Worth to the Atlantic, an Iberian covent-cum-castle with a forty-car garage, patios, a swimming pool illuminated from underneath and a private zoo. Mizner was not a wholly experienced architect, so he forgot to include a kitchen. The Stotesburys didn't mind, and he duly built one. For the Rasmussens, he forgot a staircase, so at the last minute he stuck a turret on their house and built a spiral staircase around it. Unkind critics called such Mizner cottages, which mushroomed, examples of the Bastard-Spanish-Moorish-

16. Amory, *Last Resorts,* p. 351.
17. Pratt, *That Was Palm Beach,* p. 56.
18. Alva Johnston, *The Legendary Mizners* (New York: Farrar, Straus and Young, 1953), p. 23.
19. Amory, *Last Resorts,* p. 356.

Romanesque - Gothic - Renaissance - Bull - Market - Damn - the - Expense style. Floridians stared. Outsiders who came to Florida for the winter were regarded as "sick Yankees," and now look at what the sick Yankees were doing! Whole towns in Spain began getting unroofed for the likes of A. J. Drexel Biddle, Jr., Major Barclay Warburton, Rodman Wanamaker, and Harold Vanderbilt. Mr. Stotesbury was so happy in his new abode that he regaled guests with his favorite song, for which he accompanied himself by banging on a small drum:

> The old family toothbrush,
> The old family toothbrush,
> The old family toothbrush
> That hangs on the sink;
> First it was father's,
> Then it was mother's,
> Then it was sister's,
> Now it is mine.[20]

Stotesbury, a banker, was known to his intimates as Little Sunshine.

Addison Mizner had his rivals; one of Florenz Ziegfeld's designers, Joseph Urban, reacted with Boom Spanish of his own, though he did not go so far as Mizner did in "antiquing" statues by hacking off their noses and arms or aging furniture by searing it with a hot paper fire. Urban designed the Bath and Tennis Club and also the residence of the late Mrs. Merriweather Post, the Postum heiress. Mrs. Post's Mar-a-Lago was also aided by the ministrations of a Venetian artist named Ju-Ju de Blas, who decked it with murals. The dining-room table cost one million dollars, and guests compared the house to Versailles. The door was decorated with golden cupids. According to Palm Beach tradition, when Harry K. Thaw—who had killed architect Stanford White over the Girl in the Red Velvet Swing, Evelyn Nesbitt—saw Urban's handiwork, he exclaimed, "My God, I shot the wrong architect!"

Paris Singer, Addison Mizner, and Joseph Urban had created the "Golden Littoral," and it remains today a staggering tes-

20. Amory, *Last Resorts,* p. 381.

tament to what America did with its wealth in an era when the word *ghetto* meant a quaintly cobbled enclave of Polish Jews— in Poland, faraway and undisturbing.

When the Crash descended, in 1929, Paris Singer and Addison Mizner crashed with it; when both men finally did die, they died in debt. But Palm Beach did not perish. In the next two decades, a new generation arrived; young John Kennedy went swimming in the Atlantic, and Wrightsmans and Pulitzers graced opening nights at the local theater along with the Walter Chryslers and Barbara Hutton, the Woolworth heiress, then the Countess Haugwitz-Reventlow. Mrs. Stotesbury still presided over her El Mirasol, though she was watching her budget a bit more earnestly than she ever had. Joan Crawford and Beatrice Lillie and the Windsors burst upon the scene. That generation was succeeded by Kleenex Kings and Baby Jane Holzer, erstwhile darling of *Vogue;* when Consuelo Vanderbilt Balsan died in 1965, everybody knew an era had ended. Society, according to Cleveland Amory, had long since been killed.

But some things in Palm Beach do not change. Lorelle Hearst, a social columnist for the *Palm Beach Daily News,* describes a local hostess and her projects in the year of Madame Balsan's death:

> She is now doing her house over, she will have a lemon yellow tile driveway to the front entrance door, which will be round, the roof will be like a Thailand Temple, also the large porch where she has breakfast and lunch, and will have lemon yellow tile on the floor. There are blue and white porcelain elephants at the edge of the porch leading on to the terrace. The colors there are Avocado green and again lots of yellow. She says yellow is like having sunshine at all times of the day.[21]

Where Spain once reigned, Thai and Hindu models are taking over, with perhaps just a touch of Angkor Wat.

One of the most famous observers of Palm Beach was Henry James, who described it in *The American Scene,* written in 1906. Palm Beachers say his comments are still pertinent:

21. Ney, *Palm Beach,* p. 265.

The interest of the general spectacle was supposed to be, I had gathered, that people from all parts of the country contributed to it; and that the value of the testimony as to manners was that it brought to a focus so many elements of difference. . . . The distinction that was least absent . . . was that of the . . . ability to spend and purchase; the ability to spend with freedom being . . . a positive consistent with all sorts of negatives. This helped to make the whole thing documentary—that you had to be financially more or less at your ease to enjoy the privileges.[22]

The mansions remain; so do their formidable seawalls, their marble tables laden with issues of *Town and Country* magazine, their red-tiled roofs and their turrets and golden cupids and their general air of adamant exclusion. Newport and Bar Harbor— what is left of them—still sneer, and the descendants of north Florida planters gaze in amazement from their beautiful-man-nered poverty, which they must accept if they have not held on to great-grandfather's pastures long enough to turn them into apartment complexes. The Royal Poinciana has been dis-mantled; but on soft winter nights, when the Palm Beach surf is singing and the misted stars are shining palely and the darkness-muted red and yellow and salmon hibiscus blossoms are quiver-ing in faint winds, it is possible for the imaginative and the nostalgic to hear old echoes floating out to sea: "Ta-Ra-Ra-*Boom*-De-Ay, Ta-Ra-Ra-*Boom*-De-Ay!" Once again, Vander-bilts have come to watch the cakewalk, chandeliers are flashing, Little Sunshine's cronies wish he would bang his drum after the party and sing "The Old Family Toothbrush," and Mary Lily Flagler, thanks to Standard Oil and the Florida East Coast Railway, has changed and discarded her clothes six times in the last twelve hours.

22. Ney, *Palm Beach,* pp. 269–270.

13

Hurricane Harvest

AND all the while Palm Beach was reveling, its razor-slim matrons strolling along Worth Avenue and Via Mizner in search of Nina Ricci perfumes and Italian silks and lemon-yellow tiles for the driveway, there was an alien green orchid-festooned world westward. Of this world Palm Beach had and has little knowledge. Palm Beach orchids are mostly conservatory plants (rarely corsages, since the American middle class can now afford an occasional lavender Cattleya for a date, a bride, or Mom). There is no record of any Palm Beacher ever being fluent in the Seminole dialects of Hitchiti and Muskogee, and the sleekly coiffed wives who buy Sulka ties for their profit-making husbands are innocent of what it means to be a migrant worker. Many, of course, have seen migrant camps; still more saw the famous CBS documentary of the 1960s, "Harvest of Shame," and at a safe distance they agonized with the late Edward R. Murrow over poverty, disease, and despair among a rootless people. Murrow devoted much of his air time to Florida. The state—especially its fruit- and vegetable-growers—is still smarting with indignation because the problem of migrancy is national, economic, and agricultural, not exclusively Floridian.

If the environment of Palm Beach is far from that of north Florida, it is still further from that of the country surrounding Lake Okeechobee, the Big Water, once a perfumed wilderness of custard apples (*Annona squamosa,* or sweetsop) and wild, bright vines and now, according to Okeechobeeans, the Winter Vegetable Capital of the World. The Everglades remain. Seminole dugout canoes still move slowly down labyrinthine ebony waters; Seminole wives and daughters still stir pots of *sofkee* in their *chikees.* The Indians are in the deepest wilderness below the lake. North of it lies the land of agribusiness, where the migrants toil, students in social work write theses on migrants' sufferings, and the conscientious grower wonders how he can house and feed the human beings, mostly black, who are his laborers and still manage to keep down the price of food. Palm Beach likes escargots and Beluga caviar; the Indian still lives off the fish and game and plants of sawgrass prairies and hammocks; American dining-room tables in winter offer corn, green peppers, and tomatoes grown in reclaimed Everglades muck; and the migrant still eats chitterlings, field peas, and crackling bread laced with too much molasses and not enough nutrition.

There are 730 square miles of Lake Okeechobee, dotted by the four small islands of Observation, Kreamer, Torry, and Ritta. No conquistador ever saw the Big Water, though the Calusas knew it well. It has been described by engineer Isham Randolph, whose engineering wears better than his metaphoric prose, as "the great liquid heart of Florida . . . at the focus of the greatest agricultural drainage problem in our country." [1] Ten thousand years ago, the Big Water was a hollow in a teeming prehistoric sea. Time, sediment, and erosion have made it the shallow basin that it is today, rarely deeper than seventeen feet. The land surrounding it receives approximately fifty-five inches of rainfall per year and loses the same amount by evaporation. The whole area has a timeless history of cycles of flood and drought; one of the ironies of this history is that each generation castigates the preceding one for having caused the problem. Possibly the Calusas castigated their gods.

In 1877, Hamilton Disston, of Philadelphia's Keystone Saw, Tool, Steel and File works, came to Florida in search of good

1. Alfred Jackson Hanna and Kathryn T. Abbey Hanna, *Lake Okeechobee* (Indianapolis: Bobbs Merrill, 1948), p. 17.

fishing. When he saw Lake Okeechobee and the Everglades, he became overnight a man obsessed. Before he was forty, in 1884, he had bought four million acres of the Lake Okeechobee country from the state of Florida, with an idea of "remodeling the place." Hopeful Floridians intoned, "With Napoleonic instinct and foresight he has seen an opportunity to promote his country's welfare by the reclamation of a more than kingly domain." [2] Disston's schemes for draining south Florida were soon attracting European investors: Sir Edward Reed of England and a Dutchman named Jacobus Wertheim. Disston dredges appeared to hew out canals. Disston saws cut down jungles of custard apples. Pioneers from the North and Midwest began to drift in, in search of Utopia. The possibility of Utopia on Disston land lasted until 1896, when Disston died suddenly. He had "seen too far into the future and died too soon." [3] But engineers still planned canals, would-be Lake Okeechobee farmers kept coming down to Florida, and other investment companies sprang up to publish brochures glowing with visions of glory.

Yet, in 1898, explorer Hugh Willoughby—there is no other word for any white man who dared the Everglades then—could write:

> It may seem strange, in our days of Arctic and African exploration, for the general public to learn that in our very midst, as it were, in one of our Atlantic coast states, we have a tract of land one hundred and thirty miles long and seventy miles wide that is as much unknown to the white man as the heart of Africa. [4]

Who had wandered in the Big Cypress swamp southwest of the Lake? How many had followed the Caloosahatchee River west from the Big Water to Fort Myers and the Gulf? Thomas Alvah Edison had built the first modern swimming pool in America on his Fort Myers estate, where his incandescent lamps lit homely sitting rooms as well as laboratories. Thirty miles east of him lived Seminole Indians who knew nothing of elec-

2. Hanna and Hanna, *Lake Okeechobee*, p. 95.
3. Hanna and Hanna, *Lake Okeechobee*, p. 104.
4. Hugh L. Willoughby, *Across the Everglades* (Philadelphia: J. Lippincott, 1898), p. 13.

tricity's existence. Only the hardiest of souls, like Hugh Willoughby, assaulted the country to the lake's south.

> A rubber ground sheet was of course indispensable. For a pillow I
> used my coat, which I found better than rubber pillows. A full suit
> of rubber mackintosh made by a Boston firm, in the same shape as
> "oilskins," which keep you dry all day in a pouring rain, I always
> kept loose in the canoe, this being the only extra outer clothing car-
> ried. The suit I habitually wore consisted of a brown tweed Norfolk
> jacket with knickerbockers, brown flannel shirt, leather leggings to
> protect as much as possible from snakes and mosquitoes, and heavy
> leather shoes, with tennis shoes to wear in the canoe, which slip off
> easily when preparing for wading, when rubber hip boots are put
> on.[5]

Some of his equipment was curious; he carried a game bag full
of letter paper, for example. To whom was he writing, and
where did he mail the letters? He also had notebooks, rubber
surgical plaster, "cholera mixture," castor oil, quinine pills,
"aristol and colocynth pills, carbolized sinew for sewing
wounds, zinc ointment . . . and a clinical thermometer." [6] The
clinical thermometer cannot have been totally comforting; what
good would it do a man in an Okeechobee custard-apple jungle
known only to elusive Seminoles to learn that he was running a
temperature? But Willoughby loved the watery reaches of the
lake and the River of Grass, the 'Glades. At the end of his trip
through the Everglades, he reached Biscayne Bay, where he
found a hotel. It saddened him; he had hoped for empty sand
and coconut palms. He stated the dilemma of modern south
Florida well: "In the nature of things the wilderness must be
gradually encroached on. What would the settler and the farmer
do without the railroad that now gives him rapid communication
with the North for his winter products?" [7] The Seminoles did
not yet know that *pot-see-lon-ee,* the Carolina parrakeet, and
wa-to-law, the whooping crane, were passing from earth forever. But Hugh Willoughby had intimations of their mortality.

5. Willoughby, *Everglades,* p. 50.
6. Willoughby, *Everglades,* pp. 50 ff.
7. Willoughby, *Everglades,* p. 63.

What did the early settlers of the Okeechobee region find? Water shimmered in tropical sunlight. Rookeries were full of great blue herons and snowy and American egrets, rare white herons, wood ibises with their immense wingspreads, small white and glossy ibises, whooping cranes, limpkins whose eerie calls rent nights when hammock jungles dripped out their music and the wild orchids bloomed unseen. Okeechobee's southern shore was sawgrass, tall and spiked, ready to cut to ribbons the skin of a human being who tried to penetrate it. On East Beach, there were hard sands where high waves broke when winter northers came. The northern shore was covered with a dense forest of pop ash, palmetto, and fig trees. Elders and willows had taken over some of the shore line, where redwing blackbirds sang their reedy songs. Blooming pickerel weeds formed acres of soft blue. And between the south and east shores, there was the custard-apple forest, a dense and impenetrable barrier. "Custard apple, moonvine, catfish and moonshine": that was how the first white settlers saw Okeechobee.[8] They also watched in astonishment as the Big Water lost by evaporation more than an inch of level on a hot summer day. In back country, to the north, there were pinewoods and sedge prairies and small ponds ringed with maiden-cane and white arrowhead flowers. But what fascinated the first whites most were those endless miles of custard apples:

> Under leafy branches covered over with a solid blanket of white-blossomed vines which made twilight at midday, you might walk for miles and scarcely glimpse the sky. . . . There was a peculiar fascination in walking through this murky forest, zigging and zagging between outreaching roots, dodging under crooked branches which tangled overhead . . . Sometimes you'd be stopped by a barricade of wind-felled trees with their meshing branches bound by vines and laced by spiderwebs . . . Between the close-growing trees the ground was bare except for lacy ferns among the angles of the roots, or again, some giant fern, head high to a tall hunter, which unrolled its brown-backed leaves . . . Gourd vines with their green pendant fruit, looping and lacing from branch to branch, were

8. Lawrence E. Will, *A Cracker History of Okeechobee* (St. Petersburg, Fla.: Great Outdoors Publishing Company, 1964), p. iii.

duced seven killing frosts. Recurring floods lasted anywhere from 142 days to 194. Boom towns like Fellesmere became ghost towns. But many sufferers hung on, hoping that nature in Florida could somehow yet be tamed.

On Friday, September 14, 1928, a farmer named A. J. Little went to Belle Glade for supplies. He was told a hurricane was on the way and would probably hit the Little homestead at Lake Harbor by Sunday night. On Saturday, Lake Okeechobee fishermen towed their boats into a drainage canal for shelter. By Sunday morning, the rain had started; the sky was dark, and a steady, strong north wind was gradually becoming stronger. During the afternoon, the Littles heard shouts; when they went outdoors in the streaming rain, they saw a family trying to cross the drainage canal nearby. Little managed to get out his skiff and ferry them across in repeated trips. The lake was already overflowing, the refugees said. Now the wind was roaring; the terrified Littles and their guests huddled together in the Littles' parlor. Little saw the galvanized iron sheets being stripped by the wind from a storehouse. Suddenly, the whole building vanished. As darkness fell, they could see the water covering the ground like foam. The wind was driving the water onward. Little nailed his doors shut while the wind keened on. Then with horror he saw water seeping underneath them. Little hacked at his ceiling with a hatchet while his guests piled a table underneath with a box and on top of that a chair. When the water in the house was waist-high, everyone climbed up into the attic via box and chair. In the attic space, three feet high, a total of ten adults and three children had to crouch on a two-by-four ceiling joist. The rain was striking the roof overhead with tremendous force. The roofing paper hung down in tatters; everyone was soaked. Then the house was torn by the wind from its foundations and began to jerk along in the floodwaters. When day broke, the Littles heard people screaming for help, but they were powerless. When the house finally came to the end of its macabre journey, it was in the Negro quarters of another farmer. All of the tiny houses except one in the quarters had been swept away, and that was filled with terrified blacks. When the wind finally died down, the blacks held a prayer meeting and the Littles and their refugees joined them. No one had food or water. When the rain stopped, blacks and whites climbed the spoil bank of a drainage ditch until they reached the highway canal. When a boat picked them up, they made for a local hotel, where they learned that many of their friends, "the pioneers," had perished.

After the storm, it became plain to survivors that south Florida nature would have to be interfered with more drastically than before. There were no vocal wilderness buffs on Lake Okeechobee in 1928. People wanted the lake diked, they wanted more canals, and they laid the foundations for the development of the Central and Southern Florida Flood Control District, later the whipping boy of ecological purists who wished the lake and the Everglades to stay as nature had made them. But nature had made them with floods, and within them there was now human life to be protected. Zora Neale Hurston wrote movingly of the hurricane of 1928 in her novel, *Their Eyes Were Watching God*. Florida's climate affects even—perhaps especially—the state's literature.Today, because of the Herbert Hoover Dike, one cannot see Lake Okeechobee from the road; in this respect, the lake resembles the Mississippi, which cannot be seen at New Orleans because of the same type of huge levee. The country around the lake produces sugar in limitless green canefields. The reclaimed Everglades muck produces vegetables and fruits. Whereas the sugar fields are worked by West Indians, the vegetables and fruits are the special province of American black migratory farm workers. At night, in the sugar camps, there are soft West Indian laughter and guitars. In the camps of the American blacks, there is less joy; these people have been watching American television longer than have the West Indians, and they know exactly what the rest of America has that they do not: stability, conspicuous consumption, and housewifely enthusiasm over enzyme detergents and Lady Grecian Formula, which washes away only the gray. "Move up to Cadillac!" "Treat yourself to the very best!" The constant commercial grinding of the television mills underscores the migrants' poverty.

Social observers have called the migrants rented slaves. This is unfortunately the case. But if migrants are to be given the wages of industrial workers, new dilemmas arise. Some Americans may be willing to pay seventy-five cents for a tomato, but not many. The same housewives who watched Murrow's "Harvest of Shame" in tears have staged grocery boycotts. Meanwhile, the migrants fiercely resent their label. They speak of themselves instead as being "on the season." There are two parts of on-season existence: Florida, and The Stream. In Florida, the period extends over fall, winter, and spring. Many migrants in the Pahokee-Belle Glade area near Lake Okeechobee are not strictly migrants, for they are residents in their own or rented shacks. They enter The Stream only in summer, when they work their way up to Maine and blueberries. But Floridians consider migrants a race apart. An illuminating glimpse into migrant culture is provided by a public health manual published in Florida in 1961:

> The migrants were encouraged to plan a safe method for preserving their birth, health, and school records, insurance policies and other types of documents. . . . A number of families were given plastic record containers for this purpose. It was found, however, that the containers were used for diaper bags more frequently than for preserving records . . . Communicating with migrants is often a slow and difficult process. During interviews, migrants seem to answer *specific* questions, not seeing the questions as being related, i.e., they do not anticipate questions generally. For example, if asked "How many children do you have?," the migrant mother may reply "Six." The interviewer may assume that the migrant mother lives in a household where she has six children of her own. But if the question is followed with, "Do all of your children live in the house (or room) with you?" the reply may be, "No'm, four of 'em lives with dey grandma." Again, the interviewer may assume that the migrant mother lives in a household with two children, her own. But if she is asked, "Do any other children live with you?" the interviewer may learn that there are children in the household in addition to the mother's children. The additional children may be her stepchildren, her boyfriend's children, her nieces or nephews or her own brothers or sisters.[13]

13. R. H. Browning and T. J. Northcutt, Jr., *On the Season* (Tallahassee: Florida State Board of Health, n.d.), p. 47.

In spite of the seemingly condescending flavor of this manual, it was written by public health personnel deeply involved with and concerned for the welfare of migrant labor.

The migrant system has its roots in Old World Spain; it has been strengthened by the passing of the American family farm. "American Gothic" is a thing of the past. Agriculture has become an industry in itself. And though it feeds a nation and more, it is also a devourer of human beings. Often the migrant gets into The Stream because he has lost a tiny farm in Georgia or the Carolinas. He sees on a card in his general store that there is work in Homestead, Florida. He piles an ancient, rusty automobile with his belongings and heads south. Before he reaches Homestead, he discovers work in Belle Glade; why go farther south? And when the ex-farmer realizes that employment is not permanent in Belle Glade, he can do nothing but enter The Stream when the Florida harvest is over. When he enters the Bluebird bus that will take him north—perhaps it is gaily painted with signs like "Beanpicker Special" and "Jesus Loves You"—he has entered a prison from which few escape. His boss is now the crew leader, who may or may not be honest. In May 1963, a crew leader named Poor Boy Slim herded forty-two workers onto his Bluebird outside Belle Glade. A truck being driven by a white man started to pass the bus; the bumpers locked, and the bus was thrown into the waters of the Hillsboro drainage canal where it sank. Twenty-seven harvesters were drowned; twelve were children, who should have been in school.

The Stream abounds in tragedies. There was the crew in Long Island that left behind an old woman too sick to travel back to Florida. When she woke up, after a half-delirious sleep, she saw snow falling. She was alone in the unheated migrant camp. Heeding some homing instinct, she got up, wrapped herself in a blanket, and stumbled through the deserted camp as the snow fell harder and colder. Finally, she reached the main street of a Long Island suburb; here she sat on the curb in the snow until she froze to death. Others have died, not of snow and cold, but of the insecticide parathion, in a pre-Rachel Carson era.

What incenses Florida fruit- and vegetable-growers is that

they have more often than not been blamed for the disgrace of the migrant economy in America. The grower must compete; he must produce; he must stay solvent. Some growers are crass profiteers, and some are sensitive, intelligent men who deplore an evil they cannot stop singlehandedly. Edward R. Murrow—a local Okeechobee author refers to him as Edgar, and then says he wasn't accurate—filmed what he saw. Sometimes the problem of communication between reporters and migrants resulted in distortions. One woman interviewed had lost seven of her fourteen children. Murrow—and America—assumed that this was because the children had had no medical attention. An irate Florida Fruit and Vegetable Association came up with figures showing that the family had received more than two thousand dollars' worth of medical care from local hospitals and doctors; what had felled the children was lack of domestic hygiene. Yet it is difficult to maintain hygiene in a shack. It is also difficult to teach it in modernized or modern camps. When Murrow was selected to head the United States Information Agency—the Voice of America—he tried, a wiser man, to prevent the documentary's sale to European television. CBS, he said, was "wholly irresponsible" in making such a sale. Former Governor LeRoy Collins also tried to stop the transaction; he had no more success than Murrow. "Harvest of Shame" was shown, and any American visitor to Britain in the autumn of 1961 heard talk of little else. In the United States, the film had been sponsored by Philip Morris. (It was several years before any Philip Morris cigarettes were available in the Lake Okeechobee country.) America had gasped; then she had done nothing, and her agriculture slipped further and further into crisis. And Florida was saddled with blame for a human trap not of her own making, since the problem cannot be solved at state level, but is a federal concern.

If there is tragedy "on the season," there is a paradoxical fascination in the Florida fruit-and-vegetable industry itself. The firm of A. Duda and Sons in Belle Glade farms eighteen thousand acres in cane, cattle, and vegetables, where once there were otters. Anyone who has ever bought a tomato in January has probably eaten Duda produce. Deseret Ranches is an aus-

terely Mormon beef-cattle operation; a large number of cowboys
are home on the range down South, within its confines. The
town of Kissimmee has hotels full of cowpunching pictures of
the genre of Frederic Remington; rodeos abound, to the irrita-
tion of humane societies. The cattle world, the fruit world, the
vegetable world are all worlds of formidable mechanization and
immense volume. A quarter of a million crates of Florida celery
went to Europe in 1967.

Agribusiness also has its own caste system among the workers. A "ladder man" working on oranges has more prestige
than a "stoop man" working on celery. And all the while, over
the lush fields whereon is enacted the drama of men, machines,
and the profit motive versus humanitarian scruple, the yellow
Florida sun shines down—or pouring grey Florida rain falls, to
create an agricultural miracle. Near-tropics have been domes-
ticated. Freezes happen, but they are rare. Conservationists rage
against man's control of water entry into the Everglades, National Park officials war with the Florida Water Users' Association, poets lament the passing of the primeval, labor unions try
to organize the farm workers into a cohesive group, and American wives and mothers fight the rising price of food. Out of the
hurricanes came the unending harvest; what may well also come
from the unending harvest is the kind of social chaos that initiated the Watts riots of the 1960s in California; or, perhaps,
what may come in place of that chaos is further apathy and economic depression. Florida's agriculture, though it is special because of its latitude, is also a mirror of America's, and sooner
or later the tortuous labyrinth of agricultural economics and artificial controls will have to be reshaped. To some Americans,
The Stream is a river of sorrow; to others, it is a river of gold.
To still others—perhaps to any grower with a conscience—it
is a river of moral dilemma. And these contradictions are too
disparate to endure forever.

14

Marshes and Moonports

"NO ship escapeth which cometh thither," wrote an Englishman named John Sparke the Younger in 1564, about Cape Canaveral.[1] It had been the Cape of the Currents to Ponce de León; other Spaniards had called it the Place of the Tall Reeds and the Plantation of Canes. To the Ais, it was a word interpreted by early whites as Canaveral. Sparke had sailed from England with Capt. John Hawkins, who had been ordered by Queen Elizabeth in the sixth year of her reign to explore the southern coast of America. Even then, Elizabeth was dreaming of challenging Spain as a world power; she cared nothing about the souls of the Indians. Hawkins had planned to put in at Cuba for food and supplies, but his fleet was blown off course and landed at Canaveral, where he and Sparke saw strong tides and treacherous shoals and felt the force of stiff winds. Clearly, it was a place no ship could ever safely navigate. Hawkins's fleet had been driven by the force of a tropical storm that built into terrifying intensity. Palm fronds lashed each other in driving rain, and the wind screamed on until finally the rain abated and the sun emerged from thick clouds to shine over a place of desolation: swamps, red mangroves, and a dense mat of reeds. Alligators and crocodiles crawled ponderously from underneath

1. Harriett Carr, *Cape Canaveral, Cape of Storms and Wild Cane Fields* (St. Petersburg, Fla.: Valkyrie Press, 1974), p. 7.

the water to bask on grassy islands. Bobcats slept in the tangles, emerging at night. Eagles circled high overhead, and also black buzzards, their wings shining ebony in the nearly-tropic light. Sparke shuddered as he wrote his report to the queen. Over Canaveral, the gulls did not screech mournfully, as they did over the cliffs of Dover. Here, they laughed a raucous cachinnation worse than silence. Canaveral was not only a wilderness; it was a wilderness full of Ais, who may have come to Florida from the Bahamas. They were backward, compared to other Florida tribes, and Sparke found them "wild and cruel. . . . The Ais build a big house like a great barne . . . The fire burneth all night to keep out the beastes." [2]

Queen Elizabeth found his report far from encouraging. Canaveral was unconquerable; its mangrove forests teemed with menace. Inland, there were the snakes—rattlers, water moccasins, and deadly coral snakes—bears and scorpions. Carolina parrakeets chattered in moss-festooned trees, and the Ais sang their raucous war songs. Both Hawkins and Sparke were devoutly thankful when their repaired fleet did manage to escape Canaveral after all, and they set forth for the haven of Huguenot colonies to the north, as yet undevastated by Pedro Menéndez de Avilés. It is an irony of history that Canaveral, the place from which Sparke thought no ship could escape, became the place from which American rockets thundered outward into space to conquer the moon, more frightening even than Canaveral ever was, because it contained not "beastes" and Ais, but starkly empty wastes.

Menéndez had known what to do with the Ais: he enslaved them. His overseers drove them with whips and threatened them with greyhounds while they were forced to cut logs for a series of forts. At the tiny outpost of Santa Lucia de Canaveral, Spanish soldiers desolately watched the wide shore full of land crabs and terns and ruddy turnstones. To comfort themselves with at least one familiar sight, they planted some orange trees, harbingers but not ancestors of the modern Indian River fruit. After the death of Menéndez, however, the soldiers deserted the fort,

2. Carr, *Cape Canaveral*, pp. 5, 8.

and their groves went wild. The pigs they had kept for pork went wild, too; their descendants remain in nearby hammocks. After Spain and the Hawkins expedition, Canaveral lay dormant. Its reputation was so bad that nobody was interested in braving the place.

But then Britain got interested once more; surely Florida could play a role in Britain's projects of world trade. During Florida's British period, the government offered land grants, yet there were few takers. The years passed on Canaveral with only the tenancy of its possums and wildcats, its panthers and bears and alligators and crocodiles and deadly snakes. The cane thickets waved like shining swords under blinding sun, and warm blue waters washed on beaches once more Spanish, where green turtles buried their eggs. Horseshoe crabs crawled undisturbed.

After the United States acquired Florida from Spain, Washington began hounding the Seminoles out of Florida. But even the Seminoles didn't want Cape Canaveral; they passed it by for a haven in the Everglades. Pirates patrolled the Florida coast in search of wrecked American trading ships, which they plundered impressively; it was baffling geography and pirates, not Indians, that caused the United States to build a lighthouse on the Cape. It was built of sturdy brick, and it stood 165 feet tall to warn ships away from Canaveral by means of a whale-oil lamp.

Several prospective American settlers came to look over Cape Canaveral in 1842, but few stayed. One who did was Capt. Mills Olcott Burnham, who had fallen in love with the Indian and Banana rivers and knew that even wild Canaveral, at the tip of the peninsula called Merritt Island, could be tamed. Burnham started a pineapple plantation and marketed Canaveral turtles in Charleston, South Carolina, to which he sailed periodically in his schooner *Josephine*. Col. Thomas Dummitt and his son Douglas began their Indian River orange groves. Little towns began to dot Merritt Island, separated from the mainland by the Indian River. Indian River citrus acquired a national reputation. The coming-to-life of Cape Canaveral was stopped abruptly by the Civil War. Confederate soldiers ordered Captain Burnham to extinguish the whale-oil lamp in the lighthouse, since it was helping Union blockaders to sight Southern ships starting at night for Nassau and Cuba and the money and medicine their cargoes of Southern cotton would bring.

When the war was over, the government put a kerosene lamp in the lighthouse; after a hurricane, the light was moved inland. Merritt Island acquired a jelly factory and guava trees. But still the country of Cape Canaveral was sparsely populated; settlers had to get their supplies from nearby Titusville by steamboat. The Cape was wilderness until World War II:

> It wasn't well known, . . . mostly only to native Floridians who lived along . . . Merritt Island, grew small orange groves, and lived a leisurely, placid life, hunting and fishing whenever they felt like it. In the marshes of the Island duck were plentiful in the winter months when they flew down in V formations from the north. In the summer months the Cape was a fishing paradise where the red bass foraged in the surf in schools and struck at anything, and where the fighting chobie lurked, ready to shatter the gear of any untutored angler who cast a line into the sea. . . . miles from anywhere, it was a drowsy world, a somnolent world of quiet sand dunes and whispering sea, of sunny days and starlit nights and lazy Sundays spent a-fishing under the warm Florida sun. That was the Cape as we knew it then, Cape Canaveral as it was listed on the charts, just a point of sand on the long, narrow spit of Merritt Island.[3]

That was how Fred H. Langworthy of the *Daytona Beach News-Journal* remembered it, when the Ais, the Spanish, the Burnhams, and the beachcombers had given way to the likes of Dr. Wernher von Braun, a frequent visitor, and Neil Armstrong, a resident astronaut and first man on the moon.

During 1939 and 1940, the United States government bought land in Florida for a naval base. World War II was ravaging Europe, and American shipping had to be protected. Cape Canaveral land was cheap; because the new base was near the Banana River it was christened the Banana River Naval Air Station. The era of biplanes and gliders had passed, and now pro-

---

3. Fred H. Langworthy, *Thunder at Cape Canaveral* (New York: Vantage Books, 1962), pp. 11–12.

peller craft reigned. During the war, the base was full of officers and men in smart navy whites, and such neighboring towns as Cocoa Beach and Titusville flourished. But when the war was over, the Banana River Naval Air Station was declared surplus and transferred to the U.S. Air Force's Air Materiel Command; it had become a "standby."

The base quickly decayed. Florida nature was too much for it. Local citizens watched, as

> old runways crumbled under the burning sun and lashing salt waves. Unsightly weeds surrounded the buildings, roofs sagged, broken windows were boarded over, tough sawgrass buckled the sidewalks. Empty hangars and deserted barracks squatted in the sun-baked, storm-swept land at the south end of 15,000 desolate acres—a place as primitive as when Ponce de León first sighted Cape Canaveral.[4]

But something had happened during World War II. Germany had fired V-1 and V-2 rockets into Britain; and, while the rockets were only the beginning of a new and intricately strange technology, their significance was understood by world science. The United States wanted to develop missiles that could be run by remote control. What the government needed was a wilderness with few human inhabitants. The Banana River Naval Air Station! There were so few people on Merritt Island itself that no cities would be in peril from missiles guided imperfectly. Cape Canaveral offered a good chance of security. Moreover, rockets could fall into the vast expanse of the Atlantic, and Merritt Island acreage was ridiculously cheap by Washington standards, if not by those of Florida. President Harry Truman, on May 11, 1949, officially signed Public Law 60 and created the Long Range Proving Ground on Canaveral. The Banana River Naval Air Station was renamed Patrick Air Force Base, in memory of a former Army Air Corps chief; America negotiated treaties with Britain, Ireland, and the South American countries for telemetric and tracking instrument installations. On a spit of land completely without paved roads, army trucks bogged down in the dunes; wooden tracks for them had to be built. Snakes

4. Carr, *Cape Canaveral*, p. 23.

and mosquitoes were everywhere; in the trailer parks mushrooming in the area, roaches had a field day, and wives moaned in the heat. But the Ph.Ds arrived, and ships full of security police came face to face with their first giant sea turtles. Once, a suspicious group of people with binoculars was sighted; who was watching operations on Cape Canaveral so carefully? The offenders turned out not to be sinister spies, but the local Audubon Society, which wanted to know what was happening to the pelicans.

People who do not believe in the adaptability of many species of wildlife gape when they visit the modern Merritt Island National Wildlife Refuge, which comprises 145,000 acres of land. Its bird and animal tenants—migratory waterfowl, raccoons and bobcats and alligators and feral pigs—have accepted rocket blast-offs with ease. (At Countdown Zero, the 'gators bellow handsomely.) Shore birds and ducks build their nests within sight of launch pads. There are even such endangered species as the bald eagle, the dusky seaside sparrow, and the peregrine falcon circling overhead. More than 195 birds were identified on one Christmas count by the Indian River Audubon Society. The alligators in the pool in front of NASA headquarters have become addicted to marshmallows, the remains of peanut-butter sandwiches, and bologna; NASA employees feed them assiduously, though not always with what an alligator ought to be eating.

The beginnings of the Space Center were slow, but Russia speeded things up when she launched Sputnik I on October 4, 1957. America was electrified. The Communists had a technology of rocketry far ahead of anything the United States had produced. Communists on the moon! Panic set in rapidly in America. It was accelerated when Sputnik II went up with a dog inside it on November 3, 1957. American comics produced a reigning joke: What is the difference between Sputnik and a hamburger? With Sputnik, you *know* there's a dog inside. Russia had participated in the International Geophysical Year with a vengeance, and the race for space was on. Congress wanted to know how the United States had fallen behind. Educators, industrialists, and newspapers demanded action. Schools of Engineering sprang up in American universities at an unprecedented rate. In the spring of 1958, the United States launched a forlorn little eight-pound Vanguard satellite which, like its predecessor the Explorer, was a feeble echo of the Russian achievement. American booster rockets didn't have the thrust Russian rockets had. Russia followed Sputnik with the *Luna* series; Luna II impacted the moon in the autumn of 1959. On April 12, 1961, Yuri Gagarin, the first cosmonaut, was launched in Vostok I. By this time, John F. Kennedy had succeeded Dwight Eisenhower as president, and Kennedy was a man of action. America must begin launching heavy space vehicles immediately. Kennedy summoned three men who, between them, had spent three quarters of a century in rocketry: Dr. Kurt H. Debus, Theodor A. Poppel, and Georg von Tiesenhausen. Later, others were added to the planning and counseling group; Albert Zeiler and Wernher von Braun were among them. "That good old American know-how has gone to work," satirist Tom Lehrer observed about the German scientists who were veterans of Hitler's Peenemund rocket station.

NASA had come into existence, and the Kennedy Space Center on Cape Canaveral started expanding at a breath-taking rate. Overnight, Cocoa Beach and Titusville became cities full of technological wizards and their neglected wives—Space Center widows who tried everything from playing bridge to drinking southern bourbon to soothe their loneliness. So scientific was the atmosphere that, when the inevitable call girls arrived, they set up a complex co-ordinate index of each lady's talents and preferences. Traffic in Cocoa Beach and Titusville was a maze, and once-quiet roads witnessed the construction of Satellite Motels with Universe bars. Project Apollo, the manned lunar expedition, was devouring men and materials even as it was bringing chaos into what had been the dreaming Indian and Banana River country. Now the bananas rustled their flopping leaves not only on riverbanks, but on patios where the conversation centered on miniaturizing, the thermal stability of fuels, and Who Was Who back in Germany, from which 120 of the top scientists had come. And the Germans charmed Florida; they were soft-spoken and polite, their work was the romance of the age, and everybody in the area of Brevard County and Cape Canaveral was prospering mightily. Professor Charles Fairbanks of the University of Florida noted that, near Canaveral, Western civilization had come to the new world—from the east, since western Indians were not supposed to have had much civilization, particularly not the Ais. Now that same Western civilization would go out from Canaveral to other worlds.

Today, the Kennedy Space Center is staggering. It is also terrifying, with its intricate towers and immense ocean vessels, called Guppies, which transport spacecraft components, its columns of white fire and its earthshaking roars when rockets are launched, its mazes of buildings and laboratories and simulated moons. By September 1968, NASA employed 26,000 administrators, engineers and technicians and also a Civil Service planning and co-ordinating group numbering thousands. Eight hundred million dollars of government money had made Cape Canaveral into the staggering miracle that nonpluses, terrifies, intrigues, and finally defeats, for the sensitive, all human attempts to measure it or what its possibilities mean. Life in other solar systems? Undiscovered intelligent races? The total destruction of humankind? Perhaps the people most comfortable with the spectacle are nonintellectual tourists fresh from Florida Mermaid shows who are placid enough, in their air-conditioned buses, to wonder mostly about the possibility of Little Green Men. That there are such simple souls touring the Kennedy Space Center is underscored by the most frequently asked question with which NASA public relations officers have to cope: How do the astronauts go to the bathroom? NASA, over the years of Project Apollo, has developed a standard, polite and very simple document called the Bathroom Letter. Its crux is: "little plastic bags."

The comic relief must be welcome. Otherwise, the vastness would surely overwhelm even the Space Center personnel. The main features of the complex are a hangar large enough to enclose Saturn V rockets, each of which is 363 feet tall; moveable launch platforms on which the rockets are assembled; the system of transporting rockets and launchers weighing 12,000,000 pounds to the firing site, more than three miles away; a service tower, also moveable, which is forty-five stories tall and in which technicians complete preparations on the launch pad; and a control center from which the preparations are observed. The doors of the Vehicle Assembly Building are taller than is St. Peter's Cathedral in Rome; in the statistic there is perhaps a symbolic significance.

All during the time that Project Apollo was under way, the Mercury and Gemini projects were also dazzling Floridians. There was no longer any question about the operations on Cape Canaveral being secret. The world was watching, and Florida watched with it. The state was bemused that such a thing had come to pass. It is even arguable that Florida's violent plunge into the Super-Twentieth Century hastened her accommodation to civil rights. There was so much to see, so much to think about regarding men on the moon, that Klan hoods and beleagured school buses didn't seem as real. The North had seen high-powered science before; Florida had not. She was ravished by the spectacle.

Diplomats, premiers, kings and queens and princes and assorted commissars came and went. Sometimes, especially with representatives from communist countries, the results were richly comic. When two Russian scientists arrived in Tallahassee for a conference at Florida State University, they were duly entertained by a faculty member. The faculty member had a teenage son who gave the men a long look and then told them, "Gosh! You're the first real Russians I've ever seen!" The scientists loved it. They were not even fazed when the same bright lad asked them: "Hey—how come you guys always say one thing in the U.N. and do another?" When they returned to Russia, they sent him a raft of cosmonaut souvenirs and literature, and they signed it "From your first real Russians." [5]

Florida mourned the death of astronaut Virgil Grissom and his colleagues in the January 1967 ground fire aboard Apollo I as a personal loss. And on July 20, 1969, it would have been safe to say that every Floridian with access to any television set anywhere was watching the impossible triumph of Neil

5. The author was present.

Armstrong on the moon. If the world's eyes were on Armstrong, they were also on Brevard County, Florida. From a poverty-racked state of bitter whites and desperate Reconstruction blacks, the Land of Flowers had achieved the glamour of knowledge incarnate. Her complex of technological industries was vast; her citizens were earning more money than they ever had before. And if Florida had learned things, so had the astronauts. One day, Gordon Cooper went fishing on Merritt Island and waded happily in his shorts in a little lake. When he came back, he told a friend, "Those are the biggest dang bullfrogs I ever heard." "Were you wading around in there?" the friend asked. "Yeh, up to about my waist." The friend said softly: "Those weren't bullfrogs, Gordon. Those were alligators." Dr. Wernher von Braun learned about the Southern Bible Belt when a woman wrote him that he had no business sending people into space: "We should all stay home and watch TV like the good Lord intended." [6]

Florida's honeymoon with space did not and could not last forever, of course. The cost of Vietnam diverted money from space research. Space Center personnel were laid off. Engineers lost jobs, public school enrollment dropped off, and Brevard County learned it would have to do without some of the luxuries for which it had acquired a taste: caviar, artichokes, and handmade shoes. Eventually, $150 million of federal money were poured into Brevard to help it readjust and diversify. The government insured housing mortgages, made educational loans, and assisted in the construction of hospitals and harbor facilities. Briefly, in 1971, the situation improved. Retirees were coming in, and so were small industries. Then came Watergate and a recession, which, in most of Florida, has been a depression; Cape Canaveral, Merritt Island, the Indian and Banana River shores, and Brevard County as a whole have yet to recover, though the area looks glossy enough to the uninitiated. It is hard to think of a man as suffering when he is living in a

6. John F. Kennedy Space Center, *Kennedy Space Center Story* (Cape Canaveral, Fla.: Kennedy Space Center, National Aeronautics and Space Administration, n.d.), pp. 209, 210.

house on a waterway and maintains a boat. But the apparently prosperous suffer differently from the downright poor; they suffer in debts and hidden economies and marital quarreling over checkbooks and the costs of psychiatric therapy and the relentless demands of children made tyrants by erstwhile abundance, as wives have been made tyrants, too. The children want portable television sets, and the wives cannot imagine life without a garbage disposal unit in the kitchen, even if electricity costs have soared. Why can't America get interested in space again as she was after Sputnik? She is, naturally, more than interested; she is committed. But journeys to Mars have been delayed by journeys to Saigon and to American ghettos.

On Canaveral, however, the towers still flash in the sun, the white buildings gleam, the computers run their magnetic tapes in eternal revolutions, and NASA dreams big dreams. There are rocks from the moon to analyze, now; Floridians have become space-geology buffs. They have been catapulted into the future. They will never be the same.

15

How to Spend Your Golden Years Enjoying Fun and Relaxation in South Beach

I F Florida is the Great American Escape, it is also something else less enticing: the Great American Dumping Ground. It is where Mom and Pop go to die, while Son and Daughter mingle socially with their own contemporaries but rarely with those of parents. In many cases, Mom and Pop are fairly well-heeled, in which case they become Mother and Father. They come for sunlight, patios, fishing, and dignified residence in expensive houses along the palm-fringed shores of such places as Naples, on the west coast, and Vero Beach, on the east. Mother and Father do not join clubs with names like The Funsters and The Gayeteys; they are to be found on the Symphony Board and in the local Friends of the Library. Mother and Father are realists, usually. They know they are going to die, and they keep a well-bred stiff upper lip about it. In this, they differ enormously from Mom and Pop, for Mom and Pop not only do not mention death (retirement is the New Life), they spend an impressive amount of time denying that their old age will have infirmities.

The literature of Florida retirement—those Golden Years in the Sunshine State—is vast. Some of it is unbelievably inept; for, some of the time, a Mom or a Pop with nothing but good will sits down at the typewriter and later cherishes his or her opus enough to pay to have it published. (The Vantage and Exposition presses, of New York, print many such manuscripts.) Most have the unmistakable sound of whistling in the dark. Some purport to be novels:

> "Herman," asked Edith, "have you been happy today and pleased with the things you have done?" "Yes," replied Herman, "I have enjoyed every minute. I have been comfortably busy with many little things I have found to do around the house, the yard and garage, and there are still countless things I want to do. . . . There is no danger of idleness. I do not know how to be idle." [1]

In a later passage of this work—the title is *You Can Live Longer in Florida* (you certainly can, but not necessarily will)—Herman wants Edith to go to the library to check "Florida Health Publicity" facts and figures. Naturally, she assents with delight. Both Herman and Edith are avid readers, as well as researchers; their favorite book is *Floridays,* by Don Blanding, a self-styled "Vagabond Poet." Blanding's illustrated hymns to the Sunshine State were commercially published:

> A book of sounds and scents and sights,
> Of Flori-days and Flori-nights,
> Flori-stars and Flori-moons
> And Flori-suns of Flori-noons.
> Flori-fragrance on the breeze
> And blended blues of Flori-seas.
> Patterns drawn with pen and words
> Of Flori-folks and Flori-birds.
> An hour of friendly chit-and-chat
> Of Flori-this and Flori-that
> With pictures when you care to look.
> I hope you like this Flori-book. [2]

Mom and Pop loved it.

There are many retirement travelogues. In one, *Skippy Rides through Florida,* the author is ostensibly a Boston bull terrier, his mistress his amanuensis: "I have not met any more nice girl

1. William H. Bates, *You Can Live Longer in Florida* (New York: Exposition Press, 1950), p. 14.

2. Don Blanding, *Floridays* (New York: Dodd Mead, 1946), p. 9.

Bostons; maybe I shall before the trip is over. The drive to Tallahassee is beautiful over Route 90. . . ." [3] Some of the literature has more than one illusion; not only is man immortal in the Land of Flowers, but Floridians are perfect. One vanity-press author reported, in 1957, when no black could get a drink of water in any white public establishment:

> In a broad sense, there certainly is no discrimination against the colored people in the south, even though segregation practices may infer otherwise. After living in Florida for many years, one begins to understand the reasons and justice of the white people's handling of the problem. They do not antagonize the Negro nor hold any malice toward him. In fact, the people of Florida and, I am sure, the entire South, treat the Negro extremely well. [4]

There is only one fly in the ointment: "When we first came to Florida, the Negro was more conscious of his proper place in Southern society than he now seems to be." [5] The day was soon to come when Rosa Parks, of Montgomery, Alabama, refused to move to the back of the bus.

Up-to-date commercially published retirement guides are few; Norman Ford, of *Norman Ford's Florida,* is probably the reigning king of the genre. A once-excellent guide, *How to Retire to Florida,* by George and Jane Dusenbury, has been hopelessly outdated; it appeared in 1947, not without its own impressive tales from former invalids: "I came to Florida with a 20-year arthritic condition. Now I no longer need crutches and can care for my place. I am now taking dancing lessons." [6] Not that such testimonials are not genuine; arthritis *may* abate, and high morale may well send oldsters to Arthur Murray. They may indeed enjoy the time they spend in the Prudential Insurance Retirees Club of St. Petersburg, and may even agree with the American Association of Retired Persons that they are not Sen-

3. A. P. Wilks, *Skippy Rides through Florida: as Told to Lady Peg Wilks* (New York: Vantage Books, 1959), p. 109.

4. Max E. Bulske, *Florida Isn't Heaven!* (New York: Vantage Books, 1957), pp. 86–87.

5. Bulske, *Heaven,* p. 87.

6. George Dusenbury and Jane Dusenbury, *How to Retire to Florida* (New York: Harper and Brothers, 1947), p. 64.

ior but Mature Citizens. Some of them, according to veteran Florida retirement columnist Burt Garnett, can be feisty "nymphs and satyrs . . . there are 'goings-on' at some hotels and retirement villages." [7]

The one feature of retirement in Florida that few people in the state or out of it mention is that it is segregation as blatant as any racial segregation. It may, too, be filled with the deep but unspoken knowledge that one's children back home are glad to be rid of a parental burden, and it can be anything from a time of final fulfillment in a land of verdant beauty to a horror story in an old-age ghetto like Miami's South Beach. Floridian Donn Pearce, author of *Cool Hand Luke,* ex-convict turned Academy Award winner, has had the courage to look at the Golden Years in Florida squarely and without evasion. His book about them, *Dying in the Sun,* was not a bestseller, for it is not a pleasant book. It is even terrifying. But it should be read by every American who has parents in Florida. Jessica Mitford concentrated on financial cost in *The American Way of Death;* Pearce concentrates on the more awful cost in human dignity and even sanity when segregation of the old is a way of life. It is Pearce who writes of the commonplace Miami dying-style of the Café Coronary (choking on a piece of meat), of St. Petersburg youngsters who make bets among themselves on how many seizures they will witness in a given time period, of the junk-auctions where gullible elderly are persuaded they are buying Waterford and Meissen when they are buying dime-store excess, of one-legged old women with brave blue ringlets and palsied old men in gold caps and palm-tree shirts, of bridge fishermen trying to catch a free main course for the dinner there is not enough pension to buy, of days-dead bodies found in locked apartments when neighbors complain of the smell, and, most especially, of the South Beach Rescue Squad, whose reports are a litany of senility:

> "Subject complained of being nauseated. Age eighty." "Subject was sleeping. Roommate said she complained of colon trouble. Age

---

7. Burt Garnett, *How to Retire in Florida and Trade Old Lives for New* (St. Petersburg, Fla.: Great Outdoors Publishing Co., 1966), p. 114.

ninety-three.'' ''Subject was lying on floor. Small cut on foot from broken glass tabletop. Belts tied together. Apparent suicide attempt. Moaning and screaming. Had apparently slipped out of noose. Age seventy-four.'' ''Blood pressure 210/100. Abdominal pain. Age eighty-one.'' ''Subject complained of pain in her chest. Age seventy-eight.'' ''Subject took sleeping pill and didn't know it. Couldn't stay awake. Had thimble still on her finger as sleeping.'' [8]

During the peak winter season in South Beach, the Rescue Squad has an average of thirty emergencies a day; during 1971, the crises totaled 10,373—this in a small corner of Miami Beach, within sight of Key Biscayne. South Beach is also called, by the initiated, Varicose Beach. In Dade County there are nearly 200,000 people over sixty-five. In South Beach, the special feature of the aged is that they are almost invariably Old-Country Jewish. Men wear skullcaps, *yarmulkes;* women remember Ellis Island and Delancey Street. My Son the Doctor and My Son the Lawyer have made it, in the North; they attend symphony balls in their spare time; and, when they entertain in carpeted homes, who wants an old man in a *yarmulke* around, his broken English laced with Yiddish and Polish and God knows what else?

The Jews in Florida are anything but homogeneous, considered as a whole. In north Florida, they are socially powerful old families, southern for generations. A pioneer chronicler of the Second Seminole War was Myer Cohen; David Levy Yulee was Florida's first U.S. senator. One of her present U.S. senators is a Jew from a part of Miami light-years away from South Beach. There are legions of Florida Jews with social and political clout; they intermarry freely with gentiles; harried rabbis moan about maintaining Jewish identity. (Tallahassee has Jews allied with Icelanders; children whose names end in *-sky* read sagas about Grettir the Strong.) Central and south Florida Jews who are not recent immigrants are usually not of Confederate stock; what they are is seasoned avid patrons of the arts and citizens who not only participate fully in community life but actively, in many cases, lead it. Compared to South Beach, all this is an-

---

8. Donn Pearce, *Dying in the Sun* (New York: Charterhouse Books, 1974), p. 68.

other plane of existence. In South Beach, Fanny Reichgott makes her living writing letters in English for clients who want to write My Son the Doctor in Bridgeport, Connecticut, in a language he can understand. And he certainly does not know how it was "under the Czar."

To see South Beach is to be forever haunted. Old men shuffle along in sneakers, baggy pants, open cotton shirts wet with sweat. There are wheel chairs and paralytics, shabby canasta players in tiny parks, down-at-heels 'thirties hotels converted into rooming houses, small synagogues with chipped bricks. Window signs are trilingual: Spanish, Yiddish, and English. The women fight their decay with purple wigs, sequinned chiffon scarves from the dime store, heavy rouge, and harlequin glasses with sparkle-frames. But their feet are encased in solidly ugly oxfords when they are not in sandals. South Beach has its evening promenade: when rich shoppers have left the Lincoln Road Mall, on the edge of Miami Beach to the north, the ambulatory old come to see the palms and the dazzling store windows, to sigh over portly mannequins in the Lane Bryant window, to stare at hobby-shop collections of coins, to see the lush tropical plantings in front of glossy banks. But Lincoln Road belongs to the old only for a brief hour or two; by the next morning, it bustles once more with tourists and with Miami Beach matrons. Nearly all the salespeople are Cubans.

The contrast between South Beach, where Miami Beach started, and Miami Beach itself is almost obscene. Miami Beach is the Fontainebleau and the Montmartre. It is Miss Universe contests and Polynesian sword dancers in dark night clubs where diamonds glitter—too many of them, of course. Miami Beach has never been known for restraint. It is possible to see gold female mouths there, and also the longest false eyelashes on record, affixed with globs of glue blackened by heavy doses of eyeliner. Miami Beach has, some say, the Mafia. But there is no Mafia in South Beach, where the entertainment is apt to be municipally sponsored Disney nature films or else that eternal Florida staple, shuffleboard. The South Beach old who are not walking around are condemned to plastic living rooms and perpetual Archie Bunker, Rhoda, and "As the World Turns."

Some of the invalids do not take in what they are seeing, but the noise comforts them. Strokes, heart attacks, cancer—all take a staggering toll. Ambulances come and go. There are suicides by gas, suicides by rope.

And yet the question arises: Is it South Beach only, or is this what all America does to its aged? On the Anglo-Saxon frontier, the aged were kept alive by heavy jobs: milking cows, hauling lumber, gathering hay. South Beach, like migrant camps, has no inheritance of American Gothic. It is exemplified in Yetta R., aged ninety, her sight failing and her dentures badly fitted. Her childhood was passed in Romanov Russia, in fear of pogroms and persecution. Then came the Lower East Side of New York, marriage to a tailor, children who left Delancey Street, grandchildren who left the city for the suburbs. And now Yetta has great-grandchildren (whom she never sees) who are *goyim* because there have been mixed marriages. The great-grandchildren call themselves Unitarians, and they drive Mercedes-Benzes, and one of them has a doctorate from the University of Iowa. It is hard for Yetta to assimilate these facts. All she knows is that, whereas she began life in a world of pogroms and matchmakers, she is ending it alone (except for the care of a Cuban doctor) among palm trees and rubber Mickey Mice.

Such stories are not, obviously, the whole picture. There are plenty of retirement communities in Florida where the old enjoy their gardens, form clubs, go on junkets to Cypress Gardens or Marineland or St. Petersburg Beach's Aquatarium, and stage neighborhood cookouts. The women wear white slacks and pseudo-Pucci tunic tops, and their men are in seersucker and khaki. They dance, they bowl, often they live together without marriage so that separate social security benefits won't be lost. On St. Petersburg's green benches, they flirt; they go to church, they fish, and they walk in a dream of loveliness along Gulf Coast beaches. They feed pelicans, collect shells, take courses in decoupage, and adore bingo. Undoubtedly they are better off than if they lived with children in the North, for there they would be supernumeraries, and in Florida they are a market, however modest. The New Life is actually that—now. But a lot of that New Life depends on owning a car, and here the statistics are disheartening. Florida's public transportation is almost a joke. And as of March 1971, 48 percent of all individuals aged sixty-five years and over and 61 percent of all individuals seventy-five years old and over were not licensed to drive. Recent stringent vision and hearing tests have reduced the number of older drivers still further. Of state agencies trying to serve the elderly, 86 percent indicated their clients were isolated by poor transportation. For an oldster to get from Tampa to Clearwater can take the best part of a day. He cannot shop in quantity at the supermarket and take advantage of the special sales he needs. His best friend in St. Petersburg is Doc Webb, who runs "The World's Most Unusual Drug Store." That it is, since it possesses costumed moon-maids, chickens that perform on a high wire, and sometimes Doc himself in a parking lot vaudeville act. Webb's City is vast, block after block of it, and it features blood-pressure machines. But not many store owners have the genuine love for the elderly that Doc Webb incontestably has.

Nearly 30 percent of the people in the following Florida counties are over sixty-five: Pinellas (with St. Petersburg), Sarasota, Manatee (with Bradenton), and Pasco, with its mushroom tract houses near New Port Richey. In Dade County, with Miami, the percentage is about fourteen, the same as for all of Florida. The number of Floridians over seventy-five is climbing steadily. And when people over seventy-five cannot shop, cannot visit their friends in another part of the city, cannot go to church, and, in short, cannot belong to the human race, senility is inevitable. There are no outside stimuli. Buses and private charities have not, as yet, met the problem. And thus it is that Florida has earned the sobriquet "God's Waiting Room." On the whole, however, waiting in the sun seems to most of the Florida retired to be better than waiting in the snow. And to a large extent, a retirement must psychologically be what one makes of it: heaven or hell, according to spiritual and intellectual resources. But on nothing except social security, retirement in Florida, as elsewhere, is humiliation utter and complete.

16

When You Wish
upon a Mouse

*T*HERE is one Mature Citizen in Florida who obviously
has neither pension nor transportation problems—yet—since he
has visited Walt Disney World 207 times since 1971, even
though the Magic Kingdom is an eighty-four-mile round trip
from his home in Lakeland. He is, perhaps, the very incarnation
of the Kingdom's attraction for Americans in search of play and
solace in a complicated era. It is much more comforting to think
about Mickey, the redoubtable rodent, than about political scandals and espionage intrigues that would have curled the hair of
the Founding Fathers and *are* curling the hair of most of the
contemporary uninitiated.

Millard Jones is eighty-three, and he is remarkable among the
thirty-three million tourists who have made pilgrimages to the
land of the monorail, the Tiki Room, and parking lots named
Minnie and Pluto and Goofy. When Jones's wife died in 1971,
he decided to visit Disney World because he was lonely. The
visits became a habit; Disney World turned into home, a place
where something was always happening and where new friends
were to be made. Mickey's empire reciprocated, with a plaque
appointing Jones a "Citizen of Disney World" and a pass as a
"Very Special Visitor," to be used without limit. Jones takes
repeated pictures and presents them to the management; he pays

pretty compliments to the scrubbed young girls acting as tour guides. They, and the rest of the staff, love him. For Millard Jones the ultimate American fantasy has turned into a reality that sustains.

The Magic Kingdom has transformed central Florida in general and the city of Orlando in particular into a teeming maze of tourism, high-rise hotels, exorbitant prices, and a nightmare of billboards. Florida wanted Disney World badly, and so did America, each for different reasons. Mickey Mouse fills Florida pockets; he makes Americans laugh, and he also reinforces a national proclivity for believing that the United States is the best of all possible worlds. Critics of Disney World have poured out tons of acerbic ink deriding what they judge as phony wholesomeness, synthetic joy. It is true that the Magic Kingdom abounds in the type of non-art called kitsch. Plastic hippopotami surface in a streamlet whose waters reflect plastic flowers. A plastic Abe Lincoln moves and talks on regular schedule, while a complete assemblage of plastic United States presidents listen and murmur. Plastic shrunken heads delight patrons of the Jungle Cruise, and so do plastic crocodiles. The plastic ghosts in the Haunted Mansion are transparent. The aural background of all this plasticity is everything from genuine Dixieland jazz to ear-shattering, high-decibel rock. Mission Control Center simulates a moonshot; the patrons' chairs shake with rocket power during lift-off, and space itself has been populated with plastic stations and buses. Tourists gaze raptly at televised close-ups of the lunar surface. "Emergency!" cries a sudden voice. "We have entered a meteorite shower area!" But never fear, the reigning astronaut can cope. During re-entry, everybody shakes again. Then, perhaps, it is time for a hamburger; crowds wait happily for the better part of an hour to be fed. Lines are staggering. On some days, the Magic Kingdom must close early; it has slowed traffic on Interstate 4 to a crawl. Even a bag of popcorn means a standstill line and at least twenty minutes.

Monsanto's America the Beautiful exhibit offers a cross-country journey that takes in everything from Mount Rushmore to the crookedest street in San Francisco. Cinderella's Castle towers into the blue Florida sky, while plastic parrots sing tropical serenades. For those weary of the exotic, there is a Main Street that is hardly a re-creation; it is, instead, a dream—America's dream of what it once was, clean and shiny and totally without beggars or ghettos. If Disney World in general makes cynics of some of its beholders, the Country Bear Jamboree is pure Disney charm. You don't mind those robot bears, because they play bass fiddle, mouth harp, violin, banjo, and a bottle (into which the bogus ursine performer blows). Liver-Lips McGrowl sings "Blood on the Saddle," and Trixie, a monstrous lady bear in a pink tutu, descends on a swing to enthrall; country-and-western music, bear-style, is Disney World's affectionate joke on Nashville—"Music City, USA." How enchanting to hear Tex Ritter's soulful voice emanating from something that looks like Smokey!

The Magic Kingdom has its hits and its misses. The Contemporary Resort Hotel is so vast that it has been christened the Grand Canyon. And the whole realm is a huge American Saturday-afternoon-and-Saturday-night epitome. Fireworks blaze up into the humid Florida evenings. Donald Duck complains his way into children's hearts, and their parents are not untouched. In local motels, it is not surprising to encounter waiters who can play Donald or Goofy or José Carioca; many moonlight at the Magic Kingdom. Is it all a catastrophe? A triumph? Pundits in general have opted for the former verdict and Disney publicists for the latter. Probably the truth is somewhere in between.

From the kitsch and the overcrowding, one thing emerges clearly: America's capacity for simple joy, which for the two centuries of her existence has been one of her greatest strengths. Who is to say that Millard Jones, veteran of 207 visits, ought to be writing a treatise on Rembrandt or composing symphonies instead of easing his last solitary years with monorail rides and strolls past the tri-cornered hat shop in Liberty Square? Asian, Persian, and Venetian resort hotels are coming, says the Disney World management, for America wants fantasies of other parts of the world beside her own. Disney World, the escape, chose wisely when it chose Florida. The Magic Kingdom, like Florida itself, is a national emotional safety valve: it makes back-home routine newly bearable, it cuts the Kennedy Space Center down to manageable size, and it insulates, however briefly, from global woes. Disney World tourists do not see migrant workers; they do not see death in South Beach. But many of them are leading quietly heroic lives as breadwinners and housewives tied to monotony, and perhaps they deserve to be delivered from pain while they mill in Adventureland, Fantasyland, and Tomorrowland to the accompaniment of brass bands and never-never Gay Nineties steam trains that toot and puff.

Without question, Walt Disney World is the most gothic of the gothic assemblage the Florida Chamber of Commerce calls Florida Attractions. There are car museums and circus concessions, western towns and Spanish jails, wax museums and eternally affable jumping porpoises, a stunning variety of aquariums, Seminoles who have learned to amuse the public by wrestling alligators, re-created African plains full of lions and giraffes, parrot jungles and monkey jungles and orchid jungles and brilliant tropical gardens heavy with strange perfumes. (One of these, in Sarasota, has posted a patron's testimonial: "I don't think Heaven can be any more Beautiful!" Next to this encomium, a sign announces, "Trained police dogs patrol these grounds by night.") And the phenomenon about it all is that natural Florida herself has miracles to be seen that dwarf anything man has created within her boundaries. Elysian Florida has pinewoods and bogs in the north, dazzling with spiderwebs in morning dew; she has blue lakes and dreaming cypresses just beyond the Magic Kingdom's doors; and most especially she has the Everglades, the great River of Grass, where pale white herons feed among lily pads and oncidium orchids bloom huge in the tops of hammock trees while giant wood storks fly overhead in soft rushes, their black-tipped wings gleaming in gold sunlight. There are no billboards in the Everglades.

There is Women's Liberation, however. The current chief of the Seminoles is Betty Mae Jumper. They are still a silent people, the Seminoles; in the old, hatred of the white man goes deep. Seminoles still have their medicine men, their Green Corn ceremonies, their sacred visions. Especially are they untouched by what is happening in Miami, where 350,000 Cubans have come to live since Fidel Castro marched out of the mountains of Oriente province.

Miami is bilingual (South Beach, with its Yiddish, is trilin-

gual). The Cubans are everywhere. "We are changing from
exiles to immigrants," says Marino Lopez Blanco, a lawyer
who has been in Miami for six years. "The hope of returning—
much as I hate to admit it—is growing dimmer and dimmer and
dimmer." [1] By day, he works in a drug rehabilitation center; at
night, he is studying American law to prepare himself for the
Florida bar examination.

There are racial tensions in Miami. There are also warm cafés
serving thick black coffee and yellow rice and garbanzo beans
and turnip-green soup. Plaintive Latin songs drift into summer
darkness, and on the sidewalks, old men play street games of
dominoes. It is the third wave of Cubans in Florida history; the
first came in the wake of the conquistadores, to establish fishing
ranchos; the second arrived with Vicente Martinez Ybor; and
the most recent are those whose lots had been cast, in Havana,
with Fulgencio Batista. Suburban Hialeah is 55 percent Cuban,
and inner-city Miami is 51 percent. There are Cubans in service
occupations, and there are also Cuban bank presidents. *"No
fumar,"* read the no-smoking signs on Miami buses. Cubans are
pouring into the already crowded Florida Keys, one of many
current conservation battlegrounds in the state. When they reach
Key West, they will find other Cubans waiting, many of them
descendants of cigar workers located in Key West before the industry moved to Tampa.

Florida's ethnic hodgepodge is mind-boggling. In Tarpon
Springs, the music is Greek *bouzouki,* hawkers shout in front of
bazaars on Dodecanese Boulevard, the dome of a Greek Orthodox cathedral gleams in the sun, and on Epiphany young boys
dive into a lagoon for a sacred cross, usually in the presence of
Greek archbishops. The Greeks came to Tarpon Springs to harvest Gulf sponges, and today they run businesses and seafood
houses and gift shops as well. They have built a museum dedicated to their past, and in any drugstore it is possible to buy the
works of Aristotle and Plato. Tarpon Springs is rich with the
smell of Greek pastry and *avgolemono* and *feta* cheese, and
brightly trimmed sponge boats rock at anchor in the Anclote
River.

1. *Tallahasee Democrat,* March 30, 1975.

In the Hernando County settlement of Masaryktown, south of Brooksville, Czechs dance the *beseda*. The heart of Masaryk-town is the Masaryktown Hotel, which hasn't rented a bed in years but is famous for its roast duck and dumplings and sauer-kraut. Twice a week in Masaryktown, the women stage a com-munal strudel-bake, pounding the dough into paper thinness. Masaryktown began when homesick Czech immigrants in the crowded northeastern states came to Florida to try growing oranges in an effort to recapture the pastoral life they had known in the Old Country. The land proved to be too low for successful citrus culture, so the Czechs turned to chickens. Mas-aryktown now holds a Guinness World Record for chicken-plucking speed. Older residents complain that the trouble with the place is that one forgets one's English; at the Kovarcik Motel, Beneviches and Hrubas and Slaviks and Stastnys eat goulash, and many exercise at a Czech gymnastics club. When Masaryktown dances, it is in bright beads and embroidery and exquisite lace and stiffly starched caps, the assembled costume called the *kroje,* which was brought to Florida fifty years ago and has been carefully preserved. Masaryktown is changing, of course; its young don't want to learn Czech, and they often know more about baseball than about the ancient *beseda*. There are even Italians and Irish, now. Masaryktown has been touched by Florida in other ways; at the annual Super Pluck, a man ap-pears in a red rooster suit—Evel Kchicken, who sails over a small lake in a pedal-powered "sky cycle" with flopping ply-wood wings. But Evel Kchicken isn't a Czech any more; his name is Tony Pepenella.

Cubans, blacks, Czechs, Greeks, Florida crackers, retired Scandinavian-Americans from the Midwest who have come to St. Petersburg for the sun, French counts (in Tallahassee) and German rocket engineers, Dutch nurserymen and old-guard Confederates and Southern belles who parade beneath the mag-nolias of commercial gardens in hoopskirts; Icelanders and or-thodox Jews and Reform Jews, Jews whose Florida ancestry dates back to before the Seminole wars and Jews who have recently arrived from the Bronx; cowboys and Indians; Hindus who teach transcendental meditation classes in the cities, saf-fron-robed *hare krishnas* and followers of Guru Maharaj-ji and

Sun Moon the Korean Prophet and Hardshell Baptists—Florida
has them all and more. In 1940, Florida ranked twenty-seventh
among the states in terms of population; she had fewer than two
million souls. By 1970, the state was ninth, with nearly seven
million. Until the Recession of 1974–1975, some communities
were growing at a pace of 10 percent per year. Most of the new
residents were northerners; this in turn made Florida still more
different from her southeastern neighbors. Yankee-style shopping malls now dot the land. Ethnic foods are a commonplace.
So is expanded involvement in Congress; fifteen Floridians sit in
the House of Representatives. Even the Vietnam disaster has
left its mark on the state.

On the morning of May 4, 1975, when Panhandle beaches
glared whitely beyond their rosemary dunes, the first 254 Vietnamese refugees arrived at Eglin Air Force Base. They came to
a tent city, a massive feeding operation, a north Florida appre-
hensive that, in a recession, they would be taking jobs away
from Floridians, and clergy neither Buddhist nor Catholic like
most of themselves but Methodist and Presbyterian and Assembly of God and Church of Christ and Baptist. In Tallahassee,
children sat down to Sunday-school desks to letter huge flash
cards that would be used in the teaching of English: HOW DO
YOU DO? I AM WELL, THANK YOU. AND YOU? Fundamentalists
worried about the possible building of mini-shrines to Buddha
on U.S. government soil. Mrs. Mai Garner of Tallahassee,
Vietnamese herself, began a heroic shuttling operation between
the state capital and Eglin to act as a voluntary interpreter. In
June, the refugee population at Eglin reached 5,997. By July 1,
160 Vietnamese were already in Tallahassee finding jobs as bus
boys, maids, and maintenance men; the new chef at Pasquale's
Pizza Parlor hailed not from Italy but from Saigon. Many did
not find jobs, but persisted with English and the effort toward
employment. Those who had worked with Americans in Vietnam had the advantage; for others, the climb into Florida's full
sunshine will be long. Yet they will inevitably feel a fellowship
with every American who came in flight, or whose ancestors
came in flight. What unites the diverse groups in Florida—and
will eventually unite the Vietnamese with such groups—is the
weather and the tourists.

At the annual Florida Folk Festival in White Springs, on the banks of the Suwannee, English Morris dancers mingle with long-gowned Seminoles and with backwoodsmen who play bass fiddles made from washtubs. Over the festival, a Florida institution presides: "Cousin Thelma" Boltin, of the Stephen Foster Memorial in White Springs. Her costume is a long-skirted gown and a pioneer sunbonnet. You don't see many sunbonnets any more in the country fields, but they have become a hot item among the casual young.

The accusation most often leveled at Florida is that of being synthetic, an apogee of bad taste. The architecture of Miami Beach, the billboards, and the real estate seem to bear this out. When young writer Alex Shoumatoff came down from the North to explore, a developer "looked me dead in the eye and said, 'We figure you can get 25,000 homes in here without destroying the natural character of the place.'" [2] Shoumatoff watched strippers perform in Miami for an audience of retirees; he interviewed north Florida fundamentalists, and he slept in a migrant flophouse and drank Thunderbird wine with Florida bums; he rode airboats and explored nursing homes where the senile babbled at him vacantly; he checked out the Magic Kingdom, and he sorrowed for the polluted rivers he saw. (He did not see the sparkling Wakulla, which empties into the Gulf below Tallahassee, or the Chipola, in northwest Florida, where old-timers say there are still ivory-billed woodpeckers high in the virgin forest.) Florida has been devastated by man; much of the devastation was inevitable because Florida in nature could not be lived in except by Indians inured to it. Heat and mosquitoes and tropical diseases killed even Indians. The kitsch that white men brought is something else, again; yet is it uniquely Floridian? Does it not exist in Chicago and in Connecticut? Was there not a Disneyland before there was a Disney World? Florida has learned that, when you wish upon a mouse, you get many of the things your heart desires—jobs, for instance—and plenty it doesn't: traffic jams, inflated hotel rates, and pickpockets. But it is too late to turn back to the primeval. What can

2. Alex Shoumatoff, *Florida Ramble* (New York and Evanston: Harper and Row, 1974), p. 4.

be turned to is a major conservation effort unfettered by ecology amateurs who mean well but do not always know what they are talking about. Poets cannot, by themselves, save Tampa Bay.

Alex Shoumatoff was deeply disturbed by Florida. One morning as he lay in his motel room in Coral Gables, he

> gradually realized it was time for me to split. It was time to clear out of this hot-dog circus world, so exotic in some ways and so contemptibly familiar in others. Sixty-two days on the road was plenty, and I was beginning to wake up in the morning with cold shudders. I missed my dog. I missed winter, stone walls, and a sense of the past. I know a woods near my hometown where you can sit at dusk and listen to the liquid fluting of wood thrushes, watch fireflies light up, and smell wild azaleas at the same time.[3]

He saw a lot of Florida, and he writes of it with engaging perception. He saw—and often he did not see. For highway Florida is not Florida. Mickey is not Florida. The tourists are not Florida. Florida is her permanent inhabitants, whose ancestors hailed from every corner of the globe. Some of those ancestors, the red ones, came from Siberia in pursuit of wild game. Black ancestors came as slaves. White ancestors came in pursuit of prosperity. Vietnamese came as pawns in a bitterly useless war, trying to rebuild shattered lives.

To be Floridian, you need not have lived long in Florida. But you must know its seasons and its wild places, the white little town squares beyond the superhighways, the clear-windowed Baptist churches in the pinewoods and the bougainvilleas in Hobe Sound gardens and the palms in Jacksonville's Hemming Park, where the sparrows chatter at night. You must have drunk thick Cuban coffee, listened to the music of visiting Polish composers in Tallahassee, and seen broad Ocala lawns where solid citizens in Bermuda shorts are mowing the grass. You must have smelled tea olives and jasmine and night cestrums. (And you can smell wild azaleas all over north Florida, though there are no stone walls there, and the resident singers are mockingbirds instead of thrushes.) South Florida has less sense of the past because it has less nonwilderness past; in north Florida, the

---

3. Shoumatoff, *Ramble*, pp. 175–176.

sense of the past is everywhere—in Tallahassee, for instance, where Civil War trenches remain open in a city park.

I would like to have asked Alex Shoumatoff into my own garden, with its banana trees and twittering purple martins (in summer), its nesting mockingbirds and cardinals and jays and woodpeckers and yellow-shafted flickers and small bluebirds that come and go. All winter, the camellias bloom rose and white; in spring, Indian azaleas turn into blankets of magenta. Because there is so little cold, tropical plants grow in our mimosa tree for most of the year. Fireflies glimmer in the southern night, and the air is heavy with pine resin. At dawn, you can hear the mourning doves; then the sun comes up to shine on wisterias and dogwoods and firethorns, and in the empty field behind the house, bobwhites call. Next to that empty field, there is a high-rise apartment complex where once there was nothing; but the quail have stayed, and in Florida privacy is a matter of quick-growing pines and freshly transplanted palms. Florida, like America, is inescapably full of people; but Florida cities have the special magic of their latitude.

"Florida," announces Alex Shoumatoff's publisher on the book jacket, "is the most complex and the most excitingly improbable of the United States." Perhaps—though for complexity, California is no piker. Improbable? As improbable as the lack of snow, the nearly eternal sun, and the presence of pilgrims who have come in search of various Utopias. The thought of Florida, for much of the rest of America, is heaven; and since human beings need to believe in heaven, America will always need Florida in a way that is different from her need of most other states. Arizona is hot, but has no ocean; Hawaii is far; California is industrialized. The United States dreams its dreams of paradise against a backdrop of sea and palms and pines. Some of the dreams are impossibly garish; some are announced by billboards—illegal since Lady Bird Johnson's highway law was passed, but triumphantly intact; some are utterly unreal because they seek to deny such realities as pain and death; some are vintage lower-middle-class mistakes: real estate saleswomen in outdated boots and hotpants, postcards with outhouse humor, plaster flamingoes for the front yard. Wild Marco Island, near

Naples, is gone. Once it was mangroves and buttonwoods and dark water and shade; now it is the Mackle Brothers and golf courses and ranch houses framed by the ritual multicolored croton bushes that abound in south Florida. One dream has passed; another has replaced it. Each must judge for himself the value of dreams he sees—those belonging to others, those one fashions himself. Florida is a country of American emotions, a mirror of American souls. It may not be best to wish upon a mouse, but to wish on *something* is essential to human spirit everywhere. Even cynics dream; the fault they find with life is that it does not conform to the private vision. Without the wish, the dream, there are atrophy and death. Florida is a living testament to the American belief that there will always be a tomorrow, the clouds will roll away, and a stunning sun will shine. After all, it was in such a belief that most of the races of man arrived in the New World, in the first place, and those who arrived in chains dreamed of flight into the nation that lay beyond the plantation. What has created Florida has also created the entity of the United States of America.

It is simply that, in Florida, the weather is very much better.

Suggestions for Further Reading

Bartram, William. *Travels of William Bartram*. Edited by Mark Van Doren. New York: Dover Publications, n.d. Not only a comprehensive work on Florida's natural history at the close of the eighteenth century, but a hymn to her beauty and people.

Bickel, Karl. *The Mangrove Coast*. New York: Coward McCann, 1942. Treats Florida's west (and Cinderella) coast in terms of natural and human history.

Douglas, Marjory Stoneman. *The Everglades: River of Grass*. New York: Rinehart, 1947. An American classic of south Florida nature and men.

Douglas, Marjory Stoneman. *Florida: The Long Frontier*. New York: Harper and Row, 1967. Florida from geologic formation to the present; modern years are filled with delightful personal recollections.

Gannon, Michael. *The Cross in the Sand*. Gainesville: University of Florida Press, 1965. The story of Florida's Roman Catholics.

Hanna, Alfred Jackson, and James Branch Cabell. *The St. John's: A Parade of Diversities*. New York: Farrar and Rinehart, 1943. A distinguished volume in the Rivers of America series. Treats northeast Florida in detail.

Hanna, Kathryn T. Abbey. *Florida, Land of Change*. Chapel Hill: University of North Carolina Press, 1948. An over-view of Florida history, with emphasis on human and industrial development.

Hurston, Zora Neale. *Their Eyes Were Watching God*. Philadelphia: Lippincott, 1936. A novel of the Okechobee hurricane by one of Florida's foremost black writers.

Jahoda, Gloria. *The Other Florida*. New York: Charles Scribner's Sons, 1967. An account of north and west Florida, their history, customs, and people today.

Jahoda, Gloria. *River of the Golden Ibis*. New York: Holt, Rinehart &

Winston, 1973. The story of the Hillsborough River, which empties into Tampa Bay, and the worlds through which it has flowed.

Kofoed, Jack. *Moon over Miami*. New York: Random House, 1955.
The glitter and the gold, along with some flotsam and jetsam.

Laumer, Frank J. *Massacre!* Gainesville: University of Florida Press,
1968. As vivid an account of the Dade Massacre as has ever been
written.

Lowery, Woodbury. *The Spanish Settlements within the Present
Limits of the United States*. 2 vols. New York: Russell and Russell, 1959. The definitive treatment of Spain in Florida.

Mahon, John K. *History of the Second Seminole War*. Gainesville:
University of Florida Press, 1967. Contains the latest scholarly
findings on the war, well and simply told.

Neyland, Leedell W. *Twelve Black Floridians*. Tallahassee: Florida
Agricultural and Mechanical University Foundation, Inc., 1970.
A splendid glimpse of black Floridian history for laymen of all
races.

Olsen, Stanley J. *Fossil Mammals of Florida*. Florida Geological Survey, Special Publication #6. Tallahassee: Florida Geological Survey, 1959. This paperback may be ordered from the Florida Geological Survey at the Florida State University, Tallahassee, Fla.
32306.

Patrick, Rembert W. *Florida under Five Flags*. Gainesville: University of Florida Press, 1960. This is *the* book for readers unfamil-
iar with Florida's past.

Pratt, Theodore. *The Barefoot Mailman*. New York: Duell, Sloan and
Pearce, 1943. A novel, later a film, of postmen and pioneers on
the lower east coast.

Rawlings, Marjorie Kinnan. *Cross Creek*. New York: Charles Scribner's Sons, 1942. Life on a central Florida orange grove, told by
a poet.

Rawlings, Marjorie Kinnan. *The Yearling*. New York: Charles Scribner's Sons, 1939. The immortal Jody Baxter and his yearling
deer; an authentic view of yesteryear's Florida crackers.

Redford, Polly. *Billion-Dollar Sand Bar*. New York: E. P. Dutton,
1970. Miami Beach, from the sublime to the ridiculous.

Swanton, John R. *Early History of the Creek Indians and Their Neighbors*. Washington, D.C.: Bureau of American Ethnology, Bulle-

tin 73, 1889. Florida's Muskogee and Hitchiti-speaking peoples, including the subtribes who later formed the Seminoles.

Tebeau, Charlton. *A History of Florida*. Coral Gables: University of Miami Press, 1971. The most contemporary and exhaustive work available, written by a master.

Index

Actinic therapy, 5, 12, 38, 115
Acuera (Indian chieftain), 23, 24
Adams-Onís Treaty, 49
Agribusiness: land of, 159; caste system, 170; mentioned, 13. *See also* Citrus industry
Agriculture, 14, 15, 70, 163, 169
Air conditioning, 125. *See also* Gorrie, John
Ais Indians: name Canaveral, 171, 172; enslaved, 172; uncivilized, 178; mentioned, 16, 147, 148, 174
Alligator (Seminole Indian), 60–61
Amory, Cleveland, 144, 156
American Revolution, 40–41, 70
Apalachee Indians, 16, 19, 21
Apalachicola, 30, 69, 125
Armstrong, Neil (astronaut), 174, 179–180
Army Corps of Engineers, 13, 14, 15
Askew, Reubin (governor), 7, 142
Audubon Society, 134, 176

"Baby Corps, The," 76, 77
Ball, Edward: legislation against, 131, 132; financial empire, 131–136 *passim;* federal investigation, 133; and wildlife, 134; opposes Pepper, 135
Ball, Jessie Dew, 132, 133
Balsan, Consuelo Vanderbilt, 146, 156
Banana River, 173, 174, 177, 180
Banana River Naval Air Station, 174, 175
Bartram, William, 58, 105
Bethune, Mary McLeod, 85–87
Bethune-Cookman School, 86–87
Billy Bowlegs (Boleck), 64, 65, 78
Biscayne Bay: dredged, 114; land boom, 120; growth of, 123; storm clean-up, 126; Willoughby at, 161
Blacks, 78–90, 184
Blanco, Marino Lopez, 194

Blountstown, 137, 139, 144
Boltin, "Cousin Thelma," 197
Bradley, Edward Reilly, 152, 153, 154
Bras Coupé: legend of, 79, 82
Broward, Napoleon B. (governor), 13–14
"Buckeyes," 94, 95, 101
Burnham, Capt. Mills Olcott, 173–174
Burns, Haydon (governor), 140

Call, Ellen, 67–68
Call, Richard Keith: on slavery, 71; and secession, 72; mentioned, 61, 63, 67
Calusa Indians: and Christianity, 29; prey to diseases, 34; knew Big Water, 159; mentioned, 16, 19, 123, 148
Canals: finger canals, 11; Cross Florida Barge Canal, 12, 13; mentioned, 160
Cape Canaveral: and de León, 19; shoals of, 171, space rockets, 172, 177, 179; settlers, 173; and Seminoles, 173; land, 174; security, 175; prospering, 178; operations, 179; depression in, 180
Central and Southern Florida Flood Control District, 12–13, 14, 166
Cherokee Indians, 56
Chickasaw Indians, 56
Choctaw Indians, 56
Christianity, 23, 27–28, 29
Cigar factories. *See* Ybor City
Citrus industry: capital, 103; fruits of, 104–108, 109 *passim;* milestones in, 109–110; by-products, 110–111; helps state, 137; taste-testing, 138; of Indian River, 173
Civil Rights, 78, 85, 88, 179
Civil War: beginnings, 70–73; in Tallahassee, 73, 76–77, 114; campaigns and skirmishes, 74–78; in Jacksonville, 74, 84; and Cape Canaveral, 173–174. *See also* Ku Klux Klan; Reconstruction era

205